Coping with Gender Inequities

Coping with Gender Inequities

Critical Conversations of Women Faculty

Edited by Sherwood Thompson and Pam Parry

ROWMAN & LITTLEFIELD
Lanham • Boulder • New York • London

Published by Rowman & Littlefield
A wholly owned subsidiary of The Rowman & Littlefield Publishing Group, Inc.
4501 Forbes Boulevard, Suite 200, Lanham, Maryland 20706
www.rowman.com

Unit A, Whitacre Mews, 26-34 Stannary Street, London SE11 4AB

British Library Cataloguing in Publication Information Available

Library of Congress Cataloging-in-Publication Data Available

ISBN 978-1-4758-2645-6 (cloth : alk. paper)
ISBN 978-1-4758-2646-3 (pbk. : alk. paper)
ISBN 978-1-4758-2647-0 (electronic)

∞ ™ The paper used in this publication meets the minimum requirements of American National Standard for Information Sciences Permanence of Paper for Printed Library Materials, ANSI/NISO Z39.48-1992.

Printed in the United States of America

We dedicate this book to the female pioneers who blazed trails in the academy and to those women today who make a difference on their campuses, particularly Rose Ann Robertson of American University, who gave the second editor her first job in higher education. And to Jacqueline Chatman, the first author's aunt who served as a dedicated educator for fifty-three years motivating, inspiring, and helping students meet their everyday challenges.

Contents

Foreword

While women have come a long way in the realm of higher education, we still have so much progress to make. According to the report, *Pipelines, Pathways and Institutional Leadership: An Update on the Status of Women in Higher Education* (2015), as of 2014 female faculty held the highest number of positions at some faculty ranks, but male faculty continued to hold a higher percentage of tenure positions at every type of institution. In addition, a significant pay gap remains between male and female faculty. Despite it all, women continue to excel and shine in academia by making important contributions across ranks and disciplines.

As women we have the capacity to be strong, nurturing, and collaborative. The diversity we bring to our campuses makes them greater in so many respects. When I was told this book was in the works, I was reminded of another book that I read in graduate school, *Women's Ways of Knowing: the Development of Self, Voice and Mind*. In the original version, written in 1986, Belensky and colleagues explored how women come to "know what they know" by way of their environment and their interactions with others. While acknowledging the diversity and intersectionality of the female experience at various phases and stages in life, the authors asked women to explain how they came to know themselves and their purpose.

In sum, the authors identified five specific frameworks through which women came to know and understand themselves and the world around them. Although many of the individuals included in this study never set foot on a college campus, the researchers suggested that colleges and universities (which had majority male faculties at the time), might use these frameworks to think differently about education. Perhaps a more "maternal model" might enhance student development both personally and intellectually. This is just one example of the many ways women have enhanced education in this country and worldwide.

The authors who have contributed chapters to *Coping with Gender Inequities: Critical Conversations of Women Faculty* share honest vignettes, point out inequities that still exist, and give context to the challenges female faculty face currently and historically.

There are stories of courage and strength, but also glimpses into the inherent obstacles women faculty members have to overcome in a male-dominated field. Perhaps these reflections will resonate with anyone working in higher education and give them perspective on supporting and developing female faculty at all levels within the academy. Having worked my way through the faculty ranks, I am thankful for the support that I have received from both male and female mentors, colleagues, and mentees. But if I am honest, there have also been times when I was shocked to see women challenge and oppress other women. I felt sorry for them because I often found that their actions were a direct reflection of negative treatment that they personally faced along the way.

I find myself in a unique and fortunate position at my current institution where our president and provost are both female. As a relatively new university administrator, I find it inspiring when they share their experiences with me. It helps me put my own journey into perspective. It also motivates me to "fight the good fight" especially when I feel that my gender may be a factor in a difficult situation. They made it . . . and so can I.

The editors and authors of this book have taken the time to share the individual and collective voices of faculty of both genders. Perhaps the research and narratives shared here will inspire not only conversation, but also action. It will take work from all of us to come together to eliminate any remaining barriers that women face in higher education and beyond.

Kim M. LeDuff, PhD
Dean and Associate Vice Provost of University College
University of West Florida, Pensacola

Acknowledgments

We would like to thank several individuals for helping us compose this book. Most important are our families, friends, and colleagues who tolerated our missing-in-action absence during the editing of this book. We extend our deepest gratitude to the Honorable Aminah Thompson, who volunteered her time to serve as an extra set of eyes on the book proposal and who gave creative suggestions on how to market the book. We were very fortunate to have the professional assistance of many staff members from the Eastern Kentucky University Library. They frequently recused us from despair with their talented ability to locate hard-to-find references. We want to thank those outside readers who supplied us with honest and genuine feedback on our book project; their valuable feedback was tremendously helpful.

We would also like to thank Susanne Canavan, the acquisitions editor with Rowman and Littlefield, who encouraged this project and gave treasured suggestions that guided this book to its successful conclusion. And we especially would like to thank the contributors to the book, who opened their hearts and spent dauntless hours reflecting and transcribing their authentic autobiographies. We extend our gratitude for their willingness to share their stories with us.

Finally, we would like to thank Paula Hansford and Samantha Dodson, our colleagues at Eastern Kentucky University (EKU), who supported our efforts, and five EKU students, Kendra Gower, Tamara (Tammy) Kossatz, Casey Lance, Lexi Walters, and Kali Watson, who proofread the manuscript. We appreciate their contributions to this book.

Introduction

Sherwood Thompson and Pam Parry

An extensive search of the academic literature for information about the first known women faculty pioneers in higher education led to documents in the Antioch College archives in Yellow Springs, Ohio. These documents revealed that Rebecca Pennell, one of Antioch College's original faculty members upon its inception in 1850, was the first woman college professor in the United States (*Yellow Springs News*, 1937). According to news accounts, she taught for six years and received the same rank and pay as her male counterparts.

Pennell paved the way for other women like Lutie A. Lytle and Dr. Alice Hamilton, to name only a couple. Lytle graduated from the Central Tennessee College's "Law Course" in 1897 and returned a year later as a member of the law school faculty. Newspaper accounts claimed that she was the only woman law instructor in the world. She served one session in that position, from 1898 to 1899 (2016).

Dr. Hamilton was the first woman to join the faculty of Harvard University in 1919 when she was appointed an assistant professor of industrial medicine at Harvard Medical School (Thomas, 2014). She became famous for her work as a bacteriologist, with specialized research in the field of industrial poisons. Her research proved to be an invaluable contribution to the U.S. Department of Labor.

Despite the extreme pressure not to engage in formal education, these women became trailblazers; they refused to be discouraged from becoming contributors to higher education and society as a whole. These women seized the times and thrust their way into the higher education landscape with a commanding presence. One can only imagine the struggles they faced as they plowed toward their goals.

With these particular struggles as a backdrop, we believe it is appropriate to ask the following questions about women faculty experiences in today's academe: Is the academe a welcoming place for women faculty? Can women faculty succeed in their chosen fields with support from their male counterparts? Are there barriers to women faculty in the academe, and if so, what are the greatest obstacles and challenges they face? Are women faculty wrestling with issues of gender bias, inequality, racism, and structural barriers? Do women faculty believe they have benefited from affirmative action? Are women faculty, especially women of color, transcending obstacles in the academe? What would women faculty's personal narratives say about their experiences?

This book provides answers to these and other questions, through the chronicles of several women faculty on college and university campuses—public and private. It provides a discussion about their roles, responsibilities, thoughts, perceptions, and statuses in various settings of higher education.

Most specifically, this book explores the differences between male and female faculty in the academe; female faculty insight into teaching, research, and service; how female faculty members perceive their work environment; and the stress of faculty evaluation regarding tenure and promotion. Finally, we also aim to share success stories and lessons learned.

As we examine the experiences of women faculty, we discover that they see the academe as a place that they are forced to transcend barriers to make important contributions in their fields. Many express that their colleagues are not laudatory of the achievements and work. We share with readers the authentic narratives of women faculty members, in their own voices. The voices that are selected for this book are from different disciplines and at different stages in their careers. All of the participants will share personal accounts of how they successfully navigated the road to the professorate.

The narratives present a focused look at the intersection between women and their male counterparts and their pathways to success as they steer through land mines of harsh discrimination. It is clear that women faculty members are integral and contributing members of their departments. They are productive and willing to make differences in the lives of students and to their academic disciplines, evidence of which is demonstrated in the stories they share.

This discussion is critical at this juncture in the annals of higher education. Women faculty provide a very visible and meaningful role on campuses. Namely, they provide the vital function of mentorship of an ever-increasing number of women students, helping such students to understand the culture and the climate therein. Still, with all of the positive roles that women faculty play, they report that they continue to experience, to some degree, less satisfaction and greater challenges than their male counterparts in many aspects of the profession.

Many of the contributors expressed that they constantly fight to protect their sense of personal value. Studies show that women faculty are often confronted with experiences of exclusion, isolation, alienation, racism, sexual harassment, and other inequalities. MacLachian (1993) in a *Christian Science Monitor* article, reported that Stella Nkomo, a professor of management at the University of North Carolina, expressed that African American women are facing a concrete ceiling. In the Sanchez-

Hucles and Davis (2010) article titled "Women and Women of Color in Leaderships: Complexity, Identity, and Intersectionality," they indicated that women of color face a sticky floor as described by Bell and Nkomo (2001). And Eagly and Carli (2007) advanced the discussion about the glass ceiling, the concrete wall, and the sticky floor by introducing the term *labyrinth* to describe the uneven path of promotability and upward advancement for women in organizations.

Women faculty and the treatment they receive at their respective institutions ranges in degree according to the culture of their departments. These women, their experiences, their assessments of the commitment that is made, and the standards that are in place can determine if there is a sincere attempt to provide wholesome and nurturing working conditions that will enhance job satisfaction. They are akin to their male counterparts in this regard; they want to make a positive contribution to the academe and reach the highest possible level of achievement in their disciplines.

It is our hope—and the great ambition of this book—that these authentic stories by female faculty will inform and transform the discussion about gender equality in the academe. A secondary purpose and intent of this book is to learn from female faculty how they perceive their personal and professional lives on and off campus. This book will stimulate a lively discussion about creating a more supportive climate for female faculty members.

REFERENCES

Bell, E. L., and Nkomo, S. M. (2001). Our separate ways: Black and White women forging paths in corporate America. Unpublished book manuscript.

Campbell, B., and Manning, J. (2015). Microaggression and changing moral cultures. *The Chronicle of Higher Education.* Retrieved March 8, 2017, from http://www.chronicle.com/article/MicroaggressionChanging/231395/.

Christman, D. E. (2003). Women faculty in higher education: Impeded by academe. Retrieved March 8, 2017, from http://advancingwomen.com/awl/winter2003/CHRIST~1.html.

Council of Economic Advisers. (2014). Women participation in education and the workforce. Retrieved March 8, 2017, from https://s3.amazonaws.com/s3.documentcloud.org/documents/1350163/wom-en_education_workforce.pdf#page=1&zoom=auto,-226,549.

Eagly, A. H., and Carli, L. L. (2007). *Through the labyrinth: The truth about how women become leaders.* Boston, MA: Harvard Business School Press.

Kansas Historical Society. (2016). Lutie Lytle: First African American to be admitted to the Kansas bar. Knsapedia. Retrieved March 8, 2017, from https://www.kshs.org/kansapedia/lutie-lytle/12136.

Kirkman, B. L., Lowe, K. B., and Gibson, C. B. (2006). A quarter century of culture's consequences: A review of empirical research incorporating Hofstede's cultural values framework. *Journal of international business studies, 37*(3), 285–320.

Lederman, D. (2006). The real barriers for women in science. Retrieved March 8, 2017, from https://www.insidehighered.com/news/2006/09/19/women.

MacLachian, S. L. (1993). African-American women chip away at concrete ceiling. The *Christian Science Monitor*. Retrieved March 8, 2017, from http://www.csmonitor.com/1993/1022/22082.html.

Mason, M. A. (2010). Women, tenure and the law. Retrieved March 8, 2017, from http://chronicle.com/article/Women-Tenurethe-Law/64646/.

Patitu, C. L., and Hinton, K. G. (2003). The experiences of African American women faculty and administrators in higher education: Has anything changed? *New Directions for Student Services, 2003*(104), 79–93.

Robinson, C., and Clardy, P. (2010). *Tedious journeys: Autoethnography by women of color in the academy*. New York: Peter Lang.

Sanchez-Hucles, J. V., and Davis, D. D. (2010). Women and women of color in leadership: Complexity, identity, and intersectionality. *American Psychologist, 65*(3), 171–181. doi: 10.1037/a0017459.

Thomas, J. D. (2014). Dr. Alice Hamilton: Harvard's first woman professor. Accessible Archives blog entry. Retrieved March 8, 2017, from http://www.accessible-archives.com/2014/03/harvards-first-woman-professor-alice-hamilton/

U.S. Department of Education, National Center for Education Statistics. (2012). The Condition of Education 2012 (NCES 2012-045), Indicator 47.

U.S. Department of Education, National Center for Education Statistics, Integrated Postsecondary Education Data System (IPEDS), Fall 2013, Completions component. (This table was prepared September 2014.)

West, N. M. (2016). The African American women's summit: A student affairs professional development program. *Journal of Student Affairs Research and Practice*, 1–14.

White House Summit on Working Families. (2014). Eleven facts about American families and work. Retrieved March 8, 2017, from https://s3.amazonaws.com/s3.documentcloud.org/documents/1350164/11familyworkfacts.pdf.

Yellow Springs News. (1937). Antioch claims first woman college teacher. Antioch College Archives. Retrieved March 8, 2017, from https://sites.google.com/a/ysschools.org/rebecca-pennell-first-female-professor-of-equal-pay/home/introduction.

ONE

"Particularly" Good for the Women: "Differend" in the Academy

Ginny Whitehouse and Krista Kimmel

INTRODUCTION

At times in our academic careers, we have felt like we were standing knee-deep in a rushing river while the men—students to administrators—looked at us from the shore and asked why we were drenched from water they could not see. This feeling begins early in graduate school, heightens to a fevered pitch when we go on the job market, and enters our first classrooms. It then stays at a simmering ever-present reality as we navigate the corridors of higher education. Too many metaphors? Perhaps data will help define our experience.

Hirshfield and Joseph (2012) argue that women experience gendered identity taxation by having higher academic service expectations to achieve token gender balance in the academy. However, the taxation actually begins in the interview process when candidates are selected based on preconceived notions of what it means to have "the woman" hired. This taxation is further compounded for women of color, who might offer two demographic checks in the hiring diversity boxes.

The ultimate insult, however, is that when a scholar is hired as "the woman," she is strongly discouraged from articulating the limitations imposed by the label. She is essentially silenced from responding to statements from colleagues that her hire is "particularly good for the women students" or from course evaluations that state "clearly this professor was only hired because she is a woman." It would be rare-to-never for a man to be told his hire was good for the male students or that he was only employed because of his gender.

Women undergraduate students outnumbered men in 1988 and the ratio has grown steadily each year since (National Center for Education Statistics, 2012). The number of women PhDs edged past men for the first time in 2008 as the overall number of doctoral students rose (Kim, 2011). Women make up 43 percent of senior academic leadership positions, but notably most of those positions are as a president's chief of staff. Less than a third of the academic deans and less than a quarter of college presidents in the United States are women (American Council on Education, 2013). The ratio of women faculty varies widely from discipline to discipline. The result is that women who are new hires still may be seen as primarily an integration opportunity in their academic units, and women of color most definitely will be.

This narrative combines the qualitative reality of our experience with quantitative evidence. We approach this chapter with a certain fear: Will we appear ungrateful to our mentors, who guided us at times effectively, and simultaneously, unwittingly minimized our contributions to the field and the classroom? Will we be seen as troublemakers looking for slights when none are intended? This is the risk we take by telling our stories, and yet, tell them we will.

KRISTA'S STORY

I reside in the margins of the academy. That is, I am a member of the largest-growing segment of the faculty population, known as "contingent faculty." We contingent faculty now compose more than 70 percent of all faculty positions, according to the National Center for Educational Statistics. I officially hold the title of "Senior Lecturer," which means I am employed in a full-time, nontenure track position at a public, regional university. As a lecturer, I am primarily responsible for teaching five courses per semester. I enjoy little job security as a contractual employee because the university may terminate my position as unnecessary at any time. Prior to my appointment as a lecturer, I cobbled together an income working as an adjunct and other part-time jobs.

Perhaps unsurprisingly, the majority of contingent faculty members are women. Women account for 54 percent of full-time instructors and lecturers (Cordova, 2011). The American Association of University Professors (2009) reports 59 percent of full-time faculty are male, while the Coalition on the Academic Workforce (2012) estimates women comprise 61 percent of part-time faculty members.

As I contemplate my position as lecturer, who also happens to be female, I wonder how these statistics came to be. For women who are juggling professional and family responsibilities, perhaps the flexibility of part-time employment is appealing. Maybe it's something more sinister—remnants of a system designed to protect the patriarchy. Walby (1990) defines patriarchy as "a system of social structures and practices in which men dominate, oppress, and exploit women" (20). But perhaps it is something entirely different, something subtle and, even, unnoticeable.

For most academics, graduate school is a pivotal experience on our career trajectory in higher education. It's where we establish our scholarly agenda, obtain some of our earliest teaching experience, and learn the culture of higher education. In short, we learn what it means to be a faculty member. I wonder, then, what lessons we learn about the intersection of gender and faculty roles.

When I consider my experience in graduate school, I recall a chilly climate for women. Most of my professors were men. (The only female professors I had were those in my cognate area.) When a fellow graduate student and I applied for departmental funding for a research project, we were promptly denied. Of course, it's possible our project wasn't worthy of financial support, but instead of an offer from senior faculty to help us restructure our proposal, we were blithely dismissed. I also recall a professor who openly discussed a female student's personal and marital struggles with our entire class. At the time, I wondered if a male student's private life would be dissected so brazenly and publicly.

Further, as a graduate assistant for one of the department's male faculty members, I was routinely asked to perform such tasks as sharpening pencils, faxing letters, adding paper to the copy machine, and other clerical duties. Once, I drove my supervisor to the auto shop to pick up his car after an oil change. Interestingly, there were two male graduate students who were also assistants for the same faculty member. Not once were they asked to perform these tasks.

These experiences, like those of so many women, reinforce our status as "lesser" or "supporting players"—those who refill coffee and bring donuts, but who are often denied opportunity to grow and thrive. Over time, such messages and experiences accumulate and leave us questioning our own abilities and contemplating just how we navigate the dark waters of the academy.

THE DATA

Certainly, women have also made substantial progress in attaining faculty and leadership positions within higher education. In 2007, 42 percent of full-time faculty at colleges and universities were women (Cordova, 2011). In addition, more women are presiding over institutions than ever before. In 1986, women accounted for just 10 percent of college presidents. By 2012, about a quarter of institutions (26 percent) were led by women (Cook, 2012).

Despite these advances, however, women have yet to achieve parity in leadership positions within higher education. In the years between 2006 and 2012, the number of college presidents who were women increased by a mere 3 percent (Cordova, 2011). Women are more likely to lead institutions where teaching is emphasized over research. In 2006, women presided over just 13.8 percent of doctoral-granting institutions, while 28.8 percent of community or associate colleges were led by women (Cox and Salsberry, 2012). The numbers are similar for women holding chief academic officer (CAO) positions (e.g., provost). In 2009, women accounted for 32 percent of CAOs at doctoral-granting institutions. Conversely, women at community colleges hold 50 percent of these positions (Cox and Salsberry, 2012). In essence, women are more likely to attain leadership positions at less prestigious institutions.

Women have made substantial progress in attaining leadership positions outside the two highest-ranking positions (president and CAO). In 2007, women held about 50 percent of positions within the administrative branch, including executives, directors, and managers (Cox and Salsberry, 2012). However, the administrative branch encompasses numerous roles across several campus offices. Many of these positions are middle-management level, and those serving in these capacities often possess limited decision-making authority. Furthermore, women are less likely to hold the position of senior student affairs officer (SSAO), which is the highest-ranking administrative post in the student affairs division of an institution. Engstrom, McIntosh, Ridzi, and Kruger (2006) found women account for approximately 40 percent of SSAOs.

All of these statistics can be attributed to a number of causes. First, only 26 percent of full professors are women (Cordova, 2011). This is significant because many administrators are selected from faculty holding the rank of full professor. Second, women account for 40 percent of CAOs nationally. Presidents are often recruited from this rank, and because fewer than half of these positions are held by women, they are less likely to ascend into the role of the presidency (Cox and Salsberry, 2012). Third, more men are appointed to boards of trustees or regents than women. This may have an impact on the number of women selected as presidents because boards of trustees are generally tasked with hiring this position. Fourth, women generally do not receive the encouragement to pursue leadership roles in the manner men do (Madden, 2005). Finally, women may experience more difficulty in reconciling work and family responsibilities. For example, women presidents are less likely to be married or have children than their male counterparts. Female presidents also reported leaving the academy or taking part-time work more often than male presidents (Cordova, 2011).

Women of color often encounter significant challenges in higher education and are underrepresented in both faculty and administrative positions. Women of color account for 3 percent of full professors, 7 percent of associate professors, and 10 percent of assistant professors (Tran, 2014). Of female college presidents, women of color represent around 15 percent (Turner, 2007).

In addition to underrepresentation, women of color often experience discrimination and lower job satisfaction. Tran (2014) observes women of color in higher education frequently are discriminated against based on both their gender and race, which results in "multiple marginality" (303). Furthermore, Packer-Williams and Evans (2011) state African American women faculty are often retained at a lower rate than their White colleagues and can experience unnecessary challenges by peers and students alike. Academic administrators generally are promoted from within the faculty ranks, and consequently, the lower rates of retention and job satisfaction of women of color can adversely affect their ascent into leadership roles.

Ultimately, women may populate the base of the academic structure, but until parity is achieved at the top, the experience of all women will be one of struggle. The more educated a woman is, the greater the pay disparity may be (Adamy and Overberg, 2016). And even then, evidence shows that as women leaders gain in numbers in any field, their salaries do not rise to the levels of their predecessors, but instead fall to a new low (Blau and Kahn, 2016).

GINNY'S STORY

Not long after I left my first faculty appointment, a dear, former colleague called to tell me about my replacement. I had left a small liberal arts school to move across country to a state university closer to my family. I happened to be in the parking lot of the grocery store buying supplies for my new house. How I loved my former colleagues and respected their work. The caller and I discussed what a fine candidate the new faculty member would be. "I believe she will be particularly good for the women," he said. From a half-continent away, he could not see me blanch and only knew I had to excuse myself. There in the parking lot, I doubled over and wretched.

The obvious follow-up question was unnecessary: "What do you mean . . . particularly good for the women?" I know what he meant. I know a department with a hefty majority of women as majors should not have its entire faculty as men. The department had been in that state when I had arrived more than a decade earlier, and when I left, they were mono-gendered again. Such an emphasis on the word *particularly* . . . so loaded and coded with meaning.

When I was hired, it was made plain that the university had to bring a woman into my position because the department faculty members were all male. Nonetheless, everyone repeatedly said that I was the right woman for the job. I was told I was even the most qualified regardless of being a woman. When I asked in the job interview what it would mean to be the only woman faculty member in the department, the implication was quite clear: Why did I ask such a question that made everyone—every man—feel uncomfortable? My job was to solve the gender problem without mentioning the gender problem.

These small cuts to the soul scabbed and scarred. A student wrote on my first teaching evaluation "she was only hired because she was a woman." My colleagues told me not to take such comments seriously. When students referred to me as "Mrs." while the men were always "Dr.," I was told not to take it personally, to not correct students because that would make them uncomfortable.

Women of color face even greater challenges than I did. Over the years at that first faculty appointment, I formally mentored new faculty members, all women, as well as "inner-city" (code for not White), first-generation college students in two distinct and different programs. Late in my tenure at that institution, a new faculty member came on board and I was asked to mentor her with the assurance that I would "particularly" enjoy working with her. Again and again, members of the search committee, administrators, and other faculty told me I would "particularly" like her. I didn't get it. I couldn't for the life of me figure why over and over again this word was being used. So, I started asking: Why will I "particularly" like her? All I could get out of anybody was, "You will know when you meet her." Finally, a junior faculty member gave me the answer: The new woman was African American. Only then for the first time did I realize that *particularly* could be a code word. But a code for what?

THE DIFFEREND

The structure of women's leadership in the academy dramatically shapes how women enter higher education work. The very language used may be what creates the environment. Coded communication allows the speaker to be racist or sexist without guilt. Hillary Clinton is called shrill, secretive, and ambitious, words not applied to men (Blake, 2015). Codes create a wink-wink, Bob's your uncle language. Notorious Alabama Governor, George Wallace, claimed he supported "states' rights" when he meant he opposed federally mandated desegregation and talked about "crime" and "high taxes" as substitutes for "Black" (Swenson, 2004). "Family values" is code for anti-LGBTQ. These little cues happen so fast that subtext is encoded without the speaker or the listener having to process meaning. The code itself is created long before any conversation takes place, and the dominant players get to define the terms. Subordinates may have their own language, but those in power are not required to learn alternative meanings. Perpetuating the code is, however unconscious, a means of maintaining power (Hurwitz and Peffley, 2005).

These subtle wordings allow both the speaker and the listener to share truths without naming them. If this truth goes unnamed, all parties can pretend the hidden implications do not exist. Because there was no deliberate attempt at belittling, the slight or bruise simply is invisible. It lingers in the air, but does not fully apparat. Remember Galileo thought comets were an optical illusion, much like rainbows, because he did not observe their mass.

The word *differend* sounds and looks like the word *different* for a reason. Postmodern philosopher Jean-François Lyotard (1983, 1988) introduced the idea that two people may share a common word but view that word's meaning completely differently. Both definitions have value, but the one held by the dominant person serves as the official version.

The ones with power use language to their own end. Therefore, a word such as *particularly* can be labeled as innocuous rather than a signifier for difference. Women in a lower position of power cannot respond to such comments and identify them as sexist or racist because the speaker intends them as praise. Thus, a compliment becomes not empowering, but silencing. Because the speaker believes his or her intent to be good, offering a counterinterpretation is perceived as ungracious at best and emasculating at worst. Even expressing the differend itself becomes challenging because the harm done may be impossible to define.

Academic research or essay writing, as Lyotard refers to it, is interpreted as a masculine occupation, whereas feminine writing is most frequently relegated to the role of seduction, he explains. To attempt to make rhetoric a gender-neutral product is much like a conservative politician's claim to be apolitical: Physical evidence makes that argument invalid on its face. For a woman to write, to argue, to claim, she will do so as a woman, but feminine writing by its patriarchal definition must be the antithesis of reason (1978). Therefore, simply being a woman in the academy is fraught with differend.

GINNY'S STORY

When I was asked to write this book chapter, I jumped at the chance. Then, I became afraid: What would my former colleagues think? Would my new colleagues see me as a whiner? Did I really want to delve into my own psyche about gender? In the months that followed the initial contract, my daughter became suicidal, my family buried my mother, and I underwent a hysterectomy. Each of these realities challenged my womanhood. Over time, my daughter learned to live; my mother, a great feminist, was free from the pain of ovarian cancer; and my own ovaries were cast aside as a threat to the rest of my body. And still, to write about womanhood in the academy created such angst I could hardly begin. I feared being labeled bitter.

As a religious woman in a religious family, I turned to holy texts for support and guidance for all these challenges in my life. There, I discovered a meditative practice of creative journaling in scriptures. Women were drawing in their Bibles as a form of prayer. The designs ranged from an elaborateness that rivaled the *Book of Kells* to the simplicity of stick figures. They were each beautiful expressions of faith, and yet on social media, these women reported repeatedly being asked: What right do you have to draw in your Bible? No one added "particularly as women," but the subtext was evident.

With these messages, I had an epiphany: The history of women's roles in the academy runs parallel to the history of women in religious leadership in the United States. Women, only in the last century, have widely gained the right to be in the bimah, minbar, or pulpit of many faith groups, and still not at all in other major groups. Few, if any, of these traditions barred women preaching and teaching to women and children, but nearly all have a long history of barring women preaching to men. Certain interpretations of scriptures have made it blasphemous for a woman to be placed in such authority (Mountford, 2005).

Meanwhile, women have long been teaching other women in female seminaries, girl's academies, even the finishing school where my great-grandmother taught music. Helen Magdill White became the first woman in the United States to earn a PhD in 1877, but even she was only asked to teach girls (Eisenmann, 1998). Having a woman teach men was perceived as unholy as having a woman preach.

Therefore, to suggest that a female academic would be "particularly good for the women" is to undermine her authority in the classroom before she walks in the door. Having a female role model obviously is important to female students. That fact cannot be understated. Requiring male students to recognize a woman as an authority, to call her *professor* and *doctor*, further requires men to see women as persons having something important to say.

Validating women's voices is crucial for the faculty women themselves. For so many of us, teaching helps us find our voice and express our passions. Being heard, really heard, by all our colleagues and all our students is essential to our well-being and credibility. Here lies evidence of male privilege. To suggest that our well-being might be vulnerable places us in the camp of "Lady Professors" just as women's university sports teams are at times still called by a feminine version of the home team, the "Lady Tigers" or the "Eaglettes." Even if we win the game, we are still not the main event.

I am not the only scholar who has felt the sting of the phrase "particularly good for the women." I have heard stories again and again from women hired at public universities and private, secular and sectarian, large and small: A well-meaning colleague quietly speaks the phrase sincerely believing it to be a validation. It is said almost off-handedly, but with a certain amount of collusion, as though the speaker is part of a grand plan to empower women and wholly unaware that this statement is belittling all the women in the frame. Just because there is no intent for sexism, or racism, or any other -ism, the effect of those words is still the same. In fact, if the speaker had intended harm, the harm would be easier to address. As Lyotard observed, the differend cannot be resolved and is as much felt as heard.

Silencing then occurs systematically. The dominant player, who Lyotard calls the *addressor*, does not find the words to feel belittling. For example, when I expressed frustration to a colleague, he responded, "That hasn't been true in my experience." The wrong, or referent, incident then is downgraded to something that simply could not have taken place because it was outside the addressor's frame of reference. To add insult to injury, I could not respond, "Well, this isn't about you or your experience," because that statement would have made me uncollegial and shrill.

RESOLVING THE DIFFEREND

Lyotard (1983, 1988) offered little hope for resolving differend but suggests at least three possible remedies. Those in power must first "bear witness" of those who do not have it. Simply, they must listen. This means really listening, not to plot a counterargument, not to attempt to analogize others' experience to their own, but instead empathetically hearing others' experiences as valuable, recognizing that the frames and language can and will be different. Hearing each story as a unique contribution to the academy is crucial, rather than trying to create a meta-narrative that oversimplifies and restricts individual women's experiences. Listening, however, requires a certain passivity because it is most often seen as a precursor to the primary event of action. The very act of listening, however, must be, in and of itself, a crucial activity.

For an addressor, someone in power, to listen and bear witness requires him or her to give up some power. The one speaking is presumed to be the one in authority. Too often, academic administrators claiming to go on listening tours through their campuses are actually on "talking at" tours. We've already established that women need to be validated as authorities in the classroom as having credibility for both men and women. These same women need to be validated as credible interpreters of their own experience. All too often we have witnessed male administrators in meetings explain our own disciplines to us as though we needed to be informed.

The second remedy to differend requires solving the underlying problem: instead of hinting at correcting inequity, actually creating equity. Increased numbers of women are needed in the top dean, vice president, and president slots so that all women throughout the academy are viewed as authorities in their fields. At the same time, the gendered implications of enlarging the contingent faculty pool need to be recognized, as does failing to create opportunities for contingent faculty to enter the tenure track. Bringing anyone with any difference into a homogenous community requires honest conversations about what that difference will mean.

This recognition brings us to the third remedy, one that Lyotard arguably advocated: the creation of a new discourse that empowers all voices and encourages self-reflection, so that people are more likely to become aware when they are silencing each other. Creating this discourse will be incredibly challenging. Repeatedly we hear students, both male and female, state that gender-related problems would be far less if we didn't talk about gender all the time. That makes about as much sense as saying you won't be hungry if you don't think about it; eventually you are going to have to eat or you will die. Saying nothing about gender is not a remedy. To resolve conflict, we must actually communicate, but that communication points back to the first remedy discussed here: listening.

KRISTA'S STORY

Often, when engaging with a combative or antagonist student, I silently ask myself, "Would this student be challenging me this way if I were male? Would he or she undermine my authority in the classroom?" Conversely, as I review student evaluations of my teaching, I question whether my male counterparts are rated as "sweet" or "nice." Accurate or not, I generally conclude the answers to both of these scenarios as "probably not." In the twenty-first century, it's perplexing, as well as frustrating, that we are still grappling with gender disparity.

When examining gender in the academy with a critical lens, we must consider the subtle reinforcements of gender roles and stereotypes, including those perpetuated by ourselves. If faculty and administrators fail to challenge these rigid standards, then we cannot expect our students to respond differently. For example, do we take notice when female colleagues volunteer to take minutes during meetings? Do we observe the woman who always recognizes everyone's birthdays with cards and baked goods? Do we praise the male colleagues who leave the university early to pick their children up at school as exemplary fathers, while sniffing just a bit at women who bring children to a hastily scheduled meeting because a sitter couldn't be found?

I believe these slight, seemingly innocent behaviors highlight gender stereotypes and the inequality in the academy. If we are to comprehensively remedy gender disparity, we must first look inward and examine our own actions and language.

Do we encourage other women professionally? When we hear an inappropriate comment made by a colleague, do we address or dismiss the situation as harmless? Are we aware of our own biases and perceptions? We must first partake in self-assessment before we engage in dialogue about gender. Once, I suggested to a female colleague we meet on a Saturday to complete some rather tedious curriculum revisions. She declined because her child was playing in a soccer game that day. First, I felt disappointment, but soon realized how inappropriate my request had been. I couldn't think of a logical reason why my colleague should be expected to work on a Saturday and prioritize curriculum mapping over her family. Did I ask her simply because she was a . . . woman? My suggestion required her to defend her time and reminded everyone that she had responsibilities that could be described as gender specific.

Awareness and self-reflection are only the first steps to attaining a more equitable academy. Marshall (2009) recommends encouraging open dialogue through a variety of means, which might include forums, surveys, and focus groups. In addition, mentoring and development opportunities are essential for female faculty members. Dominici, Fried, and Zeger (2009) argue women are often disadvantaged in securing social support and informal networking opportunities in higher education because the majority of senior faculty members and administrators are men. Thus, an emphasis on more mentorship opportunities—both informal and formal—for women is warranted. A simple wish for gender equity is insufficient. We must act boldly, and we must do so together.

REFERENCES

Adamy, J., and Overberg, P. (2016, May 18). Pay gap widest for elite jobs—Women in white-collar careers see biggest gender disparity, defying legislative remedies. *Wall Street Journal*, p. A1.

American Association of University Professors. (2009, July). Characteristics of part-time faculty. Retrieved March 8, 2017, from https://www.aaup.org/article/who-are-part-time-faculty#.V0Y8OL7GCw4.

American Council on Education. (2013, May 1). By the numbers: As presidential diversity stalls, looking into the future of leadership. Retrieved March 8, 2017, from http://www.acenet.edu/the-presidency/columns-and-features/Pages/By-the-Numbers-As-Presidential-Diversity-Stalls.aspx.

Blake, A. (2015, March 26). The 13 words you can't write about Hillary Clinton anymore. Retrieved March 8, 2017, from https://www.washingtonpost.com/news/the-fix/wp/2015/03/26/the-13-words-you-cant-write-about-hillary-clinton-anymore/.

Blau, F. D., and Kahn, L. M. (2016, January). The gender wage gap: extent, trends, and explanations. *IZA DP No. 9656.*

Coalition on the Academic Workforce. (2012, June). A portrait of part-time faculty members. Retrieved March 8, 2017, from http://www.academicworkforce.org/CAW_portrait_2012.pdf.

Cook, B. J. (2012, September). The American college president study: Key findings and takeaways. Retrieved March 8, 2017, from http://www.acenet.edu/the-presidency/columns-and-features/Pages/The-American-College-President-Study.aspx.

Cordova, D. I. (2011). Moving the needle on women's leadership. *On Campus with Women, 40*(1), 8.

Cox, K. S., and Salsberry, T. (2012). Motivational factors influencing women's decisions to pursue upper-level administrative positions at land-grant institutions. *Advancing Women in Leadership, 32*(1), 1–23.

Dominici, F., Fried, L. P., and Zeger, S. L. (2009). So few women leaders. *Academe, 95*(4), 25–27.

Eisenmann, L. (1998). *Historical dictionary of women's education in the United States.* Westport, CT: Greenwood Publishing Group.

Engstrom, C. M., McIntosh, J. G., Ridzi, F. M., and Kruger, K. (2006). Salary determinants for senior student affairs officers: Revisiting gender and ethnicity in light of institutional characteristics. *NASPA Journal, 43*(2), 243–263.

Hirshfield L., and Joseph, T. D . (2012). "We need a woman, we need a Black woman: Gender and cultural taxation in the academy." *Gender and Education.* 24, 213–227.

Hurwitz, J., and Peffley, M. (2005). Explaining the great racial divide: Perceptions of fairness in the U. S. Criminal Justice System. *Journal of Politics, 67*(3), 762–783.

Kim, Y. M. (2011, October). *Minorities in higher education 2011 Supplement.* University of California Santa Cruz. Retrieved March 8, 2017, from http://diversity.ucsc.edu/resources/images/ace_report.pdf

Lyotard, J. F. (1978). One of the things at stake in women's struggles (D. J. Clarke, Trans.). *Focus on the Margins, 6/7*(20), 9–17.

Lyotard, J. F. (1983, 1988). *Differend: Phrases in dispute.* (G. Van Den Abbeele, Trans.) Minneapolis, MN: University of Minnesota Press.

Madden, M. A. (2005). 2004 Division 35 presidential address: Gender and leadership in higher education. *Psychology of Women Quarterly, 29*, 3–14.

Marshall, S. M. (2009). Women higher education administrators with children: Negotiating personal and professional lives. *NASPA Journal About Women in Higher Education, 2*, 188–221.

Mountford, R. (2005). *The gendered pulpit.* Carbondale, IL: Southern Illinois University Press.

National Center for Education Statistics. (2012). Degrees conferred by sex and race. U.S. Department of Education. Retrieved March 8, 2017, from http://nces.ed.gov/fastfacts/display.asp?id=72.

Packer-Williams, C. L., and Evans, K. M. (2011). Retaining and reclaiming ourselves: Reflections on a peer-mentoring group experience for new African American women professors. *Perspectives in Peer Programs, 23*(1), 9–23.

Swenson, M. (2004). *Democracy under assault: Theopolitics, incivility and violence on the right.* Denver, CO: Sol Ventures Press.

Tran, N. A. (2014). The role of mentoring in the success of women leaders of color in higher education. *Mentoring and Tutoring: Partnership in Learning, 22*(4), 302–315. doi: 10.1080/13611267.2014.945740.

Turner, C. S. (2007). Pathways to the presidency: Biographical sketches of women of color firsts. *Harvard Educational Review, 77*(1), 1–38.

Walby, S. (1990). *Theorizing patriarchy.* Oxford, UK: Basil Blackwell.

TWO

Achieving Tenure and Promotion

Simone C. O. Conceição

INTRODUCTION

The current scenario of higher education is volatile. Achieving tenure and promotion has become a contentious matter. There are many myths that make the profession polemic. For example, some people think that tenure means lifetime job security. In reality, tenure is the right to due process (National Education Association and American Federation of Teachers, 2015). Any faculty going through the tenure process remains accountable after achieving tenure. Institutions of higher education have post-tenure reviews, which involve periodic evaluations for promotion and merit increases, and there is no guarantee that the faculty position is a job for life.

Another myth is that faculty don't work much and have summers off. On the contrary, full-time faculty in four-year institutions of higher education work an average of fifty-four hours a week (Cataldi, Bradburn, and Fahimi, 2005). Tenured faculty must teach, publish, and serve on academic and professional committees. Summers are often spent completing research because during the academic year, teaching and service may take over the time for publishing. Another myth is that it is assumed that faculty need tenure to have academic freedom, but according to the U.S. Constitution this is not the case. Academic freedom allows for challenging conventional wisdom, but it is not an assurance that faculty will never be fired for articulating personal beliefs (National Education Association and American Federation of Teachers, 2015).

Another myth for faculty members related to tenure and promotion is that any faculty member achieves tenure. This is not true. The number of faculty who are tenured in the United States accounts for no more than one-third of all colleges and universities (Hutcheson, 1996; Lee, 2001). To add to this equation, institutions of higher education are not replacing faculty who retire with tenure-track positions today because it gives institutions increased flexibility and the opportunity to save money by replacing positions with part-time faculty (National Education Association and American Federation of Teachers, 2015). For faculty of color, the experiences with tenure and promotion can be even more challenging (Hassouneh, Akeroyd, Lutz, and Beckett, 2012).

Achieving tenure and promotion requires academic standards, focus, discipline, and perseverance. Gender-related issues in four-year research-intensive higher education institutions affect women more than men and minorities in higher proportion. In this chapter, these issues are addressed from individual and institutional perspectives based on existing literature and personal stories.

INDIVIDUAL PERSPECTIVE

Writing this chapter made me reflect on my own journey to achieving tenure and promotion. As a woman and minority faculty, I always felt that I had to work twice as hard to be recognized. This did not pull me back from a career that I value because of the opportunity to help and serve others through teaching and service and the creative and discovery nature of conducting research in social sciences, more specifically in the field of education.

My educational philosophy is based on a learner-centered approach. I believe that helping others through instruction requires designing courses in ways that allow for individual differences with a curriculum that is developmental in nature. In this context, I believe that students must be allowed to learn and grow at their own pace. In the diverse world we live in today, I also believe that teaching from different perspectives to address recurring problems in education can help learners meet their own learning needs, think and reason more broadly, and select what is most relevant to them. In my personal situation, being a teacher has allowed me to take into account the unique differences among students. Each learner is different in terms of past experiences.

Serving others involves engaging at the institutional, community, and professional levels. This engagement to service aligns with my teaching and research agenda. My research has a scholar-practitioner focus and informs my teaching and service. This educational stance has served as the framework for achieving tenure and promotion within my institution.

ACHIEVING TENURE

Going through the tenure process was like a spider web. I needed to put together the elements of my academic dossier, proceeding from step to step according to the institutional policies and guidelines for tenure and promotion. Each element had to be intertwined like a network of inter-connected nodes. This process can be overwhelming at first because of the complex elements that lead to the final tenure documentation. The elements must be conveyed together to show interconnections across the three areas of teaching, research, and service. The final product needs to clearly demonstrate scholarly independence, outcome quality, research variety, and alignment of the three areas. For me, the first step in the process was to determine a teaching, service, and research agenda. Then connect the three areas. Mentoring played an important role in the process.

DETERMINING A TEACHING, SERVICE, AND RESEARCH AGENDA

Fitzgerald, Bruns, Sonka, Furco, and Swanson (2012) stressed that a new framework for scholarship was essential to the success of higher education. This framework "moves away from emphasizing products [e.g., publications] to emphasizing impact" (11). In 1990, Boyer published *Scholarship Reconsidered: Priorities of the Professoriate*, which helped start a discussion on reframing the definition of scholarship. Boyer's definition of scholarship includes discovery, integration, application, and teaching. His work proposed to modify faculty roles in which teaching and application were equal to research.

The discussion contended that the evaluation of faculty performance should be conducted along a continuum of behaviors and social impacts instead of focusing on the number of publications in a limited set of specific journals. This discussion on the engaged university was centered on the production of meaningful research that "benefits the society and educates students for productive roles in a modern and diverse world" (Fitzgerald et al., 2012, 15). For me, Boyer's framework was the basis for meaningfully and scholarly connecting research, service, and teaching and establishing a line of inquiry.

CONNECTING THE THREE AREAS

From my experience with the tenure process, having a line of inquiry kept me focused. My line of inquiry involved three research areas: adult learning, online education, and educational technology. During the two-year contract renewal report, I created a concept map to identify the interconnections in teaching, service, and research. The courses I taught were directly related to my line of inquiry, which allowed me to stay current on concepts, theories, and research. I tried to contribute to service activities that would give greater value to my teaching and research, and at the same time, serve the department, university, and profession. For example, I was a member of the Technology and Distance Education Committee (at the school level), Information Technology Policy Committee (at the campus level), and program committee for the Annual Distance Teaching and Learning Conference (at the professional level).

My research involved discovery of new teaching and learning practices, integration of adult learning principles and distance education foundations as the department launched a new master's degree online (integration of knowledge and inquiry in context), and application of new strategies from research to teaching practice (moving beyond transmission of knowledge to joint learning with students). Having a focus and mapping my line of inquiry throughout the process enriched the learning experience of students, created results with impact and relevance at the school and university levels, and expanded innovative practices by allowing the examination of new teaching and learning designs in a real-world context (our own departmental program). The outcomes of my work stimulated creativity and innovation in our department, the university, and the profession (Fitzgerald et al., 2012). Later on, two new online programs were developed based on the practices from the initial online program.

The experience with the online program led me to participate in leadership roles within the university. I became a member of the Online Program Council on campus and later became the council co-chair. My council contributions were purely based on my research-to-practice approach. My expertise benefitted the department, university, and later, through consulting, other organizations at the local, national, and international levels.

MENTORING

Mentoring had a critical impact on my success in the academy. I was assigned to faculty mentors in my department, who helped me understand the pathway to achieve tenure and promotion. One important aspect of the mentoring relationship was to listen to my mentors. My mentors showed me the importance of understanding faculty governance, institutional policies and procedures, appropriate venues to publish my work, types of research to consider (i.e., refereed, database research), kinds of service contributions to be involved in, and workload management strategies.

According to the departmental tenure guidelines, it was important to have a balance between teaching, service, and scholarship. I shared my scholarly agenda with my mentors and sought feedback on my writing before submitting to a refereed journal. I also updated them on my progress toward tenure frequently.

My colleagues protected me during my first years as a faculty member, which is an indication of faculty support. I did not feel marginalized, as some studies have indicated for minority faculty (Turner, 2003). On the contrary, I felt I was integrated into the department and the school for the type of work I was involved in. Because my area of research had practical outcomes in higher education, I was able to easily balance all three areas of teaching, service, and research.

GETTING PROMOTED AND BEYOND

Getting promoted to the rank of full professor is another process that places the faculty member at a different anxiety level. At this point, faculty need to achieve excellence in all three areas by showing the development of a cutting-edge combination of scholarly research and theoretical and practical issues in the field, complex expertise in existing or new areas, professional field recognition through awards, and national and international advancement standing. Faculty must maintain the publication flow and acquire grant funding, expand service contributions at all levels (local, national, and international), and increase doctoral student supervision.

Upon tenure, faculty can take advantage of a sabbatical to accomplish some of these expectations. This was my case. I felt that the sabbatical was an opportunity to reflect, relax, recharge, create, and plan for the next phase of my career. During the year of my sabbatical, my publication productivity was the highest. I was able to start and complete several publications for peer-reviewed journals, finish writing one book and start a new one, and take time to recharge. The sabbatical was a time to focus on the creative and discovery nature of the profession, which can be a lot of fun. Not having to balance research with teaching and service was a relief. I had control over my time, location, and undertakings.

One of the dangers of getting tenure for some faculty is that the need to rest from the intense work tends to reduce scholarly productivity. This can be a trap due to the false sense of job security after getting tenured. With higher education being attacked with state regulations about tenure and promotion, this is a risky situation. If universities can release faculty as a result of cancellation of programs, one must be current with publications to be marketable in the workplace. Post-tenure reviews are now more than ever being demanded by higher education institutions; one more reason for maintaining scholarly productivity.

The process of achieving promotion to full professor also needs to be strategic based on timing, logistics, and networks. The timing of the promotion depends on the expectations of the institution and department. Some institutions may have a minimum number of years before someone can go for promotion. In terms of logistics, it is essential to continue updating the academic dossier on a regular basis and monitoring the impact of the publications. With databases available online, the process now is more transparent. Anyone can check on publication ranking, impact, and citations.

The narrative statement can help the evaluator identify the strengths and limitations of the scholarly record. Thus, a well-prepared account of the themes that interconnect the three areas of teaching, service, and research is imperative. The networks are the colleagues in the department, the internal and external reviewers, and the administrators who will give the stamp of approval at the end of the process. It is important to maintain good rapport with colleagues within the profession, department, and administrators in the institution who approve the promotion.

BIASES ASSOCIATED WITH WOMEN NAVIGATING THE ACADEMY

My entry into the academy occurred because I was working at an institution of higher education and modeled after my mentors who later became my colleagues. In their research, Glass, Doberneck, and Schweitzer (2011) found that success in "the tenure system is central to how early-career faculty organize their work" (p. 22). Morrison, Rudd, and Nerad (2011) found that individuals who transition from graduate school to a position outside academia are less likely to move into tenure-track employment than those in contingent jobs. Also, individuals who try to transition considerably later into a tenure-track position can only do it successfully on completing a postdoctoral fellowship or getting a nontenure-track faculty position.

One important factor that made me feel comfortable with embarking in the profession was the opportunity to see, practice, and collaborate with others even before I obtained my doctorate. By the time I became a faculty member, my mind-set was ready for the tenure process. The informal and formal support I received from colleagues helped me prepare for the rigors of achieving tenure. Two challenges affected my trajectory, but they did not prevent me from embarking in the journey: ethnic status and gender bias. These challenges are interconnected.

Ethnic Status Bias

Studies have shown that faculty of color continue to be underrepresented in the academy (14 percent); many faculty describe having racial and ethnic bias in the workplace (Turner, 2003). My own experience with bias in the workplace relates to my foreign accent and the feeling that people did not believe in my "can-do attitude" because of the ethnic status. Initially this bias affected me emotionally, but over time I let it go and started focusing on the task to be accomplished and moved the issue (from my mind) to the person who made the comment or demonstrated a negative attitude toward me. In the classroom, the issues of communication initially were resolved through strategies that provided clarification of concepts and theories through handouts or PowerPoints. When I started teaching online these issues were transparent because most of the communication was text based. When creating videos, I included closed captioning. My enthusiasm for teaching made my communication concerns invisible over time.

Furthermore, my research interest on creating a sense of presence in online environments helped me understand the cognitive, emotional, and behavioral aspects of teaching and learning and in turn led to feelings of closeness and personalization with my students (Lehman and Conceição, 2010). Eventually my work became known based on empirical studies through peer-reviewed publications and books at the international level that the sense of bias no longer felt present for me. I realized that my work had value when I started receiving invitations to give talks, provide professional development workshops, and collaborate with others in Turkey, the Dominican Republic, China, Chile, and Brazil. Gaining a sense of confidence helped me continue to be productive within my profession.

A situation involving bias that I experienced was when I received a professional award. After receiving the award, while having lunch with a colleague, I was told I received the award because I was the only candidate for the award. I initially felt like an imposter for having received the award and wondered if I really deserved it. The person who made the negative comment seemed to have had an issue with her own career advancement and showed resentment toward me. This situation made me reflect not only on my own potential, but also that I should not allow others to affect me because of their bitterness.

The challenges of the professoriate may at times build up to feelings of dissatisfaction, frustration, and dismissal of our own possibilities. One must be strong against the negativity others may direct toward us and look for the rewards of a career of multiple experiences.

Gender Bias

One major issue that affects women faculty from getting tenure is gender inequality. Although gender-based discrimination in higher education was banned more than forty-five years ago, women still suffer from gender differences related to promotion and tenure compared to men entering the professoriate in regard to ranks, advancement, and attrition (Morrison, Rudd, and Nerad, 2011). The main reason for women has been related to family roles. Marriage affects the chances of women getting full-time, tenure-track jobs in an institution of higher education (McBrier, 2003; Wolfinger, Mason, and Goulden, 2008).

On the contrary, for men marriage increases the chances of employment advancement—such as making more money, having a higher publication productivity rate, and advancing to a higher rank (Bellas, 1992). When it comes to having kids during the transition from doctoral completion to a tenure-track position, the chances for women are even worse. Though, married men (or with a partner) tend to get tenured faster than other men from prestigious institutions at a higher rate than women (Morrison, Rudd, and Nerad, 2011).

Although this issue did not affect me personally during my tenure and promotion process, I felt a sense of reverse discrimination. Not having a family leads to an assumption that you have time to take on leadership roles, coordinate programs, or take on school committees. Moreover, if you are a woman and an ethnic minority, university leadership tends to request your participation in key campus committees to show value to diversity (Padilla, 1994; Park, 1996). When you are trying to get promoted and avoid a negative attitude about you from people who will sign your promotion, this can be a challenge.

Women of color tend to be more committed to teaching and service and often find themselves lacking research productivity essential for tenure and promotion (Antonio, 2002). Part of this challenge is the teaching and learning philosophy of helping students succeed. Students of color are inclined to seek advice from faculty of color because of their apparent focus on "student first" mentality. All these have happened to me. I place personal importance on the success of my students and time engagement in my research activities. I started engaging students in my work after I was promoted to full professor. My purpose for engaging doctoral students in research activities was to facilitate their entry into the academy. Having this philosophy with students can influence work productivity or result in overwork due to the extra time with students. In my case, I leaned to the overload category. My work with doctoral students goes beyond production of publications; it also pertains to their emotional and personal development as part of their professional practice.

MAINTAINING WORK–LIFE BALANCE

Being a faculty member involves an unpredictable journey due to the complex experiences and associations with colleagues, family members, and subordinates. These experiences go from navigating the complexity of the spider web of the tenure process to handling the relationships with people along the way. This requires managing time and tasks and balancing family and professional responsibilities. It is more complicated if faculty are going through these experiences with a family due to the additional roles and responsibilities. Though a spouse can be supportive, it can also be a challenge to balance a family relationship because of the intense work needed to meet the requirements for tenure.

In a study of faculty's decision about work and family, O'Meara and Campbell (2011) found that "a sense of agency to make satisfying work and family decisions is constructed in context" (473). Institutions that have flexible institutional and individual work expectations are more supportive of work-family balance. Women do not always take advantage of institutional policies related to parental leave. Decisions about leave may be influenced by departmental norms about work and family, role models or lack thereof while still pursuing a doctoral degree, and timing of career during the decision rather than what one wants to be.

My experience in balancing work-life activities has been a favorable one. In my case, I was able to focus on my work and maintain my freedom to get things done on my own time. One drawback is that a person needs to take care of self to survive the emotional roller coaster of the tenure process. Taking care of self means taking breaks, exercising, socializing, and taking time off when possible. My strategies to balance work and life during the process involved identifying tasks and prioritizing time on when to work on writing, on teaching, and service; on exercising, eating healthy, and vacationing with family and friends.

Managing my workload involved being strategic with the choice of service contributions. I tried to be a member of committees that could culminate in research or inform my teaching. Teaching required more cognitive and emotional efforts because most of my classes were taught online. Teaching online needed to be planned in advance with scheduled times dedicated to designing the course, being present in the online course, and providing feedback, but at the same time being flexible. One must be careful when teaching online courses because courses are always available, and for the instructor it gives the sense of being accessible 24/7. For research, the best strategy is to know how to cooperate in grant writing, joint publishing, and involvement in international collaboration.

INSTITUTIONAL PERSPECTIVE

I have experienced the tenure process from my own individual perspective as a faculty, but also as a member of the executive committee that reviews tenure and promotion at my institution. Being on the other side of the process gave me a different perspective of the complex system. From my own observation, I have noticed that one of the most challenging aspects of the process is to avoid seeing the process as a checklist, and instead as a web of interconnected elements that portrays the picture of an academic life.

When viewing the process from the back end, the focus is on each piece of the dossier that shows the interconnections among the three areas. The presentation of the materials is the entry to the context of the file. With a sharp eye, each element of the documentation points to a theme. The candidate's narrative provides how the person views his or her own past, present, and forthcoming work. The assessment from reviewers provides a perspective from within the discipline. Assessment from the institutional executive committee provides an evaluation of the candidate from outside the field.

The dossier must be clear enough for someone who is not familiar with the discipline to provide a sound appraisal of the materials. One concern when reviewing the documentation is not so much the number of publications, but rather the quality based on field specific standards. The number of publications counts when reviewing for variety, independence, or single and multiple-authorship; however, quality may take different values—impact of the journal, methodology used, number of citations, or implications to theory, research, or practice.

The evaluation from impartial external reviewers has significant value in the process. For example, in my institution, external reviewers cannot be done by individuals who have published with the candidate, former and current coworkers, coauthors, major academic professors and advisors; individuals who had financial or contractual obligations with the candidate; or other persons with whom the candidate has established an extensive working relationship, currently or in the past ten years. A thorough assessment identifies and evaluates the qualified contribution of publications, service or professional work, or programs of study/scholarship of a candidate. The process may be open or closed at the candidate's choice. For the most part, processes are closed in which the candidate does not have access to external reviewers evaluation letters.

During my process as a member of the institutional executive committee for tenure and promotion, there have been instances when the documentation was incomplete and the hearing did not take place until the full documentation met the criteria. For the candidate, this can be disturbing when the person is anxiously waiting for the process to be completed. The process of gathering information can be time-consuming and must be planned strategically. Precise, timely, and organized documentation help move the process smoothly.

STRATEGIES FOR ACHIEVING SUCCESSFUL TENURE AND PROMOTION

Based on my experience as a faculty going through the process of tenure and promotion and observing others as a member of the institutional executive committee, I have identified strategies for achieving successful tenure and promotion and surviving the complex process. These strategies include learning about faculty governance, gaining skills needed to thrive as a scholar in the twenty-first century, having a mentor, identifying approaches for balancing workload and prioritizing time, and maintaining work-life balance.

Learning about Faculty Governance

One of the first steps when a faculty member enters a new tenure-track position should be to look at the rights and responsibilities that come with the territory. Often the documentation is not thoroughly reviewed until contract renewal approaches or when the dossier for tenure is about to be prepared. It is essential for faculty to become involved in the process as they start the new job. Faculty governance lays out faculty powers and responsibilities for determining curriculum or making personnel decisions (such as appointments, promotions, reappointments, and tenure). By understanding policies and procedures, faculty can better negotiate and advocate for their own rights during the process.

Gaining Skills Needed to Thrive as a Scholar in the Twenty-First Century

It is important to have technological skills to be part of the new digital academic landscape. These technological skills include creation, management, and monitoring of productivity; communication and networking; and judgment of the quality of a journal.

With a transparent process to achieve tenure and promotion, it has become more challenging today to develop an academic record, build a profile, and maintain a steady productivity record. It is essential to have technology skills to manage one's own work. Anyone can conduct an online search and see the profile of a scholar and the impact of that person's work.

A faculty's profile is no longer available to just a few people in a specific field. Thus, one common strategy for scholars is to have a profile in the many existing online databases—for example, LinkedIn, ResearchGate, Academia.edu, and Google Scholar, to name a few—to showcase their work. Online databases show the extent publications are viewed, downloaded, or cited, and provide an opportunity for scholars to communicate and network with other colleagues. Some scholars have their own websites to disseminate their work or blogs to share viewpoints or communicate with others.

Another important skill is to be able to discern the quality of a journal. One way to discriminate the quality of a journal is to identify the publication impact factor, which now plays a major role in the profile of a scholar. The impact factor of a journal reflects the average number of recent citations in a given journal. The impact shows the importance of the journal within the field. Journals with high-impact factors are more relevant than those with lower-impact factors.

Having a Mentor

Having a mentor on or off campus, in or outside of the discipline can help negotiate the spider web of tenure and promotion. A good mentor will help in understanding the institutional culture; identify venues for publishing, types of conferences to attend, and service contributions to consider; and counsel on the progress of the achievements to avoid pitfalls.

It is not uncommon to have more than one mentor depending on the purpose of the mentor–mentee relationship. For faculty of color, a mentor might help the individual feel less isolated and marginalized if the institution is composed of a small number of minorities. A mentor can also help with the promotion process by advising on leadership opportunities, encourage the application to more advanced positions, and nominate for awards (Stanley, 2006).

Identifying Approaches for Balancing Workload and Prioritizing Time

With a multitude of tasks, balancing the workload can be overwhelming for faculty. For teaching, one may need to design, administer, and deliver courses on a continuum of a semester. For research, one may need to consider a problem to be solved, develop a proposal, seek institutional review board approval, collect and analyze data, and then report findings through publications. For service, one may need to identify areas in which the contribution will make a significant impact, participate in meetings, provide insights, and potentially create reports. These are just a few examples that, if completed together, require managing tasks and prioritizing time. These tasks may happen at intermittent times outside the control of the faculty. Planning ahead and selecting and ranking tasks based on importance demonstrate a sense of agency in decision making.

Strategies for managing teaching tasks can include a range of options, such as an instructional designer. Additionally, partnering with other scholars can distribute the research workload. Contributing to low-impact service activities in the beginning of the tenure process and then moving to more demanding service contributions, as articles are published, can help in prioritizing time and tasks.

Maintaining Work-Life Balance

Maybe one of the most difficult strategies during the tenure and promotion process is taking care of oneself. There must be a balance among the cognitive, emotional, and behavioral efforts a person puts into achieving career success. Exercising, meditating, eating healthy, and spending time with family and friends are just a few examples that can help maintain work-life balance. Without a conscious effort to do things that will maintain one's sanity, a person can lose a sense of self and identity. It is important to stay "human" throughout the process.

CONCLUSION

Being a faculty in higher education requires knowledge of the expectations and opportunities to grow in a constantly changing educational environment. Navigating the complexities of the professoriate may be the reason why persisting in the journey is not for everyone. Though it can be challenging at times, a career that can serve others, contribute to the good of society, produce innovation, and help others think and reason more broadly can be the most rewarding and engaging experience.

REFERENCES

Antonio, A. L. (2002). Faculty of color reconsidered: Reassessing contributions to scholarship. *Journal of Higher Education, 73*(5), 582–602.

Bellas, M. L. (1992). The effects of marital status and wives' employment on the salaries of faculty men: The (house)wife bonus. *Gender and Society, 6*, 609–622.

Boyer, E. L. (1990). *Scholarship reconsidered: Priorities of the professoriate.* Lawrenceville, NJ: Princeton University Press.

Cataldi, E. F., Bradburn, E. M., and Fahimi, M. (2005). 2004 National study of postsecondary faculty (NSOPF:04): Background characteristics, work activities, and compensation of instructional faculty and staff: Fall 2003 (NCES 2006-176). U.S. Department of Education. Washington, DC: National Center for Education Statistics. Retrieved April 3, 2015, from http://nces.ed.gov/pubsearch.

Fitzgerald, H. E., Bruns, K., Sonka, S. T., Furco, A., and Swanson, L. (2012). The centrality of engagement in higher education. *Journal of Higher Education Outreach and Engagement, 16*(3), 7–27.

Glass, C. R., Doberneck, D. M., and Schweitzer, J. H. (2011). Unpacking faculty engagement: The types of activities faculty members report as publicly engaged scholarship during promotion and tenure. *Journal of Higher Education Outreach and Engagement, 15*(1), 7–30.

Hassouneh, D., Akeroyd, J., Lutz, K. F., and Beckett, A. K. (2012). Exclusion and control: patterns aimed at limiting the influence of faculty of color. *Journal of Nursing Education, 51*(6), 314–325.

Hutcheson, P. A. (Spring 1996). Faculty tenure: Myth and reality—1974 to 1992. Thought and Action, National Education Association. Retrieved March 8, 2017, from http://www.nea.org/assets/docs/HE/Tenure7MythReality.pdf

Lee, J. (June 2001). NEA Higher Education Research Center Update, 7(3). Retrieved March 8, 2017, from http://www.nea.org/assets/docs/HE/Tenure2ResearchUpdate. pdf.

Lehman, R. M., and Conceição, S. C. (2010). *Creating a sense of presence in online teaching: How to "be there" for distance learners.* San Francisco, CA: Jossey-Bass.

McBrier, D. B. (2003). Gender and career dynamics within a segmented professional labor market: The case of law academia. *Social Forces, 81*(4), 1201–1266.

Morrison, E., Rudd, E., and Nerad, M. (2011). Onto, up, off the academic faculty ladder: The gendered effects of family on career transitions for a cohort of social science PhDs. *The Review of Higher Education, 34*(4), 525–553.

National Education Association and American Federation of Teachers. (2015). "The truth about tenure in higher education." Retrieved March 8, 2017, from http://www.nea.org/home/33067.htm.

O'Meara, K., and Campbell, C. M. (2011). Faculty sense of agency in decisions about work and family. *The Review of Higher Education, 34*(3), 447–476.

Padilla, A. M. (1994). Ethnic minority scholars, research, and mentoring: Current and future issues. *Educational Researcher, 23*(4), 24–27.

Park, S. M. (1996). Research, teaching, and service: Why shouldn't women's work count? *The Journal of Higher Education, 67*(1), 46–84.

Stanley, C. A. (2006). Coloring the academic landscape: Faculty of color breaking the silence in predominantly White colleges and universities. *American Educational Research Journal, 43*(4), 701–736.

Turner, C. S. (2003). Incorporation and marginalization in the academy from border toward center for faculty of color? *Journal of Black Studies, 34*(1), 112–125.

Wolfinger, N. H., Mason, M. A., and Goulden, M. (2008). "Problems in the pipeline: Gender, marriage, and fertility in the ivory tower." *Journal of Higher Education, 79*(4), 389–405.

THREE

Family-Friendly Working Conditions

Karen Christopher

INTRODUCTION

In her controversial article in *The Atlantic,* Anne-Marie Slaughter (2012) concluded that in today's society, most women cannot "have it all"—if having it all includes being a hands-on parent and working unbounded hours. Her personal narrative in this article, however, reveals that when she worked in academia, she was closer to "having it all" than when she worked in the State Department under Hillary Clinton; even though she worked long hours and traveled frequently as a faculty member, she could craft her work schedule around family demands.

A growing body of research explores how women and men with children fare in academia. Some studies suggest that academia is a uniquely challenging work environment for parents—particularly those with young children. Other studies (many of specific disciplines) suggest that academic mothers can thrive under certain conditions. This chapter draws from theoretical and empirical research on gender in the academy to explore what changes could make universities more family-friendly environments for faculty.

I begin with a brief overview of how gender theory informs discussions of parenthood within academia. Then, I present recent empirical studies of work-family conflict in the academy. I draw from these literatures to explore their implications for family-friendly policies in universities and then conclude with a brief discussion of my personal experience as an academic with two young children, including several years on my university's family-friendly policy committee.

THEORY ON GENDER AND PARENTHOOD IN THE ACADEMY

Gender scholars suggest that gender inequality exists and persists on multiple levels: the individual level of gendered identities, the interactional level of different cultural expectations for women's and men's behavior, and the institutional level of policies, laws, and norms in social structures (Risman, 2004). Risman suggests that when analyzing a gendered social problem, researchers should explore all of these levels to pinpoint where social change is most needed. For example, if research shows that inequalities between male and female faculty are most influenced by the university policies, we would focus most on institutional changes. Therefore, I start by reviewing scholarship on the different levels of gender inequalities in academia and then discuss implications for social change.

Because men remain overrepresented in powerful positions (such as tenured professors, administrators, and presidents) in the academy (Mason, Wolfinger, and Goulden, 2013), many female academics enter into predominately male workplaces; the gender identities of female faculty do not seem to prevent them from entering into typically male environments. Because little research explores the gendered identities of women in academia, in this chapter I focus more on gendered inequalities in the interactional and institutional levels of academia.

Research on cultural expectations for female academics suggests that cultural beliefs and expectations, which inform all of our interactions at work and at home (Risman, 2004), still differ for female and male faculty. Mason and colleagues' (2013) analysis of University of California faculty find that female faculty with kids spend about twice as many hours a week on caregiving than male faculty with kids (and far more hours on caregiving than faculty without kids (71). This finding is consistent with research showing that although men do more household labor than in the past, mothers in dual-earner households still perform about five hours more per week on child care than fathers, and about seven more hours per week on housework than fathers (Pew Research Center, 2013).

In addition, the cultural demands of parenting have increased over time, with mothers spending more time with children in the late 1990s than the 1960s, even though their employment rates steadily increased during this time (Sayer, Bianchi, and Robinson, 2004). Many social scientists identify a pervasive intensive mothering ideology (Hays, 1996; Arendell, 2000), which posits that mothers are the best caregivers for their children, and ideal child-rearing is emotionally demanding, expensive, and expert driven.

Other scholars have uncovered important challenges to intensive mothering, particularly among employed mothers (Blair-Loy, 2003; Christopher, 2012) and mothers of color (Christopher, 2013; Collins, 2008; Dean, Marsh, and Landry, 2013). Nonetheless, the research cited previously on faculty mothers' disproportionate completion of caregiving work suggests that academics are certainly not immune to an intensive mothering ideology. Indeed, many academics—women and men—say they want more children than they have and that children are important to their life satisfaction (Ecklund and Lincoln, 2011).

When childless, more than one-third of female faculty in the University of California system reported that they regretted being unable to have children, and almost two-thirds of female faculty regretted having only one child and wanted more (Mason et al., 2013). In sum, cultural expectations that women perform more caregiving work than men affect female faculty—and many faculty want to have children and spend time with them, though demanding academic jobs may complicate these desires.

The institutional demands of academic jobs—the policies, rules, and norms—assume an "ideal worker" who can spend unlimited hours on research, teaching, and service (Mason et al., 2013; Williams and Dempsey, 2014). Although faculty typically have flexibility on when and where to complete our work, our workload is heavy and our job markets are competitive. Mason and colleagues (2013) argue that the extremely competitive process of attaining tenure-track jobs and the demanding nature of academic work—particularly when parents have young children and simultaneously face the "up or out" tenure system—make it less family-friendly than professional jobs in law or medicine.

Although the demands to acquire tenure are typically most strenuous in research-oriented universities, the requirements to engage in research, teaching, and service increasingly exist for faculty across all types of universities. Jacobs and Winslow (2004) find that the demands of faculty jobs have increased over time, with the average workweek for faculty currently more than fifty hours, and "professors often complain that the demands of their jobs never end" (107). In addition, in other professional jobs, more parents have part-time options; Mason and colleagues (2013) show that about 45 percent of female physicians work part-time—an option typically unavailable to tenure-stream faculty.

Feminist scholarship has long argued that both interactional and institutional constraints affect different women in different ways. For example, Patricia Hill Collins (2008) adds an intersectional perspective to work-family issues, asking how gender intersects with race/ethnicity, social class, and sexuality to affect women based on their multiple social locations.

Regarding women in academia, scholars show how the practice of "other mothering" in communities of color can require great demands on African American professors' time; they are underrepresented in the academy, and many students of color turn to them for mentoring and advice (Story, 2014). Given female associate professors already spend more time than male associates on teaching and service (see later discussion), we should be attuned to how female professors of color may confront higher expectations for service work and teaching.

In addition, the maternal wall may be experienced differently for women of color in academia (Williams and Dempsey, 2014); based on demographic trends in our society, women of color may be more likely to parent without partners and have fewer resources and less time than partnered parents. Likewise, we should recognize the unique demands of LGBT parents in academia; many receive fewer health, retirement, and other benefits and also face unequal treatment in informal interactions in the academy. Thus, when exploring efforts to make universities more family-friendly, we must remember that families in the academy may have different needs based on their racial/ethnic, social class, and LGBT status.

EMPIRICAL RESEARCH ON FACULTY

In their recent book on patterns that limit women's success in professional jobs, Williams and Dempsey (2014) suggest that the maternal wall—stalled progress in salaries, promotions, and status after childbearing—"may well be highest in academia" (132); among the professional women they interviewed for their book, they also found that maternal wall bias was most prevalent among women of color. Several studies explore why mothers face barriers within the academy. In their study of the work and family demands of faculty, Jacobs and Winslow (2004) identify three causes of work-family conflict: demands of jobs, such as long work hours and inflexible workplaces; family demands, such as caregiving and housework; and "normative and/or cultural expectations (e.g., the ideals of appropriate parenting and successful career achievement)" (106). These scholars suggest that institutional practices and cultural expectations disadvantage mothers in universities.

Research on the success of female faculty with children is mixed (Damaske, 2014). Mason and colleagues' (2013) study of the nationally representative National Science Foundation (NSF) Survey of Doctorate Recipients find that both "married women and women with young children are less likely to get tenure-track jobs" (59) than married men and men with young children; in addition, mothers with young children are much more likely than men with young children and non-mothers to enter into "second tier," nontenure-track faculty positions.

These researchers also show that many graduate students who want children—around 30 percent of female students and 20 percent of male students—are deterred from entering academic careers altogether (Mason et al., 2013); female graduate students most commonly cited the lack of family-friendliness in academia as the reason they left. As confirmed by other large studies, Mason and colleagues (2013) find that women with children in the sciences (including the social sciences) are less likely to get tenure than men with children: "a female scientist with a pre-school-age child is 27 percent less likely to get tenure compared with a man who has a small child" (48).

They also explore the gender gap in promotion to full professor and find that having children does not explain this gap; another study (Misra, Lundquist, Holmes, and Agiomavritis, 2011) shows that per week, female associate professors spend about five more hours on service and about three more hours with students than their male colleagues (while men spend significantly more time on research). Rather than a motherhood penalty, it seems that widespread cultural beliefs and expectations that women are more nurturing, caring, and invested in students' lives lead to these gendered outcomes for associate professors; however, Mason and colleagues (2013) show clear evidence of a motherhood penalty in attaining tenure-track jobs and getting tenure.

Other research on specific disciplines finds fewer motherhood penalties for professors. Krapf, Ursprung, and Zimmermann's (2014) nationally representative sample of professors in economics found no effects of childbearing on men's research productivity, and few effects of having children on women's productivity—if they were married and give birth to only one child. However, being a single mother and having more than one child had more negative effects: "A mother of three children has, on average, a research record reflecting a loss of four years of research output by the time all of her children have reached their teens. The respective output loss of a mother of two children amounts to about two and a half years" (30).

This study suggests that at least in economics, not all mothers are equally disadvantaged—those without partners, and those with more children are less productive in research.

Similarly, Spalter-Roth and Van Vooren (2012) find that sociologists who were mothers were just as likely as men and non-mothers to have the "ideal career path" of tenure-stream jobs in research-intensive universities; mothers were also as successful writing peer-reviewed publications (10). These scholars and Krapf and colleagues (2014) suggest that social scientists who become mothers may have figured out ways to "balance" work and family demands successfully.

In their study of male biologists and physicists, Damaske, Ecklund, and Lincoln (2014) reveal that men adopt different strategies in response to the demanding work environments in science. The slight majority of their respondents privileged work over family life and had either neo-traditional or traditional arrangements with their wives. Those who were egalitarian typically experienced the most stress and least productivity at work (but reported more contentment with their home lives). The authors conclude that, "the academy does not merely have a gender problem, but also a child-rearing problem, suggesting that it is not only women who are at risk of structural discrimination within academic science but also men who want to have and spend time with their children as well" (Damaske, 2014, 500). This research shows that the demands of lab sciences are difficult for all parents—women and men.

Jacobs and Winslow's (2004) nationally representative sample of faculty helps explain what aspects of jobs provide most stress to faculty: They find that although more than 80 percent of female and male faculty report satisfaction in their jobs, over one-third of female faculty are dissatisfied with their work load, and over half of female faculty say they cannot keep current with the research in their field. They also find that faculty who worked the longest hours (more than sixty hours per week) were the least satisfied with their jobs but were also the most productive in research. They conclude:

> The data presented here suggest that the demands of academic life are becoming excessive and are making it difficult for individuals to succeed at work while having the time to be caring and responsible parents. This suggests that efforts to promote a better balance between work and family should go beyond parental leave policies for newborns and try to establish limits on the apparently limitless demands of academic jobs. (127)

Thus, these findings suggest that family-friendly universities must also address the long work hours required to attain tenure-track jobs and receive promotions in them.

IMPLICATIONS FOR FAMILY-FRIENDLY POLICIES

Mason and colleagues (2013) convincingly argue for the need for different policies at different stages in an academic's career. Because graduate students typically earn low wages, these parents need affordable child care, health care, and housing; they also need an extension in their academic clock to PhD (Mason et al., 2013). In addition, graduate students need supportive mentors, not mentors who question their work commitment after childbearing.

Mason and colleagues (2013) argue that these policies could help diminish the number of female faculty who take the contingent route, which is more flexible for parents (but has many drawbacks, such as much lower pay and autonomy). These recommendations would entail both institutional changes through policies, as well as mentors creating a supportive (rather than hostile) culture around parenting.

In the intense "make-or-break" years leading to tenure, Mason and colleagues (2013) argue that tenure-track parents need a professional part-time option, during which time faculty can temporarily work part-time due to caregiving demands and then return to full-time work. At least six weeks of paid leave for childbearing/adoption and policies to stop the tenure clock, two of the more common policies offered to faculty nationwide (Mason et al., 2013), are also essential. The authors argue for more generous leaves from teaching: a two-semester leave from teaching for female parents, and a one-semester leave from teaching for male parents. High quality childcare—particularly for single parents in the academy—can also help faculty be more productive and less stressed. These changes are institutional: Formal policies recognize the unique challenges of caring for young children (or other dependents) and allow faculty members more time to attain tenure.

However, as suggested, cultural changes are equally necessary. Mason and colleagues (2013) and other scholars (Hochschild, 1997) suggest that faculty will not use family-friendly policies if they think colleagues will question their work commitment. Therefore, it is imperative that administrators, department chairs, and senior faculty are both knowledgeable about and openly supportive of these policies. Another important cultural change would encourage male faculty to engage in unpaid work; policies such as paternal leaves and teaching releases for male faculty could, over time, challenge the deep-seated belief that mothers should be primary caregivers of children. In couples where both partners are academics (about 13 percent of men and 18 percent of women have academic partners), these policies have the benefit of freeing up mothers' time so they can spend more time outside of the home (Mason et al., 2013). Again, male administrators, chairs, and colleagues must also support these policies because fathers are unlikely to use these policies if they believe they'll be penalized.

However, recent research suggests that department chairs may be resistant to structural change within their departments. Wharton and Estevez's (2014) in-depth interview study of department chairs (at a research university in the Midwest) found they discussed gender, family, and work with "an outmoded view of family as a woman's issue and as separate as distinct from work" rather than seeing gender as "an entrenched feature of the academy" (131). This research highlights the continued presence of gender inequality at the interactional level—and the need for faculty, or upper administration, to challenge department chairs when they refuse to acknowledge or ameliorate the gendered patterns in academia revealed previously.

Challenging pervasive cultural norms in academia—such as the "ideal academic worker" academic who works unbounded hours—may be one of the more important, and difficult, strategies for social change. Ollilainen and Solomon (2014) suggest that graduate students tend to be more critical of long work hours than faculty members (though some faculty members do engage in strategies to lower their work hours); if graduate students remain more critical over their careers, we would expect the ideal academic worker to lose ground in coming decades. Challenges to long work hours could also be promoted by a professional part-time option and leaves for caregiving because these policies signal the importance of life outside of the academy.

However, recent nationally representative, survey-experimental research shows that while the presence of family-friendly policies (paid leave, child care, and flexible work options) makes women more inclined to support egalitarian arrangements in the home, the same does not hold true for men (Pedulla and Thébaud, 2015); the authors suggest that policies designated for men (such as paternal leave) or other policies designed to diminish long work hours may be necessary before more men reduce their work hours.

The ideal worker seems most daunting in the lab sciences, which require long hours in the lab and require faculty to apply for and receive highly competitive extramural grants. These expectations help explain women's low levels of promotion in these fields. Mason and colleagues (2013) discuss positive changes in one funding agency, the NSF, which recently announced family-friendly policies allowing the postponement of grants for childbirth/adoption, the suspension of grants for parental leave, and supplements to cover staff to maintain labs when principal investigators take family leave. If more funding agencies adopt these kinds of policies, they could help lessen the steep gender gap in promotion and tenure in the lab sciences.

Regarding family-friendly policies for faculty of color and LGBT faculty, these groups may need additional policies that recognize the unique demands facing them. Given faculty of color are both underrepresented in the academy and also highly sought after for mentorship by students of color, department chairs may need to either limit the amount of time faculty can spend on service, or better yet, chairs and administrators could both count and value this kind of service in promotion decisions and pay raises.

Faculty of color who are parents and LGBT parents may face unequal treatment because of being a parent in academia and their other social locations; for example, the "maternal wall" can disadvantage mothers of color more than White mothers (Williams and Dempsey, 2014). Therefore, university policies designed to equal the playing field between parents and non-parents must be sensitive to these differences. For example, many parents of color discuss the importance of a diverse student body and a diverse curriculum in preschools (and in every stage of education); these issues need to be considered when designing child care policies.

In addition, contingent faculty typically earn low wages and have low levels of autonomy in universities; they are also disproportionately female, in part because contingent jobs (in theory) offer more flexibility than tenure-stream jobs (Mason et al., 2013). Any efforts to improve the working conditions of faculty must recognize the large percentages of nontenure-stream faculty; family-friendly options for contingent faculty include subsidized child care and paid leaves comparable to those offered to tenure-stream faculty. In addition, any efforts to increase the autonomy of contingent faculty, such as giving them more power to determine their teaching schedules, could help them better manage work-family conflict.

In sum, a family-friendly university must not only offer institutional supports for caregiving like the many policies described previously, but also challenge the culture of the ideal academic worker with no other demands on his or her time. The cultural expectations for intensive mothering must also be challenged with policies that pull men into the home, and thus allow women more time and energy for efforts outside of the home. In addition, family-friendly policies should acknowledge and aim to overcome the unique barriers experienced by faculty of color, LGBT faculty, and contingent faculty.

PERSONAL EXPERIENCES WITH FAMILY-FRIENDLY POLICIES

I am an associate professor with two children ages seven and ten, married to another academic. We were lucky to solve our "two-body problem" after only two years of working at different universities. I am White, heterosexual, and from a privileged class background; all of these social locations benefit me in the university.

I had both children during summer months; at my university, faculty are on ten-month contracts, so I received no paid leave. There was no on-campus child-care center when I had my first child, though one was created three years later when I had my second. After having my first child, I took an unpaid leave for a semester to not return to teaching when my son was six weeks old; after having my daughter, I took a year-long sabbatical. I was able to take these leaves because of my partner's salary and my tenure-stream job that grants sabbaticals.

Over the past six years, I served as chair, and then as a member of our university's Family-Friendly Policies Committee (now called the Work-Life Balance Committee). On this committee, we developed several policies that were approved and have been implemented across the university: an increase in paid leave for childbearing/adoption among faculty and staff from three to six weeks, a policy allowing faculty to stop the tenure clock for a year because of caregiving demands, slight changes to the university calendar to make it more consistent with the local public school system calendar, and a lactation policy (required by the federal government). We also surveyed faculty and staff to assess their needs for work-life policies, created awards for supervisors who support work-life balance, and updated the university website to better publicize the family-friendly policies that exist.

In our experience, the most effective strategy to persuade the university administration to implement more family-friendly policies has been to provide them with data on benchmark universities and argue that our university falls short; this was crucial in the implementing several of the policies implemented. However, our committee has long considered a part-time faculty option, in which faculty could reduce their work hours because of caregiving demands for a period of one to three years; the committee has also repeatedly discussed a "modified duties" policy that would provide a semester leave from teaching to faculty with caregiving demands. The university administration has supported neither of these policies, perhaps because these policies are not as common as short-term paid leaves and policies to stop the tenure clock. Thus, the benchmarking strategy is limited.

Based on the results on our survey of faculty and staff, our committee found that some faculty oppose part-time or modified duties policies. Survey data, combined with anecdotal accounts, suggest that older faculty members—many of whom worked for decades in an institution with very few family-friendly policies and came of age under more traditional gender arrangements in families and workplaces—are less likely to support these policies. Some faculty members see these policies as "special privileges for parents" and believe it is unfair that faculty without caregiving demands cannot qualify for them. Although our committee has been quick to point out that most family-friendly policies include leaves for those caring for spouses or ailing parents (in addition to children), it is not clear our arguments have been persuasive.

I also believe these resistant attitudes point to the need for cultural change in our definition of the academic worker; if the ideal academic worker continues to be an unencumbered (male) worker who can work unbounded work hours, part-time and modified duties policies may receive little support. On the other hand, changing policies and changes in social norms and interactions could help challenge this ideal academic worker and support a more balanced worker who is dedicated to her job and also to life outside of it.

In addition, our university has a perennial problem regarding the lack of knowledge of family-friendly policies, even though they are somewhat more publicized on the university website. A few months ago, a department chair (not mine) contacted me to ask about what policies existed for a female faculty member who was giving birth at the beginning of the spring semester, showing that department chairs have not been trained about the existence of family-friendly policies. As Mason and colleagues (2013) suggest, administrators, deans, and chairs need to not only know about policies but also publicly support them before there is wide uptake of these policies.

In sum, my personal experience with family-friendly policies supports the theoretical and empirical accounts discussed; more generous policies, and challenges to the culture of unbounded work hours among faculty (and the idea that mothers are the best caregivers for children) are necessary for a family-friendly university. As more female and male faculty use family-friendly policies and slowly challenge outdated cultural beliefs about work and family, universities will ideally become places where faculty can be both committed workers and hands-on parents who "have it all" — provided having it all requires reasonable work hours, not unbounded ones. As the work-family literature suggests and my experience affirms, both policy and cultural changes are needed for a truly family-friendly university. The most effective policies may well be those that support men's involvement in caregiving, as cross-national research on "daddy leaves" shows that when men take paid leaves, they spend more time with children during and after leaves and have more egalitarian divisions of unpaid labor than men who do not take paid leaves (Reeves and Sawhill, 2015). Family-friendly policies can foster gender-egalitarian families.

REFERENCES

Arendell, T. (2000). Conceiving and investigating motherhood: The decade's scholarship. *Journal of Marriage and the Family, 64*(4), 1192–1207.

Blair-Loy, M. (2003). *Competing devotions: career and family among women executives.* Cambridge, MA: Harvard University Press.

Christopher, K. (2012). Extensive mothering: Employed mothers' constructions of the good mother. *Gender and Society, 26*(1), 73–96.

Christopher, K. (2013). African Americans' and Latinas' mothering scripts: An intersectional analysis. *Advances in Gender Research, 17,* 187–208.

Collins, P. H. (2008). *Black feminist thought: Knowledge, consciousness, and the politics of empowerment.* New York, NY: Routledge Classics.

Damaske, S. (2014). Pregnant in a publish or perish position? New research suggests productivity levels won't suffer. Blog entry on *Gender and Society* blog. Retrieved March 8, 2017, from https://gendersociety.wordpress.com/2014/12/16/pregnant-in-a-publish-or-perish-position/

Damaske, S., Ecklund, E. H., and Lincoln, A. E. (2014). Male scientists' competing devotions to work and family: Changing norms in a male-dominated profession. *Work and Occupations, 41*(4), 477–507.

Dean, P., Marsh, K., and Landry, B. (2013). Cultural contradiction or integration? Work-family schemas of Black middle class mothers. *Advances in Gender Research, 17,* 137–158.

Ecklund, E. H., and Lincoln, A. E. (2011). Scientists want more children. *Plos One.* Retrieved March 3, 2017, http://journals.plos.org/plosone/article?id=10.1371/journal.pone.0022590

Hays, S. (1996). *The cultural contradictions of motherhood.* New Haven, CT: Yale University Press.

Hochschild, A. (1997). *The time bind: When work becomes home and home becomes work.* New York, NY: Henry Holt.

Jacobs, J. A., and Winslow, S. E. (2004). Overworked faculty: Job stresses and family demands. *The ANNALS of the American Academy of Political and Social Science, 596,* 104–129.

Krapf, M., Ursprung, H. W., and Zimmermann, C. (2014). Parenthood and productivity of highly skilled labor: Evidence from the groves of academe. Working paper of Research Division, Federal Reserve Bank of St Louis. Retrieved March 8, 2017, from http://research.stlouisfed.org/wp/2014/2014-001.pdf.

Mason, M. A., Wolfinger, N. H., and Goulden, M. (2013). *Do babies matter? Gender and family in the ivory tower.* New Brunswick, NJ: Rutgers.

Misra, J., Lundquist, J. H., Holmes, E. D., and Agiomavritis, S. (2011). The ivory ceiling of service work (AAUP Report). Retrieved March 8, 2017, http://www.aaup.org/article/ivory-ceiling-service-work#.VQnxNuHlzwg.

Ollilainen, M., and Solomon, C. R. (2014). Carving a "third path": Faculty parents' resistance to the ideal academic worker norm. *Advances in Gender Research, 19,* 21–39.

Pedulla, D. S., and Thébaud, S. (2015). Can we finish the revolution? Gender, work-family ideals, and institutional constraint. *American Sociological Review, 80*(1), 116–139.

Pew Research Center. (2013). Modern Parenthood. Retrieved March 8, 2017, http://www.pewsocialtrends.org/2013/03/14/modern-parenthood-roles-of-moms-and-dads-converge-as-they-balance-work-and-family/.

Reeves, R., and Sawhill, I. (November 14, 2015). Men's lib! *New York Times,* p. SR1.

Risman, B. (2004). Gender as a social structure: Theory wrestling with activism. *Gender & Society, 18*(4), 429–450.

Sayer, L. C., Bianchi, S. M., and Robinson, J. P. (2004). Are parents investing less in children? Trends in mothers' and fathers' time with children. *American Journal of Sociology, 110*(1), 1–43.

Slaughter, A-M. (2012, July). Why women still can't have it all. *The Atlantic.* Retrieved March 8, 2017, from https://www.theatlantic.com/magazine/archive/2012/07/why-women-still-cant-have-it-all/309020/

Spalter-Roth, R., and Van Vooren, N. (2012). Mothers in pursuit of ideal academic careers. ASA Research Brief. Retrieved March 8, 2017, http://www.asanet.org/documents/research/docs/Mothers_Ideal_Acad_Careers_2012.pdf

Story, K. A. (2014). *Living my material: An interview with Patricia Hill Collins. Patricia Hill Collins: Reconceiving Motherhood.* Bradford, Ontario, Canada: Demeter Press.

Wharton, A., and Estevez, M. (2014). Department chairs' perspectives on work, family, and gender. *Advances in Gender Research, 19,* 131–150.

Williams, J. C., and Dempsey, R. (2014). *What works for women at work: Four patterns working women need to know.* New York: New York University Press.

FOUR

Faculty Perspectives of Teaching Online

Shirley Peganoff O'Brien

INTRODUCTION

The nature of teaching at the university level is a faculty role that is shifting quickly from traditional classrooms to web-blended offerings and fully online options. Online education and teaching has changed greatly over the last decade with 90 percent of four-year public institutions offering some type of online education (Crawford-Ferre and Wiest, 2012). More and more faculty are offering courses and select programs online. The proliferation of open access courses, along with university initiatives, expanding access to students has challenged faculty to review their need for professional development, pedagogical stances, and exploration of delivery methods. Online teaching is complex and can be demanding.

Online education presents a new context in which faculty consider their work roles, particularly about decisions shaping their academic careers (Hopewell, 2012). Some faculty have embraced the opportunity to move toward online education, whereas others remain skeptical. Placing adoption of online teaching by faculty into a leadership role and change theoretical context provides a lens to understand acceptance of the delivery method. Consideration of the concepts of "how" and "why" are important in discussing faculty options for participating in online teaching (Sinek, 2012).

Rogers (2003) described in his seminal text, *Diffusions of Innovations*, a change model for adopting technological innovation. In this model the how, why, and at what rate new concepts, ideas, and technology are accepted, adopted, and propagated in social systems were explained. Rogers's first three categories in the change process—innovators, early adopters, and early majority—offer a framework for understanding in this chapter.

Innovators get the idea started, early adopters spread the word, and early majority individuals jump in to create a critical mass. Faculty members across disciplines have lept at opportunities to serve in these three categories of innovation in academic decision making for the delivery of course content, many of them females. As such, they have contributed to the critical mass acceptance of online teaching.

Further exploration about how the movement into online education has impacted faculty roles is also considered. What are the opportunities and challenges of participating in this delivery method on a faculty member's career? Where does it fit best? Another area for deliberation for faculty considering online teaching is professional development before engaging in the new teaching arena. Many faculty do not invest the necessary time in professional development activities to develop the pedagogical approach in a strategic manner (Pinchevsky-Font and Dunbar, 2015; Delahunty, Verenikina, and Jones, 2014). This often leads to frustration and lack of satisfaction on the part of both the instructor and students enrolled in the course.

Understanding the core institutional mission and a faculty member's role should be overt. However, many covert messages are shared by well-intentioned colleagues, often questioning preparation for tenure or promotion. This chapter describes the onset of online education in post-secondary education institutions, formerly referred to as distance education, skills of successful online faculty, and female faculty members' perspectives both from personal accounts and those in the literature. The cases shared in this chapter will follow Rogers's framework of the change model for technological innovation, along with an understanding of the how and why of online teaching for success in an academic career. This chapter will expand this theoretical premise into the online delivery mode, highlighting opportunities and challenges in time use, commitments, and professional scholarship. Strategies for success will be presented, from a first-person perspective.

WHAT DOES IT TAKE TO BE SUCCESSFUL
AS AN ONLINE INSTRUCTOR?

As faculty move between traditional courses and the online environment, new routines develop for work patterns. Skill sets for technology use, implementation of web-based learning strategies, and fostering student engagement can be viewed as challenges for faculty at all levels in career ages. Innovators, early adopters, and faculty in the early majority of adoption of an idea possess a growth mind-set that contributes to success in the online community (Dweck, 2006). They are keenly aware of their strengths, areas for growth, and actively seek growth opportunities in thoughts and practices.

The initial learning curve for faculty moving into online education greatly impacts workload, with increased time needed in planning and preparation (Baran and Correia, 2014; Freeman, 2015; Tallent-Runnels et al., 2006). Institutions that value the transition into developing online courses often support faculty with reassigned time or financial incentives. However, it should be noted that faculty motivation for teaching online often is more of a personal decision (Meyer, 2012; Orr, Williams and Pennington, 2009).

Some faculty have reached a career stage where they are seeking new challenges or desire to improve teaching skills. They understand the need to fundamentally change how they teach and are willing to put forth the effort in professional development. New faculty may possess a terminal degree in the respective discipline, typically beginning their first position with a student understanding of how to produce scholarship rather than understanding pedagogical methods. Moving into a teaching role requires a different skill set often developed over the pretenure years. Using past learning experiences in a traditional face-to-face classroom setting does not serve faculty well in the transition to online environments. Thus, understanding the movement of faculty to online teaching is complex.

Baran, Correia, and Thompson (2013) identified exemplary practices for faculty success in online education. These practices are possessing content knowledge to create course content, designing and structuring an online course, knowing the students, enhancing teacher-student relationships, guiding student learning, evaluating online courses, and maintaining teacher presence. One can note similarities in principles of teaching between both traditional and online classrooms; however, moving a class from a traditional format is just not about transporting content between the two contexts.

Implementation of online courses provides an opportunity for faculty to reassess what they teach, as well as how and why they teach. Course instructors must consider how the practices are employed, with the faculty assuming the role of course architect. These teaching practices require an ongoing commitment to learning and professional development about pedagogy in the online environment.

SEEKING A PERSONAL UNDERSTANDING OF FACULTY INVOLVEMENT IN ONLINE EDUCATION

I have taught using distance-learning technology (the precursor to what we now label online learning) since the mid-1990s. I could be classified as an innovator/early adopter. The "why" (Sinek, 2012) for me was about access of education for those who were place-bound in my discipline. Advanced knowledge and leadership opportunities existed, along with institutional support in the development of courses. Then with the movement to online, I saw opportunity and challenge to improve my teaching and position myself into a niche and blend professional/personal responsibilities in my roles. For me, it was a win-win. That is the short version of my story, the subjective perspective. But what about colleagues in higher education? How did they decide to move into teaching online?

An environmental scan approach gathering strengths, weaknesses, opportunities, and threats (SWOT) was employed to create discussion with female faculty members about the topic. The SWOT technique uses the concept of weaknesses, which I refer to as challenges. The use of professional social media sites were used to obtain broad thoughts. LinkedIn, The Teaching Professor, and ResearchGate provided a starting point to explore the topic. Posts elicited basic information, supporting much of the literature. Female faculty were invited to respond to interviews to add clarity to understanding of time use, commitments, and impacts on professional scholarship. Faculty (*n*=9) that offered perceptions about the topic had extensive teaching experience (more than five years) and held tenure-track positions. Three participants reported holding adjunct or nontenure-track positions. Pseudonyms are used in this chapter to protect the anonymity of participants. Their vignettes add credence to the literature on the topic.

ONLINE AS A DELIVERY METHOD IN TEACHING: THE BENEFITS

The SWOT Analysis responses were combined into two categories: Strengths/Opportunities and Challenges (Weaknesses)/Threats. Faculty responses overlapped with a blurring of internal university perspectives (flexibility and supports available) and external disciplinary understanding and socialization toward participation in online education. External factors encompassed disciplinary expectations of reward systems and tenure. All faculty members that commented were categorized as early adopters or early majority in terms of their interest and desire to engage in online teaching.

Strengths/Opportunities

Early adopters were quick to identify the need for changes in role perceptions and teaching strategies to be successful in online teaching. Those that have mastered online teaching believe they played a key role in student learning and had developed teaching practices synonymous with Scholarship of Teaching/Learning (SoTL) expectation of reflection, practice, feedback, evaluation, and modification (Bishop-Clark and Dietz-Uhler, 2012; Felten 2013). By jumping into online teaching, faculty found an internal spark for inspiring their teaching practices.

"It depends what motivates you. For me it is the flexibility of work time," said Susan, a tenured professor.

Female faculty members reported autonomy and flexibility as strengths/opportunities in why they choose to teach courses online rein-forcing literature perspectives (Conceição, 2006; Huang and Hsiao, 2012; Price, 2006; Raggl and Troman, 2008). Participating as online instructors allowed for freedom about where they lived, when they worked, and how they collaborated with a variety of institutions for adjuncts. Several women commented on how online teaching provided a sense of harmony in their professional and personal roles, allowing them to multitask and juggle responsibilities. Multitasking is a benefit of teaching online.

Family responsibilities came to the forefront in discussions, with opportunities to set their own work schedules and still be available for family as a primary reason to engage in online teaching. Fluid time use allowed for juggling of responsibilities, affording autonomy in setting schedules at the university, in the community, and in the home. Working from afar (not place bound to an institution) was also viewed as a benefit of online education. Self-discipline and motivation were underlying threads viewed in responses, reinforcing the literature about time use (Baran and Correia, 2014; Moore, 2014; McQuiggan, 2012; Windes and Lesht, 2014). Faculty commenting on the discussion threads valued preparation and were motivated by learning new tools.

Another important characteristic for success and beneficial in online education is communication. Communication can take place synchronously and asynchronously, depending on the purpose (Huang and Hsiao, 2012; Keengwe and Kidd, 2010; Moore, 2014; Tallent-Runnels et al., 2006). Asynchronous learning requires both the faculty and student to be self-disciplined in their time use and ability to communicate effectively using technology.

Faculty commented on needing to pre-plan communications, unlike those that just evolve in a traditional classroom setting. Stephanie, a non-tenured lecturer, stated, "I use the Announcement Page on our LMS and email to communicate with students. There are many ways to do it, like podcasts. I used these tools in my graduate program, so I am familiar with them. You just have to be open to the use of technology to meet your need."

Communicating with students is a needed skill for success in online education. Many options are available, depending on the purpose and the type of engagement as Stephanie alludes. Email is the typical one-on-one communication, along with the use of personal journals within a learning management system (LMS), such as Blackboard, Canvas, or Moodle. Blogs, discussion boards, tweeting, and texting can serve a purpose in communicating asynchronously. Depending on the structure of prompts, students can move from lower-ordering thinking (remembering and understanding) into applying, analyzing, and evaluating course content (Churches, 2008; Krathwohl and Anderson, 2010).

Clarity in guidelines for discussions is essential. Paula, a tenured associate professor, said, "Good teaching in an online course isn't just about making the topic palatable to students. It's also about building a sense of community and engaging the students to form relationships, not just with the instructor, but their peers and the content as well."

Paula's comment adds an important dimension to an opportunity in online education—that of building community and relatedness among the student group in the course. In the traditional classroom, this is often referred to as the use of active learning strategies in a community of learners. Just as in the face-to face setting, instructors can create an engaged environment through the use of multimedia tools for active learning.

Successful use of multimedia elements necessitates a solid purpose in the course, and an advance knowledge of how to use various tools to facilitate active learning online (Boettcher and Conrad, 2010; Baran, Correia, and Thompson, 2013; Jones, 2015). Creating a personal atmosphere is important; however, it takes a different shape, requiring effort on behalf of the faculty. Connection with the student is key to success in the course. This can take the shape of interaction in a virtual office area or group forums. Typical relational sharing is common in a traditional classroom (e.g., sharing life events and personal stories), a component needed also in the online environment. Seeing the professor as a real person who shares insights regularly reinforces the community experience. Several faculty discussed how they have learned to use podcasts and videos created on their laptop to engage students, but this training requires advanced professional development on the part of the faculty member.

Creating social presence is another element that is expected in quality online education, based on constructivist theory. Social presence humanizes the online environment. Learning to build social presence requires faculty to develop knowledge and skills with technological tools. Faculty satisfaction with online teaching is directly linked to the ability to foster interaction between three key elements: the student with the instructor, the content, and group interaction (Bolliger and Wasilik, 2009;

Keengwe and Kidd, 2010; Kehrwald, 2010; Mills, Yanes, and Casebeer, 2009; Swan, 2004; Swan and Ice, 2009). Fostering interaction requires a dynamic appreciation of how each element supports the others, with the faculty assuming the ultimate role as facilitator and curator. Karen, a tenured professor, noted:

> Online teaching rejuvenated my academic career. I am in there with my students, summarizing what I see happening on the weekly activities. I am good at it, students like it and my colleagues recognize me for my skills. Teaching online has also positively impacted my classroom teaching.

The skills used by faculty in online teaching can reinforce best practices in the traditional classroom, a benefit of teaching online. In the online environment, faculty reconstruct their understanding of how they teach, their beliefs about teaching, and how students learn. Faculty teaching in traditional classrooms may become subject to habit, using what has worked in the past, requiring minimal effort. In the online world, faculty are required to develop their repertoire of teaching tools, to infuse and inject knowledge across multiple mediums.

Having a grasp and ability to use the teaching techniques is vital. One can be an expert in their field, but if you cannot effectively impart this knowledge to the learner, frustration occurs both for the instructor and the student. Pedagogically, there is a need for the use of multimedia products, both in content delivery and in the student products/assignments. Expanding the use of multimedia, coupled with purposeful pedagogy, addresses and acknowledges broad learning needs of the online population and helps to create best practice for reaching diverse students (Delahunty, Verenikina, and Jones, 2014).

Transferring pedagogical practices used for student engagement within a web-enhanced course can reinforce and benefit face-to-face learning (Education Advisory Board, 2010; Shattuck, Dubins and Zilberman, 2011). If faculty members have a positive experience using a tool in the online world, they are more apt to implement it during a face-to-face course (Scagnoli, Buki, and Johnson, 2009). Online teaching keeps faculty cognitively engaged in an intense manner, requiring the ability to stay engaged in discussions, maintaining focus for the class as a group, while sustaining a mental picture of the unique learners in the online setting. Thus, development of online skills impacts occupational competence in teaching.

Professional development and support systems are critical to the success of online education. Professional development about teaching online is both a key strength and opportunity offered by the various institutions. The literature on faculty development of teaching practices in online education reinforces the need for institutional commitment (Baran and Correia, 2014; Farber, 2013; Schmidt, Hodge and Tschida, 2013).

University investment is consistently noted and appreciated by faculty responding to social media forums. Professional development can take many forms, both formal and informal. Examples include orientation programs, boot camps, short courses, learning communities, and teaching support groups. Professional development when missing, becomes a weakness and threat to the overall success of faculty in an online context.

Technology support is another aspect that is considered both a strength and opportunity, both for tool use and resource needs in the seamless delivery of content. This is especially true for adjunct faculty teaching a course for an institution.

Online tutorials and availability of a technology support were viewed necessary components for development. Use of instructional designers is a practice for consideration supporting faculty as they move into an online context (Conceição, 2006; Cook and Steinert, 2013; Orr, Williams, and Pennington, 2009). The blending of context experts (faculty) with technology experts (instructional designers) allows a marriage of the best of both worlds. Instructional designers often possess the knowledge of how to best engage students online and can support faculty desires for facilitating social presence. However, when instructional designers are not available, trial-and-error learning is a commonly suggested alternative. Female faculty who dabbled in online education early at their various institutions referred to trial-and-error learning as a willingness to take risks. Their feedback again reinforces the characteristics of early adopters.

Challenges/Threats

There are several clear challenges to faculty engagement in the adoption of online learning. With additional support, many of these challenges could be viewed as opportunities. These concerns offer an important consideration in a faculty role at various key career stages. Teresa, a tenured professor, commented:

> You get power, because I stepped up at a time when there was a need—I crafted it, and it allowed me an expertise. It also gave me flexibility with my family. I could teach three courses online and one on-campus course. It really gave me flexibility. BUT I was tenured when I did this.

Teresa's account addresses an important consideration: job security through tenure. Academic and professional expectations vary by discipline and institution. No agreement has been established on how online teaching should fit into promotion and tenure criteria (Hopewell, 2012; Windes and Lesht, 2014). Institutional initiatives need clarity about how participation in online teaching may impact faculty evaluation and rewards. Most tenure reviews include consideration of teaching, research/

scholarship, and service activities. The teaching aspect is an important consideration, particularly in teaching-mission institutions.

Online teaching requires an acknowledgment of effective teaching skills. Each of the women faculty discussed the importance of sound pedagogy and teaching methods as prerequisite knowledge. All had reported tinkering with web-enhanced teaching, using their respective learning management systems (e.g., Blackboard, Canvas, and Moodle) before attempting fully online delivery of course content. Style, organization, and ease of navigation all can be the source of challenges for effective participation in an online course.

Faculty development and technology support are critical in addressing this potential threat to the success of the faculty member. One of the challenges of teaching online is making your course different than in-person classes while meeting program requirements and course objectives, and creating activities and course structures in the online environment. Another weakness or potential threat is faculty staying "too basic" in their use of technology.

Faculty embrace a technique (e.g., discussion boards) without fully considering the how aspect of their use. There are easy solutions to this problem, with the integration of cognitive learning strategies, such as Bloom's Taxonomy Revised as adopted with technical media in construction of the engagement tool (Churches, 2008; Krathwohl and Anderson, 2010). Colleagues may question the legitimacy of evidence available for online teaching practices (Baran, Correia, and Thompson, 2013; Jones, 2015; Windes and Lesht, 2014). These colleagues have not yet achieved adoption of online course delivery methods and are part of the late majority or laggards (Rogers, 2003), demonstrating negative attitudes about the new delivery environment. Faculty rely on their past experiences and some are just not suited for online teaching (Chen and Chen, 2006; McQuiggan, 2012; Mills, Yanes, and Casebeer, 2009; Schmidt, Hodge, and Tschida, 2013). These individuals may continually challenge peer faculty about their pedagogical practices as evidenced by Susan's experience: "I had this colleague that questioned the evidence of online course delivery and my commitment. She just didn't get it. She lacks the desire to pursue professional development opportunities, unlike me that seeks every opportunity."

Susan highlights an important aspect of how to address the legitimacy challenge. This requires professional development and the knowledge of alternative tools that can foster engagement of students online. Faculty desire to engage in professional development may reflect where they are in their career age/stage. Those who are innovators, early adopters, and members of the early majority are more apt to engage in reflection and move toward scholarly teaching (McQuiggan, 2012). They set teaching goals and implement career strategies for success. Institutional commitment to faculty development often targets full-time faculty, which is a weakness in resource allocation.

Part-time faculty are hired to fulfill teaching needs and may possess content expertise but may not be prepared pedagogically to step into an online environment. Thus, part-time faculty continuing educational needs are a threat to effective online teaching. Adele and Rachel's comments reinforce the challenges present in professional development and teaching skill sets needed.

> I have been teaching online for over twelve years; as online tools have become available, our University Center for Teaching Excellence and Learning Technology has challenged us to use them in innovative ways. Simulating live activities can be exciting when you "think outside the box," and add to your growth as an instructor. (Adele, a tenured professor)
>
> I teach online to stay involved with my discipline and it fits with my family needs. I do miss the freedom of the classroom, you can adjust quicker there. Online takes advanced teaching skills, which are hard to develop in a part-time faculty role. I know that for a fact. (Rachel, nontenured, adjunct professor)

Peer review of teaching in the online environment is a challenge that must be addressed particularly for pretenured individuals and those planning on rank advancement. As noted, teaching online and traditional classroom teaching does require different skill sets. If peer evaluators in a discipline are not aware of the differences, preconceived notions may exist about effectiveness of engagement, content delivery, and tool use (Orr, Williams, and Pennington, 2009). Peer review of teaching is an area for advanced professional development, both at the institutional and disciplinary levels.

Teaching online offers flexibility, yet requires trust by institutional colleagues and other stakeholders of one's alternative work schedule. This is a potential threat for new faculty establishing their career. Meyer (2012) cautioned new faculty in their struggle to understand academic roles and responsibilities to approach online teaching assignments with careful consideration.

Faculty teaching split loads of traditional and online courses discussed the need to share with supervisors their work routines. Peer judgment often was negative toward faculty not available for service roles (e.g., committee meetings) at traditional times. This may reflect poorly when peers evaluate collegiality in performing one's faculty role. Karen, a tenured professor, asked, "How often do you see us asking a male faculty member why they are not at work from 9–5? Yet, my colleagues raise an eye when I am away on Tuesday and Thursday, even if I am working on my online courses at home."

Although identified as a strength, time is also a threat for faculty teaching online. It is documented that online courses are more time-consuming and require an investment by the faculty (Sword, 2012). Karen's comments demonstrate a potential discrepancy in how time is used when teaching online, particularly with a split course load. She identified a gender bias.

Women are reported to work harder than male counterparts, valuing different aspects of the work setting (Price, 2006; Raggl and Troman, 2008). Another aspect of time, engagement, requires faculty availability, monitoring and facilitating students. Learning how to use tools to evaluate engagement in many forms takes time, development, and learning. Setting time into schedules to perform competency self-assessments is part of the online role function. A successful faculty member has to "rethink" their use of pedagogy.

Faculty teaching online do have to set parameters and priorities or they have the potential to lose themselves in the teaching role; neglecting scholarship and service expectations of the university setting; a clear threat to a successful academic career. Faculty engaging in online teaching do have freedom to schedule their time, can and do continue to participate in altered work patterns, but must be cautious to prevent collegial sabotage.

Online teaching provides an opportunity for faculty to delve into pedagogical research following SoTL traditions (Bishop-Clark and Dietz-Uhler, 2012; Felten, 2013; McQuiggan, 2012). SoTL research is an evolving area, with varying levels of acceptance in traditional university reward structures. To be successful, faculty research should add specificity about instructional pedagogy in context, following best practices in SoTL.

Personalized learning needs and the dynamic nature of online education reinforce the need for professional development in not only the latest tools, but to have institutional support available from instructional designers. Mobile devices and the explosion of apps to create content are all considerations for faculty and their choice in course construction and learning products. Use of web 2.0 interactive technology, such as blogs, wikis, mash-ups, and social networking, requires greater levels of expertise and specialization; however, with more web-blended courses, this expertise is moving into the skill set of today's educator. Students look for long-standing application in collaboration and learning assignments. This is an aspect of online teaching that must receive priority at both institutional and faculty level decision making.

Given the complexity of teaching, online burnout may occur (Hogan and McKnight, 2007). Faculty needs for professional development and time are critical elements to monitor. Instructors in online education must self-assess, take into consideration the various challenges and threats along with potential solutions to preserve a productive work life.

Expectations change throughout the course of an individual's faculty career. Online teaching is not for the faint of heart; however, those who teach online consistently comment that it does help to improve their teaching. As faculty embark on a career, they need to find harmony in the intersections of teaching, scholarship/research, and service expectations in the discipline and the institution. Within university reward systems, agreement is negotiated for success, unique to the individual, his or her needs, and his or her institution.

CONCLUSION

Online courses in higher education have grown in scope and volume in the past decade. It is critical to prepare and support academicians in the movement to teaching in the online environment. Increased use of web-blended technology within traditional courses will continue to blur faculty roles and workload expectations. A one-size-fits-all approach to educational policy and delivery of online education will not serve any of the stakeholders effectively.

Faculty roles as early adopters and early majority users have created a critical mass acceptance. This group has developed effective competencies and strategies for success in online education. The time has come for the early adopters to once again contribute to advanced research in online pedagogy to assist the late adopters' movement from skepticism to levels of acceptance. Faculty development should remain a priority, addressing the varying levels of institutional adoption of online education. Academic reward structures must address the intricacies of faculty participation in online teaching to best inform future decisions impacting faculty careers within both the institution and discipline.

The decision to engage in online teaching is a complex issue. Personal choices and motivations, institutional needs, and career stage/age all impact one's desire to embark in online teaching as a part of an academic career. As female faculty members consider the journey, weighing the career opportunities along with the challenges will serve as beneficial advice for a successful career.

REFERENCES

Baran, E., and Correia, A. P. (2014). A professional development framework for online teaching. *TechTends, 58*(5), 96–102.

Baran, E., Correia, A. P., and Thompson, A. D. (2013). Tracing successful online teaching in higher education: Voices of exemplary online teachers. *Teachers College Record, 115*(3), 1–41.

Bishop-Clark, C., and Dietz-Uhler, B. (2012). *Engaging in the scholarship of teaching and learning: A guide to the process, and how to develop a project from start to finish.* Sterling, VA: Stylus.

Boettcher, J. V. and Conrad, R. M. (2010). *The online teaching survival guide: Simple and practical pedagogical tips.* San Francisco: Jossey-Bass.

Bolliger, D. U., and Wasilik, O. (2009). Factors influencing faculty satisfaction with online teacher and learning in higher education. *Distance Education, 30*(1), 103–116. doi: 10.1080/01587910902845949.

Chen, T. L., and Chen, T. J. (2006). Examination of attitudes towards teaching online courses based on theory of reasoned action of university faculty in Taiwan. *British Journal of Educational Technology,* 37(5), 683–693. doi: 10.1111/j.1467-8535.2006.00590.x.

Churches, A. (2008). Bloom's digital taxonomy. Retrieved March 8, 2017, from http://burtonslifelearning.pbworks.com/f/BloomDigitalTaxonomy2001.pdf.

Conceição, S. C. O. (2006). Faculty lived experiences in the online environment. *Adult Education Quarterly,* 57(1), 26–45. doi: 10.1177/1059601106292247.

Cook, D. A., and Steinert, Y. (2013). Online learning for faculty development: A review of the literature. *Medical Teacher, 35*(11), 930–937. doi: 10.3109/0142159X.2013.827328.

Crawford-Ferre, H. G. and Wiest, L. R. (2012). Effective online institutions in higher education. *The Quarterly Review of Distance Education, 13*(2), 11–14.

Delahunty, J., Verenikina, I., and Jones, P. (2014). Socio-emotional connections: Identity, belonging and learning in online interactions. A literature review. *Technology, Pedagogy and Education. 23*(2), 243–265. doi: 10.1080/1475939x.2013.813405.

Dweck, C. S. (2006). *Mindset.* New York: Ballantine Books.

Education Advisory Board. (2010). *Engaging faculty in online education: Rightsizing incentives and optimizing support.* Washington, DC: author.

Farber, R. S. (2013). Distance education and teaching online: My journey from mystery to mastery. *Occupational Therapy in Health Care, 27*(3), 272–279. doi: 10.3109/07380577.2013.809180.

Felten, P. (2013). Principles of good practice in SoTL. *Teaching and Learning Inquiry: The ISSOTL Journal, 1*(1), 121–125. Retrieved March 8, 2017, from http://www.jstor.org/stable/10.2979/teachlearninqu.1.1.121.

Freeman, L. A. (2015). Instructor time requirements to develop and teach online courses. *Online Journal of Distance Learning Administration, 18*(1). Retrieved March 8, 2017, from http://www.westga.edu/~distance/ojdla/spring181/freeman181.html.

Hogan, R. L., and McKnight, M. A. (2007). Exploring burnout among university online instructors: An initial investigation. *The Internet and Higher Education, 10*(2), 117–24.

Hopewell, T. M. (2012 Winter). Risks associated with the choice to teach online. *Online Journal of Distance Learning Administration, 15*(4).

Huang, X. S., and Hsiao, E. L. (2012). Synchronous and asynchronous communication in an online environment: Faculty experiences and perceptions. *The Quarterly Review of Distance Education, 13*(1), 15–30.

Jones, S. H. (2015). Benefits and challenges of online education for clinical social work: Three examples. *Clinical Social Work Journal, 43,* 225–235. doi: 10.1007/s10615-014-0508-z.

Keengwe, J., and Kidd, T. T. (2010). Towards best practices in online learning and teaching in higher education. *MERLOT Journal of Online Learning and Teaching, 6*(2), 533–541.

Kehrwald, B. (2010). Being online: Social presence as subjectivity in online learning. *London Review of Education, 8*(1), 39–50.

Krathwohl, D. R., and Anderson, L. W. (2010). Merlin C. Wittrock and the revision of Bloom's taxonomy. *Educational Psychologist, 45*(1), 64–65.

McQuiggan, C. A. (2012). Faculty development for online teaching as a catalyst for change. *Journal of Asynchronous Learning Networks, 16*(2), 27–61.

Meyer, K. A. (2012). The influence of online teaching on faculty productivity. *Innovative Higher Education, 37*(1), 37–52. doi: 10.1007/s10755-011-9183-y.

Mills, S. J., Yanes, M. J., and Casebeer, C. M. (2009). Perceptions of distance learning among faculty of a college of education. *MERLOT Journal of Online Learning and Teaching, 5*(1), 19–28.

Moore, J. (2014). Effects of online interaction and instructor presence on students' satisfaction and success with online undergraduate public relations courses. *Journalism and Mass Communication Educator, 69*(3), 271–288. doi: 10.1177/1077695814536398.

Orr, R., Williams, M. R., and Pennington, K. (2009). Institutional efforts to support faculty in online teaching. *Innovative Higher Education, 34*(4), 257–268. doi: 10.1007/s10755-009-9111-6.

Pinchevsky-Font, T., and Dunbar, S. (2015). Best practices for online teaching and learning in health care related programs. *The Internet Journal of Allied Health Sciences and Practice, 13*(1), Article 8.

Price, L. (2006). Gender differences and similarities in online courses: Challenging stereotypical views of women. *Journal of Computer Assisted Learning, 22*(5), 349–359.

Raggl, A., and Troman, G. (2008). Turning to teaching: Gender and career choice. *British Journal of Sociology of Education, 29*(6), 581–595. doi: 10.1080/01425690802423254.

Rogers, E. M. (2003). *Diffusion of Innovations* (5th ed.). New York: Free Press.

Scagnoli, N. I., Buki, L. P., and Johnson, S. D. (2009). The influence of online teaching on face-to-face teaching practices. *Journal of Asynchronous Learning Networks, 13*(2), 115–128.

Schmidt, S. W., Hodge, E. M., and Tschida, C. M. (2013). How university faculty members developed their online teaching skills. *The Quarterly Review of Distance Education, 14*(3), 131–140.

Shattuck, J., Dubins, B., and Zilberman, D. (2011). Maryland Online's inter-institutional project to train higher education adjunct faculty to teach online. *International Review of Research in Open and Distance Learning, 12*(2), 40–61.

Sinek, S. (2012) Start with Why. TED TALK. Retrieved March 8, 2017, from https://www.youtube.com/watch?v=IPYeCltXpxw.

Swan, K. (2004). Relationships between interactions and learning in online environments. *The Slone Consortium*, 1-3. Retrieved March 8, 2017, from https://pdfs.semanticscholar.org/7c1c/9f20d639c967a1ef6cf8a2c01da767208f48.pdf.

Swan, K., and Ice, P. (2009). The community of inquiry framework ten years later: Introduction to the special issue. *Internet and Higher Education, 13*(1–2), 1–4.

Sword, T. S. (2012). The transition to online teaching as experienced by nurse educators. *Nursing Education Perspectives, 33*(4), 269–271.

Tallent-Runnels, M. K., Thomas, J. A., Lan, W. Y., Cooper, S., Ahern, T. C., Shaw, S. M., and Liu, X. (2006). Teaching courses online: A review of the research. *Review of Educational Research, 76*(1), 93–135.

Windes, D. L., and Lesht, F. L. (2014). The effects of online teaching experience and institution type on faculty perceptions of teaching online. *Online Journal of Distance Learning Administration, 17*(1). Retrieved March 8, 2017, from https://www.learntechlib.org/p/155627.

FIVE

Women of Color in Higher Education

Asian, Latina, and African American Women as Teachers, Scholars, and Leaders

Carolyn A. Lin, Diana I. Rios, and Ruth Washington

INTRODUCTION

Fifty years beyond the Civil Rights Act of 1964, racial and ethnic tensions in our society spiked anew—as a result of widespread civil rights concerns—involving police treatment of minorities. The higher-education establishment, a presumed proving ground for inclusion and diversity over the decades, appears to be at a crossroads regarding racial and ethnic relations as well. Issues related to racial conflicts have led to the resignation of several major public university chancellors and presidents in the 2015–2016 academic year. The culmination of these events suggests that productive discourse on race is pressing. In the academy, this discourse should involve the roles that women faculty from racial and ethnic minority groups have on campus, as well as their contributions to improving racial climate and campus culture.

Past research shows faculty can promote interactions between students with different racial backgrounds both inside and outside of the classroom, whether through group projects or infusion of diversity in the course content (Slavin, 1985). Specifically, through peer interactions in a variety of academic settings, students from different racial groups were given the opportunities to work together and learn about one another (Hurtado, Milem, Clayton-Pedersen, and Allen, 1998; Milem, 1998).

When female minority faculty facilitate these student interactions, they not only help increase multicultural understanding between students but also serve as an immediate role model through their actions. Even so, female faculty still face a number of barriers in performing their roles and advancing their careers as teachers, advisors, mentors, researchers, and administrators (Bickel et al., 2002; Cooper and Stevens, 2002; Smith, Altbach, and Lomotey, 2002). In particular, minority female faculty experience unique and greater obstacles in achieving these career goals than do males (Glazer-Raymo, Townsend, and Ropers-Huilman, 2000).

To date, duties of female and male academics differ significantly within the hierarchy of an academic institution. It is well-documented that female faculty disproportionately perform more departmental service and university service as well as spend more time on teaching, when compared to male faculty (Bird, 2010). Male faculty, on the other hand, are overrepresented in the ranks of full professors and senior administrators (Bird, Little, and Wang, 2004). Hence, an overwhelming number of men are in decision-making roles for determining institutional policies as well as the recruitment, promotion, and tenure processes. These roles have given men and White Anglo faculty an advantage over their female and female minority counterparts (Park, 2007; Stewart, Malley, and La-Vaque-Manty, 2007).

In nature, diversity is a living organism and relies on other organisms and the affordances in the ecosystem to survive; the greater the diversity is in an ecosystem, the greater the chances are for the ecosystem to thrive (Holt, 2009). Diversity in higher education, not unlike diversity in nature or the corporate world, helps foster creative ideas, infrastructure stability, and system resilience (Allen and Montgomery, 2001). In academic settings, there are still multiple barriers to increasing gender and racial diversity. For instance, women lack mentoring and social capital for advancing their career, whereas Whites and males have difficulties mentoring ethnic minorities (Thomas, 2001). Consequently, minority women academics could become isolated and reluctant to take risks for advancing their professional goals (Etzkowitz, Kemelgor, and Uzzi, 2000).

This chapter addresses minority women academics' roles as teachers, advisors/mentors, researchers, and administrators. It draws from perspectives of three minority women faculty who represent African American, Asian American, and Latina views. All three faculty have served as teachers, advisors, mentors, and researchers in academic departments as well as held administrative leadership roles.

AN ASIAN AMERICAN PERSPECTIVE

In higher education, Asian Americans, whether they are natural born or naturalized citizens, have made significant contributions (including Nobel laureates) to advances in academia. Even so, Asian Americans are often perceived as "foreigners" because of their phenotypical characteristics. The stereotypical perceptions about Asian women are particularly daunting. They are often expected to be quiet, deferential, and dutiful. Such expectations have made female faculty of Asian descent become "invisible" and disenfranchised, which have led to missing opportunities for advancing their careers as teachers, advisors, mentors, researchers, or administrators. The following examples of four Asian American female faculty located in the Midwest and East Coast illustrate some challenges and triumphs. These are testimonies shared with the first author.

Asian female academicians must often work harder to earn trust and respect as teachers from their students (Ng, 2000). A young Asian female faculty recounted an incident of disrespectful treatment from a White male undergraduate student. Her teaching assistant (an African American male graduate student) who witnessed the event stated to her afterward, "You have a chip on your shoulder because you're neither Black nor White." In other words, she was not seen as an American. In another incident, this Asian female faculty was asked "What is your nationality?" by a White male student during a graduate seminar. Not wanting to cause any more discomfort during class, she replied by identifying her ancestral roots instead of stating that she was an American citizen. Despite these, and other examples of "micro-aggressions" from students, this faculty went on to win a teaching excellence award. Upon reflection, she realized that had most of her students not set aside the stereotypical perceptions about her, she could not have achieved success as a teacher inside and outside of the classroom.

Likewise, when it comes to advising and mentoring students, a second young Asian female faculty's concern centers on whether her students would seek or value her guidance. She recalled how her advisor role also turned into a mentor role for three first-generation and underprivileged undergrads over time. In the first case, she mentored a male student and helped him become the first person to obtain and succeed with a professional job in his family. A second student became the first African American student government president under her tutelage and was accepted into an Ivy League law school upon graduation. She tutored the third student to prepare her for a career in a major industry; the student later received a job offer from the three largest companies in that industry. She is proud of their great achievements and the role she had in nurturing them. It was notable that these students looked past a perceived social distance to reach out to a culturally unfamiliar minority female faculty member.

A third Asian American female faculty recalled that unlike the cultural majority students who did comparable work on the same projects, she did not receive authorship credit from professors for whom she served as graduate research assistant. During the same period, a White male classmate called her a "Yellow Peril" because she successfully and poignantly debated against him over a landmark U.S. Supreme Court case. As the only Asian female student in her doctoral program at that time, she understood that she would have to work alone. This pattern would then continue throughout most of her career, even when published productivity studies identified her as an influential scholar. When a little-known White male scholar defeated her in a national "junior scholar" award competition in her academic discipline, she realized that her research productivity ranking and significant service to the association had earned her insufficient recognition relative to her less productive majority counterparts.

A fourth Asian female faculty was the first Asian female department chair in her discipline. Throughout her tenure as chair, she was relentlessly challenged by several colleagues, who had refused to acknowledge her achievements in acquiring hard-fought resources. They also rejected her establishment of a transparent shared-governance structure. When she was asked to take an upper administration post, she again experienced lack of acknowledgment for both her management and leadership skills from those who oversaw her unit. Disrespect became glaringly obvious after she took over the leadership role during her supervisor's leave. Realizing an insurmountable bamboo ceiling instead of a penetrable glass ceiling, she left the position with gratitude toward the former supervisor who had recruited her into upper administration.

According to Li (2014), who documented the disempowerment of Asian-American women in the workplace, "The 'glass ceiling' and 'bamboo ceiling' are insufficient proxies for understanding the experiences of Asian American women. . . . The barriers Asian American women face are not only distinct, but also more than the sum of the discrimination faced by women and Asian Americans" (146–147). Santa J. Ono, the president of the University of Cincinnati, stated in the *Chronicle of Higher Education* (2013) that Asian Americans represent 6.2 percent of faculty but only 1.5 percent of presidents. He further noted two problems facing Asian American faculty,

> First, meritocracy is more or less assumed in academe. . . . Unconscious bias might, perversely, be harder to address. . . . Second, Asian-Americans . . . [t]hey've been in on the creation of famously successful start-ups—think Andrew Ng, of Coursera; Steve Chen, of YouTube; and Tony Hsieh, of Zappos. But this isn't an option in our profession—start your own college? So similarly gifted, frustrated people are simply lost.

In light of the bamboo ceiling that could be both opaque and resilient, Asian female faculty may have a long way to go before they can overcome the socially constructed categories that stereotypically define them. These stereotypes usually relegate them as foreigners, outsiders, lotus blossoms, dragon ladies, tiger moms, model minorities, and the like. The lessons learned from these four Asian female academicians suggest that they still need to cross a cultural divide before they can fully realize their dreams of being fully accepted as top teachers, scholars, and administrators. They lack senior faculty mentors to advise them forward and they still need to be fully and respectfully acknowledged in their disciplines and the academy as a whole.

A LATINA FACULTY PERSPECTIVE

Our information society has demanded a more skilled populace, and concomitant with improvements in generational attitudes about women, family, and work, women made incremental gains in completed college degrees since 1999. Whether driven by sheer number or new higher education opportunities, Hispanics overall made important gains in advanced doctorates (PhD, EdD, JD, and comparable) awarded between 1999–2000 and 2009–2010 (National Center for Education Statistics, 2016). Latinas have demonstrated a growing margin over male peers in earning college degrees, and a slight edge in gaining doctorates. However, Hispanics or Latinos are still behind in college degrees and doctorates in proportion to their notable size as 16 percent of the U.S. population (U.S. Census Bureau, 2010).

All these facts are important because of the demographic landscape of the nation, with aging and retiring Whites and younger non-White populations becoming the future workforce. Also, when considering the educational pipeline of Latinos to the professoriate—the academic ranks continue to be missing Latinos—who chose the academic life over better compensated careers in private industries or other professions. Latina professors, who make their lives in the academy, find themselves to be few in number across disciplines on a college campus. Furthermore, they are challenged at various times by deep-rooted societal biases about gender and race (The Latina Feminist Group, 2004; Rios, 2002). The challenges are not completely impossible to surmount, but dealing with racism and sexism wastes women's energy best applied to pedagogical and research innovations. It is a satisfying experience when one can break through environmental biases and have full academic freedom—to dedicate oneself to the educational advancements of students, research, and writing and improvements in higher education.

Teaching and mentoring students has its great rewards for intellectually curious students who are hungry for new knowledge and improving critical thinking skills. Today's students graduate and go forth into an even more diverse world than previous generations. Courses requiring or recommending students take classes about U.S. cultures and global societies ease students into controversial or sensitive topics that female faculty of color teach on ethnicity, race, gender, sexualities, and mass media. Studying abroad in unfamiliar countries, "alternative breaks" for helping build habitats or houses, out-of-state environmental clean-ups, "service learning" in soup kitchens and organic farms, have increased remarkably on my New England campus and I am glad for that. There is some merit to Mark Twain's statement about exposing oneself to new ideas, "travel is fatal to prejudice, bigotry and narrow-mindedness" (Twain, 1869, 243). The college millennials of today seem more open minded (Twenge, 2006), and education guidelines inclusive of world cultures help navigate them to becoming more sophisticated citizens.

Things get in the way of that experience when students, of any level, feel they are inherently deserving of excellent scores or grades from the professor, especially if she is female and not White. Beyond the generational tendencies of the "Generation Me" (Twenge, 2006) students of the contemporary era to anticipate high grades regardless of performance, the tendency is connected to symbolic and real power positions that women and people of color have in a relegated society. We live in a world where the social order locates females and color toward the bottom (Cooper and Stevens, 2002; Rios, 2012; Vargas, 2002). To preemptively reduce unreasonable thinking on behalf of the students I care about, I have included this statement in my online course syllabi, "This is a course that demands a great deal of your dedicated time. It is not an easy class at all. This class requires high attention and high performance. Be ready to work hard." There are still some who hold on to a feeling or bias that they know better than the seasoned woman-of-color scholar who created the course. Over the years, I have included the following syllabus statements:

> Also, did you know that sometimes students try to bully others to somehow achieve more points on their assignments? Periodically a student will demand more points for themselves on an assignment because they claim that "I have all A's in my classes except this one" or "I know how to write. You are grading me wrong. Other people told me my essay was fine!"

I recommend these examples for syllabi because they cause students to pause for a moment and consider their motives.

My research expertise on ethnicity, race, and gender came together with interests in pedagogical innovations with the establishment of a living and learning community designed for first-year students. These major or theme communities are becoming more common on university campuses today (Lenning, Hill, Saunders, Solan, and Stokes, 2013). Having a rich history inside and beyond the United States, learning communities create spaces where students learn to belong to a network of individuals focused on larger tasks of training, studies, and personal growth. In the process of belonging and claiming their rights and symbolic spaces, they gain a type of identity and social capital that they would not otherwise have. Learning communities can assist in strengthening positive self-identities and notions of belongingness (Quinn, 2010). Gaining social capital is especially important for those of working class and ethnic or racial minority backgrounds because these students often do not have the same kind of socioeconomic capital of their middle- and upper-class, cultural majority peers.

As an undergraduate in the Bay Area many decades ago, I was part of strong political, cultural communities of students who took ethnic studies courses alongside their traditional majors. We joined organized groups with legacies from the student civil rights movements and had the mindset of improving the world. I gained exposure to a well-established Chicano-Latino community "house" during my undergraduate days at University of California, Berkeley. The student groups met on campus and sometimes attended course seminars that were scheduled at the house by faculty who believed in nurturing and strengthening a sense of community among their diverse students. This house sat defiantly alongside White fraternities and sororities that were known to enforce social norms (social class, color, body type, phenotype, etc.) among their membership.

When I became a tenured faculty member, I saw that a diversity-themed living and learning community, open to all students, would add to my New England university's efforts for supporting underrepresented students who often feel alienated on White majority campuses. Also, many students of color tended to come from high schools located in large, bustling urban centers, while my land-grant New England campus is semi-rural and comparatively dull or tranquil. To this end, the learning community would help with adaptation to college living and thriving in a pastoral setting. The learning community would be another instrument for recruitment and retention of first-generation students to go to college, and all students interested in local and global Latino cultures.

After years of great exertion and complex planning, "La Comunidad Intelectual" (LCI) came to fruition with Latino and residents of diverse backgrounds. The learning community has real space in a dormitory with other themed learning communities such as Human Rights and Action. LCI would not have been possible without the combined professional capital, persistence, and continuous efforts of key Latino staff and faculty. We all held, and still hold, leadership positions in higher education. We have led seminars, workshops, and *charlas* (informal talks) as part of uplifting the community of emerging intellectuals. We take part in a variety of campus-wide events that encourage self-realization and leadership. This nascent community continues to develop with students declaring majors in many different fields of study. Some students are at junior or senior status now and are considering postbaccalaureate options such as careers in industry and non-for-profits, as well as graduate school.

Using my leadership positions, I have testified at the state level to policy makers using learning communities as one example of college and university programs that are important to adequately maintain during tough budgeting years. Higher education systems and educators are enduring an unusual epoch where highly skilled, critical thinkers need to be carefully mentored, inspired, and trained, yet there are politicos and certain public bodies who do not see the full value of adequately investing in educators and the programs they lead and teach. Rigorous areas of study and support programs cultivate young minds and promote informed citizens. In my speeches and formal statements, I emphasize that the students today are those who will be the educators, scientists, politicians, creative artists, and other professionals working in the state and region in the not-so-distant future.

AN AFRICAN AMERICAN PERSPECTIVE

Recently, the country learned that Harriet Tubman would be the new face of the $20 bill. I think about what this means for African Americans and particularly to African American females. This epic announcement resonated with me, as a person who has been labeled the Harriet Tubman of higher education because of my devoted and strategic expertise to increasing the number of underrepresented minorities in the science, technology, engineering, and mathematics (STEM) fields. Even so, the numeric disparity in minority female faculty relative to their male counterparts in the STEM fields remains glaringly large. The number of minority female faculty who occupy leadership positions at various levels also significantly lags behind male and White faculty.

African American women have been participants in higher education for more than a century. However, they continue to be seriously underrepresented among faculty and higher administration (Bradley, 2005). They serve as important mentors and role models for students (Patton and Harper, 2003; Glazer-Raymo, Townsend, and Ropers-Huilman, 2000). They take on greater teaching, mentoring, service, and committee responsibilities relative to White faculty overall and are more likely to use active pedagogical techniques that improve student outcomes (Jayakumar, Howard, Allen, and Han, 2009). Black women play a critical role in mentoring not only Black students and faculty, but also other faculty and students of color.

My academic higher education journey started with a BS from a historically Black college (HBC), a PhD from an urban public research university, and ended with postdoctoral studies at the number one public research university in the United States (National Science Foundation).

Attending an HBC as an undergraduate and returning as a faculty member shapes my mentoring model. With the absence of the hostile racial climate found at predominantly White institutions (PWIs), HBCs consistently prove to be effective in creating a nurturing and supportive environment for all students and fostering a space that is not only conducive for learning, but also makes students feel comfortable and satisfied (Hilton and Covington, 2016). Bringing this knowledge and experience to mentoring traditionally underrepresented students at PWIs is my magic formula for nurturing, guiding, and counseling an impressive number of underrepresented minority students to academic success.

Most underrepresented minority students arrive on a college campus looking for people who they feel share some of their same experiences. In essence, the students are seeking a safe space as illustrated in this excerpt taken from my nomination letter for a National Faculty Mentor of the Year Award:

> This letter could have been written by any number of students across the university. I have gone to her office and seen her mentor students from Chemistry to History, from Engineering to Education. They enter her office as I did getting on that bus so many years ago, weary with the weight of academia, and leave rejuvenated. Her office is like a mini-COMPACT conference. In the South they have Father Abraham, in the North, we have Sister Ruth.

At the graduate level, many students feel they cannot freely show their vulnerabilities in a traditional faculty advisor-student dyad without this affecting their advisor's evaluation of their academic and professional performances. Therefore, many students seek mentorship relationships outside of their department:

> Dr. Washington sat beside me as I wrote my first abstract to a national conference, as I created my first poster and as I wrote my first grant proposal. In the summer she invited me to be part of a writing group with the goal of publishing and presenting work on underrepresented minorities in the STEMs. All of these things sound like the role of a normal advisor. However, Dr. Washington is not my advisor. She is not even in my department or my field. For all the work she has helped me with, she has helped me with behind the scenes, never asking for recognition.

As mentioned in this chapter's introduction, diversity is a living organism and all living organisms require some form of food for energy, which allows the organism to grow. In higher education that food comes in the form of raw mentoring. Raw mentoring is a form of rugged mentoring needed to inspire others to dream more, be more, and do more. A student mentee shared the following after participation in a National Science Foundation summer undergraduate research program I created and directed:

You have had a huge positive impact on my life completely. Graduate school was far from my reach, but thanks to the NEA Program I feel confident that I will have better chances of getting in graduate school. I really believe in the program and because of this if you need my assistance in any way possible, please let me know. Also I want to say thanks for accepting me, I know I am not the greatest candidate.

Raw mentoring encourages students to move beyond their perceived limits and beliefs, as reflected in these words of another student mentee from the same program:

I would like to personally thank you for giving me the opportunity to participate in the 2011 NEA program. I learned a plethora of new techniques and lessons. I personally think I've grown immensely over the course of the summer. This program has opened my eyes to pursuing a Ph.D., a degree "golden ticket" that I've never thought about pursuing before.

Establishing early mentoring relationships during the undergraduate years may lead to the most successful outcomes (Kelch-Oliver, Smith, Johnson, Welkom, Gardner, and Collins, 2013). Early mentorship may increase retention, the probability of degree completion, and meet the mentee's psychological needs (Kelch-Oliver, et al., 2013). Further, early mentoring can be a transformative journey for both mentee and mentor. It sets the stage for the mentee to go on and help other students. The following paragraph comes from the acknowledgment section of the dissertation proposal of a student that I started mentoring as an undergraduate freshman (iv–v). The student recently received their PhD:

Dr. Washington nurtured my scientific mind as a freshman in college. She introduced me to an environment for me to excel socially, mentally and physically. One of the most fond moments I remember with Dr. Washington is when I realized I was so close to not knowing how to better my life by education. Dr. Washington stated to me "You don't know, what you don't know, until someone shows you!" I only hope to embody what she has taught me. I cannot thank her enough for the opportunity to learn and experience what it means to be a great leader, mentor and more importantly, a great person. Dr. Washington has been the overarching key to my success and I wished that everyone was as blessed as me and could have a "Dr. Washington" of their own. She will never truly know the impact she had had on my life. (James, 2015)

During the regular academic year and during concentrated summer programs, I constantly remind and say to students, "I know psychologically what you are going through. There are bridges you must cross. I know how to get you to the other side. I will get you across if you listen to me." Over the years, I have learned because of the problems encountered by African Americans and specifically African American women in higher education, I need the students just as much as they need me. We inspire one another to move forward and advance in our careers.

DISCUSSION AND IMPLICATIONS

In this chapter, minority female faculty from three different ethnic groups shared successes and challenges as well as lessons learned. This group of multiethnic faculty have also discussed and contrasted issues relevant to the multiple roles that they perform. They shared cross-disciplinary insights and perspectives from higher education institutions with differential missions and student characteristics. Furthermore, these minority female academics described dynamic relations between minority female faculty and college students, in addition to the positive impact these women have on their students.

It is clear that the presence and role of minority female faculty on student life reflects several different aspects. First, these women are teachers, advisors, and mentors and are vital role models in their interactions with minority students because they do not often see people who look like themselves roaming the ivory tower. Second, minority female faculty provide students opportunities to learn from their diverse intellectual perspectives and accept them as faculty members of the larger academy. They reduce students' perceived social distance between different racial and ethnic groups. Third, minority female faculty in leadership positions can impact unique viewpoints on how best to foster the growth and maturation of college students' learning and career advancement after graduation.

There are still pending challenges in the academy. Ford (2011, 445) summarized fundamental and unresolved issues that many women of color (WOC) faculty encounter:

- The "Chilly Climate" Problem: Universities and colleges are isolating environments for WOC faculty; lack of institutional support subsequently affects hiring, retention, mentoring relationships, promotion, and tenure (Antonio, 2002; Olsen, Maple, and Stage, 1995; Turner, 2002);
- Issues of Legitimacy: WOC report difficulty gaining respect and credibility as qualified teachers and scholars from students and faculty Harlow, 2003; Johnsrud and Sadao, 1998);
- Tokenization and Cultural Taxation: Expected to teach about issues of race, mentor students of color, and serve on diversity committees, WOC are over-burdened as token representatives for their respective racial groups (Baez, 2002; Thompson and Sekaquaptewa, 2002);
- Balancing Personal and Professional Roles: WOC faculty have to learn to effectively negotiate family life, commitments to service in the community, and their career goals (Mason, Goulden, and Wolfinger, 2006; Turner and Myers, 2000);

- The Glass-Ceiling Effect: WOC faculty encounter race and gender gaps in wages and slower promotion rates than their [w]hite and male colleagues (Balderrama, Texeira, and Valdez, 2004; Lee, 2002, 445).

Despite these roadblocks, minority female faculty continue to push ahead, so often rejuvenated by the successes of the students they teach, mentor, guide through many hallways, and navigate across metaphoric rivers of the ivory tower. The influences of female academicians on their students and institutions—and hence society as a whole—are considerable. Women faculty from underrepresented groups have been an integral part of university and college campus progress by mentoring and teaching students across disciplines and demographic backgrounds.

Valuing women's contributions to all facets of human history is the foundation of a civil society. In the United States, women have made great professional inroads into higher education. Women have been historic partners in the development of higher education, at all levels. Given today's racial and political climate, where we as a nation are still reminded of deeply rooted biases based on race, minority female faculty must continue to be strategic and vigilant about overcoming the challenges and breaking glass ceilings to receive their due respect and gain acknowledgment for long-standing achievements.

REFERENCES

Allen R. S., and Montgomery, K. A. (2001). Applying an organizational development approach to creating diversity. *Organizational Dynamics, 30*(2), 149–161.

Antonio, A. L. (2002). Faculty of color reconsidered: Ressessaing contributions to scholarship. *The Journal of Higher Education, 73*, 582–602.

Baez, B. (2000). Race-related service and faculty of color: Conceptualizing critical agency in academe. *Higher Education, 39*(3), 363–391.

Balderrama, M., Texeira, M. T., and Valdez, E. (2004). Una lucha de fronteras (A struggle of borders): Women of color in the academy. *Race, Gender, and Class, 11*(4), 135–153.

Bickel, J., Wara, D, Atkinson, B. F., Cohen, L. S., Dunn, M., Hostler, S., Johnson, T. R. B., Morahan, P., Rubenstein, A. H., Sheldon, G. F., and Stokes, E. (2002). Increasing women's leadership in academic medicine: Report of the AAMC project implementation committee. *Academic Medicine, 77*(10), 1043–1061.

Bird, S. R. (2010). Unsettling universities' incongruous, gendered bureaucratic structures: A case study approach. *Gender, Work and Organization, 18*(2), doi: 10.1111/j.1468- 0432.2009.00510.x.

Bird, S. R., Little, J., and Wang, Y. (2004) Creating a status of women report: Institutional housekeeping as women's work. *National Women's Studies Association Journal, 16*(1), 194–206.

Bradley, C. (2005). The career experiences of African American women faculty: Implications for counselor education programs. *College Student Journal, 39*(3), 518.

Cooper, J. E., and Stevens, D. D. (2002). Tenure in the sacred grove: Issues and strategies for women and minority faculty. Albany, NY: State University of New York Press.

Etzkowitz, H., Kemelgor, C., and Uzzi, B. (2000). *Athena unbound: The advancement of women in science and technology.* Cambridge, UK: Cambridge University Press.

Ford, K. A. (2011). Race, gender, and bodily (mis)recognitions: Women of color faculty experiences with White students in the college classroom. *The Journal of Higher Education, 82*(4), 444–478.

Glazer-Raymo, J., Townsend, B. K., and Ropers-Huilman, B. (2000). *Women in higher education: A feminist perspective.* Boston: Pearson Publishing.

Harlow, R. (2003). "Race doesn't matter but . . . ": The effect of race on professors' experiences and emotion management in the undergraduate college classroom. *Social Psychology Quarterly, 66*(4), 348–363.

Hilton A. A., and Covington, M. (2016, February 2). Learning from HBCUs to increase mentorship and representation of black women at PWIs. Blog post. Retrieved April 29, 2016, from http://www.huffingtonpost.com/dr-adriel-a-hilton/learning-from-hbcus-to-in_b_9120116.html.

Holt, R. (2009, November). Bringing the Hutchinsonian niche into the 21st century: Ecological and evolutionary perspectives. *Proceedings of the National Academy of Sciences, 106*(2), 19659–19665. doi: 10.1073pnas.0905137106 PNA.

Hurtado, S., Milem, J. F., Clayton-Pedersen, A. R., and Allen, W. R. (1998, March). Enhancing campus climates for racial/ethnic diversity: Educational policy and practice. *The Review of Higher Education*. doi: 10.1353/rhe.1998.0003.

James, E. N. (2015). Post-transcriptional regulation in osteoblasts using localized delivery of micrornas from nanofibers (Doctoral dissertation). Retrieved March 8, 2017, from http://digitalcommons.uconn.edu/dissertations/897

Jayakumar, U. M., Howard, T. C., Allen, W. R., and Han, J. C. (2009). Racial privilege in the professoriate: An exploration of campus climate, retention, and satisfaction. *The Journal of Higher Education, 80*(5), 538–563.

Johnsrud, L., and Sadao, K. C. (1998). The common experience of "otherness": Ethnic and racial minority faculty. *The Review of Higher Education, 21*(4), 315–342.

Kelch-Oliver, K., Smith, C. O., Johnson, K., Welkom, J. S., Gardner, N. D., and Collins, M. H. (2013). Exploring the mentoring relationship among African American women in psychology. *Advancing Women in Leadership, 33*, 29.

Lee, S. M. (2002). Do Asian American faculty face a glass ceiling in higher education? *American Education Research Journal, 39*(3), 695–724.

Lenning, O. T., Hill, D. M., Saunders, K. P., Solan, A., and Stokes, A. (2013). *Powerful learning communities.* Sterling, VA: Stylus.

Li, P. (2014). Recent developments. Hitting the ceiling: An examination of barriers to success for Asian American Women. *Berkeley Journal of Gender, Law and Justice, 29*(1), 140–167.

Mason, M. A., Goulden, M. and Wolfinger, N. (2006). Babies matter: Pushing the gender equity revolution forward. In S. J. Bracken, J. K. Allen, and D. R. Dean (Eds.), *The balancing act: Gendered perspectives in faculty roles and work lives* (9–30). Sterling, VA: Stylus Publishers.

Milem, J. F. (1998). Attitude change in college students: Examining the effect of college Peer groups and faculty normative groups. *Journal of Higher Education, 69*(2), 117–140.

National Center for Education Statistics. Fast Facts. Retrieved from March 8, 2017, http://nces.ed.gov/FastFacts/display.asp?id=72.

Ng, R. (2000). A woman out of control: deconstructing sexism and racism in the university. In J. Glazer-Raymo, B. K. Townsend, & B. Ropers-Huilman (Eds.), *Women in higher education: A feminist perspective* (360–370). Boston, MA: Pearson Publishing.

Olsen, D., Maple, S. A., and Stage, F. K. (1995). Women and minority faculty job satisfaction: Professional role interests, professional satisfactions, and insitutional fit. *The Journal of Higher Education, 66*, 267–294.

Ono, S. J. (2013, October 28). Why so few Asians are college presidents. *Chronicle of Higher Education, 60*(9). Retrieved March 8, 2017, from http://chronicle.com/article/Why-So-Few-Asians-Are-College/142567.

Park, C. (2007) Gender in academic career tracks: The case of Korean Biochemists. *Sociological Forum, 22*(4), 452–473.

Patton, L. D., and Harper, S. R. (2003). Mentoring relationships among African American women in graduate and professional schools. *New Directions for Student Services, 2003*(104), 67–78.

Quinn, J. (2010). *Learning communities and imagined social capital: Learning to belong.* New York: Continuum.

Rios, D. I. (2002). A U.S.-born Latina professor: Cultural stranger in my own classroom. In L. Vargas (Ed.), *Women faculty of color in the white college classroom* (257–275). New York, NY: Peter Lang.

Rios, D. I. (2012). A Southwest Chicana in the Connecticut Yankee realm: A cross-cultural feminist critique on gender, ethnic and racial inequities in higher education. In M. Meyers and D. I. Rios (Eds.), *Women in higher education: The fight for equity* (97–115). New York: Hampton Press.

Slavin, R. E. (1985). Cooperative learning: Applying contact theory in desegregated schools. *Journal of Social Issues, 41*(1), 45–62.

Smith, W. A., Altbach, P. G., and Lomotey, K. (2002). *The racial crisis in American higher education: Continuing challenges for the twenty-first century.* Albany, NY: State University of New York Press.

Stewart, A. J., Malley, J. E., and LaVaque-Manty, D. (2007) Analyzing the problem of women in science and engineering. In A. J. Stewart, J. E. Malley, and D. LaVaque-Manty (Eds.), *Transforming science and engineering: Advancing academic women* (3–20). Ann Arbor: University of Michigan Press.

The Latina Feminist Group. (2004). *Telling to live: Latina feminist testimonios.* Durham, North Carolina: Duke University Press.

Thomas, D. A. (2001). The truth about mentoring minorities: Race matters. *Harvard Business Review, 79,* 99–107.

Thompson, M., and Sekaquaptewa, D. (2002). When being different is detrimental: Solo status and the performance of women and racial minorities. *Analysis of Social Issues and Public Policy, 2*(1), 183–203.

Turner, C. S. V., and Myers, Jr., S. L. (2000). *Faculty of color in academe: Bittersweet success.* Boston: Allyn and Bacon.

Turner, C. S. V. (2002). Women of color in academe: Living with multiple marginality. *The Journal of Higher Education, 73,* 74–94.

Twain, M. (1869). *The innocents abroad or the new pilgrim's progress.* New York: Harper and Brothers Publishing.

Twenge, J. M. (2006). *Generation me: Why today's young Americans are more confident, assertive, entitled—and more miserable than ever before.* New York: Free Press.

U.S. Census Bureau. (2010). Briefs. Retrieved March 8, 2017, from http://www.census.gov/prod/cen2010/briefs/c2010br-04.pdf.

Vargas, L. (2002). *Women faculty of color in the white college classroom.* New York: Peter Lang Publishing.

SIX

Faculty of Color and Student Relations

The Role of Intersectionality on Classroom Interactions for Female Faculty of Color

Edith Fraser

INTRODUCTION

A female faculty of color and a male colleague were meeting in her office to discuss future plans. Her office door was open, as she was an administrator and wanted to be accessible to the students. A student came into her office and said, "Hi Mrs. X (Female faculty member and administrator) and Hi Dr. Y (Male faculty member)." The male faculty member said, "Isn't she a doctor too?" The student's response was "Huh" and seemed confused. Both the female faculty member and male faculty member had their doctorate degree. In fact, she had her degree several years before him.

As a female faculty of color, I have had this experience even as my male colleagues do not have the same experience. This is true even in institutions that traditionally serve students of color.

As a female faculty member of color, I have taught at several institutions, both historically Black colleges and universities (HBCUs) and majority institutions. I have also discussed this issue with other female faculty of color. These interactions, my personal experience, and research will provide the context for this chapter.

Female faculty of color are underrepresented in the number of full-time faculty positions held in the United States. They are more often employed by two-year institutions, community colleges, and minority serving institutions (Pittman, 2010). This underrepresentation has an impact on relationships with colleagues, professional development, and with student relationships.

Some of the resultant challenges, which confront female faculty members of color, include the following: isolation from other faculty, increased expectation of service for students, and oppression in the classroom (Pittman, 2010; Hartley, 2008; Chesler and Young, 2007). This chapter will explore these challenges, discuss the cost to female faculty of color, and provide some skills used by faculty of color to address these challenges.

FEMALE FACULTY AND ISOLATION

One of the challenges for female faculty of color is isolation, especially if they are in STEM areas of the academy. Although nearly 30 percent of undergraduate students around the nation are considered minorities, slightly more than 12 percent of full-time faculty members are minority (Lynch, 2013). The figures are equally bleak when you consider that only about 2 percent of women of color are tenured full professors compared to 17 percent of women in dominant culture (Evans, 2007).

The low percentage of other faculty of color, especially women of color, aggravates the isolation these women experience. This isolation is multilayered based on both gender and race resulting in isolation from male faculty (regardless of race) because of color and female faculty because of race (Pittman, 2010). Too often faculty members of color are viewed as affirmative action hires; this means other faculty and even students question their credentials and preparation for faculty position. Like apartheid, this isolation subtlety places the female faculty member on the fringe and even students may perceive the status of these faculty members as marginalized, resulting in questions about competence.

According to Dr. Stephanie Evans, women of color are hired into lower ranks, their scholarship is questioned, "taken for granted, discouraged and not valued" (Evans, 2007, 133), which results in lower levels of tenure and increases the possibility of isolation. The importance of mentoring is essential for female faculty of color to successfully navigate the tenure process, but this isolation has consequences for future advancement and professional development. Some researchers have noted that one of the top four barriers to career success for women of color is the lack of access to mentors. These women are confronted with the frustrations of navigating in a system that is not inherently congruent with their cultural norms.

FEMALE FACULTY AND TRAP OF SERVICE

Frequently, female faculty of color have increased expectation of service especially with students of color. Hartley (2008) describes this service by female faculty of color as "maids of the academe." In this analogy, the female faculty are expected by the academic departments, students, and colleagues to assume greater service for students that can impact time allocated for research leading to tenure. Thus, these faculty members may suffer from race fatigue (Hartley, 2008). For example, faculty of color at an institution in Northeast were expected to be members of committees like other faculty members plus sponsor student of color organizations, mentor students of color, and serve as buffer for students of color attending their institution. Thus, these faculty members had additional service expectations. These additional responsibilities could at times interfere with research and scholarship preparation for tenure.

FEMALE FACULTY AND CLASSROOM INTERACTION

Faculty of color often experience oppression in the classroom by students, especially White male students who find the introduction of female faculty of color unsettling (Pittman, 2010). This is reflected in this personal example:

> Dr. Z was an experienced professor who was hired to teach at a Southern rural university. During her tenure at the university, she experienced many students' challenges. It began with students ignoring her while she taught and not respecting her as a professor. Soon students were refusing to take her class and taking other professors with less experience and credentials. Students consistently complained to the chair about her: she was unfair in her grading; she did not know the content, etc. One student even told her "we are going to do everything we can to get you out of here." Students rated her poorly on rate my teacher and eventually began a campaign against her, which ended up in the president's office. This professor eventually left this institution. However, her tenure would have been even shorter if the chair had not been supportive. (Anonymous, personal interview, March 6, 2015)

Student relationships are complicated by gendered racism, which challenges the authority of the female faculty of color and questions their teaching competence. "Younger faculty, younger female faculty, younger faculty of color, and especially younger female faculty of color consistently report more challenges to their substantive expertise and more pain and discomfort (sometimes anger as well) in dealing with those challenges" (Chesler and Young, 2007). This attempt to readjust the classroom to the majority social status is frequently reflected in racial microagression for female faculty of color (Pittman, 2010). A professor who taught in a small private college in a Western state described her experience in these words:

> I have found that many students (especially in undergraduate situations) are wholly unnerved by the prospect of their competency— whether in writing, in speaking, in processing information or demonstrating knowledge and skills—being called into question by someone who often represents "inferiority" in their sometimes limited experience with people of color. The dual factor of being a woman and a person of color can often create great distress for students who have a sense of privilege based on their heritage (Anonymous, personal communication, March 8, 2015).

Many scholars view challenges and conflict as major factors impacting faculty retention and student relationships (Meyers, Bender, Hill, and Thomas, 2006). Thus, female faculty of color have challenges that exceed other females as well as men of color. Institutions that are interested in enhancing the rate of retention should recognize these challenges, provide mentors, and provide support to counteract negativity from students and other faculty members.

REFERENCES

Baez, B. (2000). Race-related service and faculty of color: Conceptualizing critical agency in academe. *Higher Education, 39*, 363–391.

Brown, K. (2002). Useful anger: Confrontation and challenge in the teaching of gender, race, and violence. In L. Vargas (Ed.), *Women faculty of color in the white classroom* (pp. 89–108). New York: Peter Lang.

Chesler, M., and Young Jr., A. (2007). Faculty members' social identities and classroom authority. *New Directions for Teaching and Learning, 111*, 11–19.

Diggs, G., Garrison-Wade, D., Estrada, D., and Galindo, R. (2009). Smiling faces and colored spaces: The experiences of faculty of color pursing tenure in the academy. *Urban Review, 41*, 312–333.

Evans, S. (2007, Fall). Women of color in higher education. *Thought and Action*, 131–138.

Griffin, P., and Ouellett, M. (2007). Facilitating social justice education courses. In M. Adams, L. Bell, and P. Griffin (Eds.) *Teaching for diversity and social justice* (89–116). New York: Routledge.

Hartley, D. (2008). Maids of academe: African American women faculty at predominately white institutions. *Journal of African American Studies, 12*, 19–36.

Hendrix, K. (2007). "She must be trippin": The secret of disrespect from students of Color toward faculty of color. *New Directions for Teaching and Learning, 110*, 85–96.

Lynch, M. (2013). Diversity in college faculty just as important as student body. *Diverse: Issues of Higher Education*. Retrieved March 8, 2017, from diverseeducation.com/article/52902.

Meyers, S., Bender, J., Hill, E., and Thomas, S. (2006). How do faculty experience and respond to classroom conflict? *International Journal of Teaching and Learning in Higher Education, 18*(3), 180–187. Retrieved from diverseeducation.com/article/52902187.

Perry, G., Moore, H. A., Edwards, C., Acosta, K., and Frey, C. (2009). Maintaining credibility and authority as an instructor of color in diversity-education classrooms: A qualitative inquiry. Sociology Department, Faculty Publications. Paper 85. Retrieved   March   8,   2017,   from   http://digitalcommons.unl.edu/cgi/viewcontent.cgi?article=1084&context=sociologyfacpub.

Pittman, C. (2010). Race and gender oppression in the classroom: The experiences of women faculty of color with white male students. *American Sociological Association, 38*, 183–196.

Turner, C., Gonazlez, J., and Wood, J. (2008). Faculty of color in academe: What 20 years of literature tells us. *Journal of Diversity in Higher Education, 1*, 139–168.

SEVEN

Establishing Effective Mentoring Relationships, Part I

Donna Gibson McCrary

INTRODUCTION

Mentoring in the corporate world in areas like business and management has long been recognized as the answer to improving productivity and longevity in the workplace (Gibson, 2006). Mentoring is used in more than 70 percent of *Fortune 500* companies for the sole purpose of attracting, training, and retaining employees (Bynum, 2015). It has been studied and promoted for years with extensive literature on the subject, mostly in reference to men.

There is a need for more women, and especially women of color, for academia to become more diverse (Thompson, 2008). Minority students in higher education, particularly those in predominately White institutions, lack having faculty of color as role models and mentors as they matriculate through college.

It is imperative for universities to hire, promote, and retain diverse faculty including women and women of color to meet the continuing needs of the student population and lessen the gap between males and females in reference to tenure track and higher academic administrative positions (Holmes, Land, and Hinton-Hudson, 2007; Blood, et al., 2012). African American female students also benefit tremendously with a diverse faculty population. These students will have access to positive role models they can relate to, and it provides the students with a sense of empowerment and determination. These attributes instill and increase one's values, ambitions, and feelings of promise that can positively influence educational and career goals. It can be difficult for universities to recruit and retain faculty of color. In the early 2000s, only 5 percent of full-time faculty in the United States were Black, and this is extremely low when compared to the percentage of White faculty in the United States (Diggs, Garrison-Wade, Estrada, and Galindo, 2009).

According to the National Center for Education Statistics (2015), there are approximately 1.5 million faculty working in higher education. More than half of these position are full-time and are mostly held by White males (43 percent). Around 35 percent of the positions are held by White females with a total of 79 percent of faculty positions held by Whites, 6 percent of faculty were Black, 5 percent were Hispanic, and 10 percent were Asian American.

These statistics are alarming with faculty and administrative positions lacking in diversity across the United States in reference to ethnic groups. Black women are underrepresented in academia due to various barriers, such as isolation and racial discrimination that hinder their success at predominantly White institutions (PWI). At other institutions, including historically Black colleges and universities (HBCUs), females are often faced with gender discrimination (Crawford and Smith, 2005). Females are not considered for administrative positions and tenure at the same rate as males. Females in administrative positions are often placed or promoted to these positions on an interim basis for extended periods. Females have to work harder and produce at higher rates before they are recognized for promotion and tenure.

Starting a new position in academia can be a daunting experience for a new faculty member to fulfill all of the required obligations associated with teaching, scholarship, and service without proper guidance from seasoned faculty. This can be especially challenging for females, with additional obligations expected in their personal lives with family (Wilson, Pereira, and Valentine, 2002).

Many females not only work outside of the house, but they come home to additional responsibilities, such as wife, mother, cook, and housekeeper. These titles come with so many other responsibilities, chores, and deadlines. Therefore, being linked with a seasoned faculty member for the first three years of employment establishes a pattern for growth and productivity for the mentee (Borders et al., 2011).

HISTORY OF MENTORING

Mentoring dates back to Homer's poem, "The Odyssey." When the king left for war, he appointed Mentor, an elderly, wise man to care for and counsel his son, Telemakhos, during his absence (McLaughlin, 2010). Athena provided guidance and cared for the king's son (Corbett and Paquette, 2011); however, Mentor received the credit. Hence the term *mentor* has taken on the meaning of a wise and trusted teacher in our day and time (McLaughlin, 2010). Mentoring is defined as a relationship between two people with a goal of providing the mentee with career development in the absence of any formal evaluations. According to Schrodt, Cawyer, and Sanders (2003), mentoring is a relationship between a senior and junior faculty, where the senior faculty acts as a role model by providing guidance, tutoring, and support in relation to the junior faculty's career development. The process of mentoring is a way of socializing junior faculty, which involves how faculty develop knowledge, skills, and values that are critical to being successful in academia (Griffin, 2012). Mentors are thought to be elderly, wise, act as a substitute parent, teacher, or a guide (Bynum, 2015).

DIFFERENT TYPES OF MENTORS

There are four different types of mentors—the friend, career guide, information source, and the intellectual guide. A mentor that takes on the role of a friend spends quality time with the junior faculty, socializing and getting to know one another. In this role, giving advice, and when necessary, providing assistance with personal problems, is also expected. Female faculty often have demanding responsibilities at home and need guidance in managing home and work life. As a career guide, the mentor actively guides research activities and works to bring attention to the mentee's professional accomplishments within the university setting. A mentor who acts as an informational source furnishes the mentee with information on promotion, tenure, scholarly work, and various committees. Knowing what is expected on a job is critical to maintaining employment; however, it is also important to have an understanding on how to accomplish this task. The intellectual guide develops an equal relationship and collaborates with his or her mentee on projects and offers constructive feedback (Zellers, Howard, and Barcic, 2008).

THE MENTORING PROCESS

The mentoring process requires both parties to be fully committed to this learning process (Boddy, Agllias, and Gray, 2012). Seasoned faculty often avoid mentoring because of time restraints. Mentoring takes up additional time, which can interfere with other job responsibilities (Girves, Zepeda, and Gwathmey, 2005). Effective mentoring provides an avenue for the mentee to participate in research with a seasoned faculty and it contributes to retention. This is especially important because faculty are expected to participate in scholarly activities, such as research, grant writing, and presentations.

Mentoring also prevents feelings of isolation with junior faculty by providing a colleague who will be a constant support system (Jones and Osborne-Lampkin, 2013). Every faculty has had a first teaching position, and without a mentor providing guidance, the journey can be intimidating. It places the junior faculty at a disadvantage because of a lack of understanding and limited knowledge encompassing job responsibilities.

The requirements associated with faculty job responsibilities help determine whether a faculty receives tenure and promotion. Failure to receive tenure can result in termination of employment. According to Crawford and Smith (2005), women of color in academia report having only family members and teachers from primary and secondary education as role models while in the academy. These identified support systems for African American faculty provided the only means of professional guidance in academia. Being compatible, having access to a mentor, sexism, and cross-gender influences, seriously impact women and mentoring in academia. There are more barriers for women to overcome in academia than their male counterparts. There are fewer women in academia, and they often are not afforded the same opportunities as men when it comes to mentoring and advancement (Simon, Roff, and Perry, 2008).

There are different types of mentoring—formal, informal, self-selected, and group mentoring—all of which can be advantageous for junior faculty. Formal and informal mentoring can dramatically enhance faculty retention and productivity in academia, which can lead to attaining promotion and tenure status. Often, mentoring is conducted informally, without an arranged agreement being implemented between the two participants, which can result in a positive match for both parties. A junior faculty may find common interest with another more experienced faculty and a mentoring relationship develops by chance (Leslie, Lingard, and Whyte, 2005). Mentoring programs at universities can assist the junior faculty in settling into their new positions and the demands that come with it (Savage, Karp, and Logue, 2004).

For formal mentoring to be successful, programs usually encompass mandatory training for both the mentee and the mentor (Corbett and Paquette, 2011). There are a number of institutions that do not realize how important it is to have a formal mentoring program, whereas others might see the benefits, not having the resources to support a formal mentoring program might prevent the implementation of a mentoring program (Jones, Osborne-Lampkin, Patterson, and Davis, 2015). Formal mentoring allows both parties to gain an understanding for what is to be expected during the mentoring process. Information that should be covered by the mentor is provided. Both parties are also provided with general guidelines (Corbett and Paquette, 2011), goals to be accomplished, objectives, and the outcomes associated with the mentoring program. The time frame in reference to the program, when meetings should take place and the length of meetings, along with training to include interpersonal skills, and other workshops the mentee should attend.

The program should also keep track of data associated with the program for evaluation purposes, along with surveys to be completed yearly, depicting the status of the mentee on completion of the program (Vega, Yglesias, and Murray, 2010). Universities that incorporate formal mentoring programs are bound to reap the benefits associated with pairing junior faculty with senior faculty (Corbett and Paquette, 2011). Recent research found faculty who were mentored experienced satisfaction with their job, opportunities for advancement, and developed professional relationships with colleagues, and those relationships promoted the initiation of scholarly writings (Borders et al., 2011). Mentoring also shows faculty how much they are appreciated, and it reenergizes complacent attitudes, while boosting the self-esteem of seasoned faculty (Carmel and Paul, 2015). It is also an opportunity to collaborate with faculty and promote research among members in a department.

It seems as if the bulk of the responsibility for the mentoring relies on the seasoned faculty; however, the junior faculty are charged with being committed to the entire process. It is imperative the junior faculty enter into this agreement with dedication and a strong desire to maintain the relationship to gain the knowledge needed for success. Recognizing the value of the mentors' years of expertise in teaching, research, advisement, and all aspects of academia brought to the table proves to be an asset for the mentees. The mentees can find comfort knowing the credentials of their mentors, which can inspire the mentees to be productive (Son and Kim, 2012).

POSITIVE ASPECTS OF MENTORING

Characteristics of a successful mentor include being dedicated to the program through its entirety, having a clear understanding of his or her role, and possessing the skills needed to perform job responsibilities. A mentor should be capable of providing needed support based on the changing needs of the mentee. Possessing excellent communication skills, including being a good listener and respected by colleagues, is also a good trait (Young and Wright, 2001). A mentor devotes a significant amount of time and energy into developing the career of the junior faculty (Corbett and Paquette, 2011) and will also use the power associated with his or her position to help nurture and develop the mentee's career (Young and Wright, 2001). Mentors, whether mentoring by choice or because of job responsibility, are expected to provide guidance and advice to junior faculty (Son and Kim, 2012).

PERSONAL EXPERIENCE WITH MENTORING

At one time our department lacked a formal mentoring program; however, the guidance and support needed to succeed could be obtained from senior faculty within our department and across the university. The years of experience held by all faculty within our department, as well as their various areas of expertise, affords junior faculty the opportunity to partner up with a seasoned scholar. This informal mentoring relationship often requires junior faculty to seek this type of guidance from his or her desire to excel in academia. One must have the motivation and drive to continue on this path. It appears as if senior faculty need to know there is interest from the junior faculty in publishing, grant writing, as well as, service for the mentoring relationship to be successful.

My experience has blossomed over the years. Initially, mentoring was informal; however, my first chair, Dr. Shelley Wyckoff, urged me to further my education to advance while employed at our university. This was a challenge that I decided to embrace in 2007. Determined to achieve this goal, knowing that on completion of this terminal degree more would be required of me. Which reminds me of one of my favorite passages from the Bible, "For unto whomsoever much is given, of him shall be much required; and to whom men have committed much, of him they will ask the more" (Luke 12:48 KJV).

According to Menges (2015), this type of mentoring, encouraging me to further my education, is defined as providing the junior faculty with psychosocial support, which includes encouragement and counseling. It took six years to complete my doctorate, and during that time, Dr. Edith Fraser advised me to turn my dissertation into an article. This form of mentoring is known as providing career support (Menges, 2015). During our meetings, she informed me that about three articles could be developed out of my dissertation to submit for publication. That was the beginning of my journey to publishing, for which I am eternally grateful.

My current chair, Dr. Charnetta Gadling-Cole, has been instrumental in mentoring her staff. She has provided several opportunities to myself and all faculty in our department to submit chapters in several of her books, as well as her journal, *Journal of Gender: Information and Development in Africa (JGIDA)*. With the guidance I have received from Dr. Gadling-Cole over the past three years, I have three publications in peer-reviewed journals and one chapter in her edited book. At the present time, I have two additional publications in print and two publications in progress. Dr. Gadling-Cole has been instrumental in coaching me in reference to authoring a book, which is my next project.

Dr. Gadling-Cole has incorporated a formal mentoring program in our department, where new faculty are paired with an experienced faculty member. My mentee and I have scheduled meetings where we discuss teaching, various aspects of the job, scholarly writings, and research on topics that are of interest to my mentee. We are also in the process of working on a research study together. Being a part of a large department has also afforded me the opportunity to collaborate with faculty within our department that share the same interest in research. This is true with my colleague, Dr. Upchurch; our dissertations were similar, which led us to collaborating with one another on several projects independently and in conjunction with other faculty in our department. We bring different talents to identified projects and succeed in our research by not only being committed but also focusing on our strengths. Once we start a research project, we are determined to stay on task until completion. In academia, team work is vital to assist faculty in meeting job requirements.

Support received by one's chair and dean is necessary for retention of faculty, and feelings of respect are of equal importance to retention (Thompson, 2008). Universities that implement mentoring programs benefit greatly along with the faculty.

The new faculty who are mentored are more likely to be committed to learning opportunities associated with teaching and scholarly writing (Corbett and Paquette, 2011). They are also less likely to feel isolated and alienated as they attempt to become acclimated to a new career. Having a mentor has been found to help reduce stressors related to the job, like teaching load, time restraints, and the review and promotion process, possible discrimination, and limited personal time. These stressors can negatively affect one's job performance (Thompson, 2008). Chandler (1996) found having a mentor is directly related to success with African American women in academia.

A study conducted by Tareef (2013) found 92 percent of faculty reported their job performance was positively influenced by a mentor. A major problem with mentoring in academia involves the severe shortage of women of color in faculty and administrative positions. This paucity of women in academia has been linked to a lack of advancement in administrative positions in academia.

Most Common Form of Mentoring

The most common form of mentoring involves informal mentoring, where the mentor and mentee initiate a relationship without the aid of the university (Menges, 2015). This type of mentoring is considered a good fit due to the relationship developing naturally. The problem with this type of mentoring involves the mentee's lack of knowledge in regard to selecting a mentor with similar interests, goals, and personalities (Leslie, Lingard, and Whyte, 2005).

As a new employee, junior faculty lack knowledge surrounding personality traits of their colleagues and are at a disadvantage when it comes to selecting an appropriate mentor. Gaining knowledge surrounding colleagues takes time by interacting with them on a daily basis. During this interaction, the junior faculty can get to know their coworkers to determine professional commonalities in research, teaching, and scholarship, and personal attributes and idiosyncrasies. With self-selected mentoring, the mentee is aware of the skills and personality traits of the prospective mentor (Carmel and Paul, 2015). This can create a problem once the mentoring process begins because it is important for the mentee to seek guidance from their mentor (Young and Wright, 2001).

With informal mentoring, both parties decide on the time frame of the mentoring process and what goals they plan to work on (Menges, 2015). Neither party is bound by a written or verbal commitment; therefore, the mentoring process can end at the discretion of either party. Self-selected mentoring is a form of informal mentoring. The mentee selects a mentor based on the qualities of the mentor and the mentee's needs. The mentee looks for a good match in regard to his or her professional goals and the known credentials and expertise of the mentor. The mentee initiates this arrangement without the assistance of the assigned department or human resources (Carmel and Paul, 2015). It is important to establish relationships at the workplace; however, there are no guarantees with this type of mentoring in regard to the duration and goals. With it being voluntary, either the mentor or mentee can dissolve the relationship at any time.

GROUP MENTORING

Group mentoring is being explored as a viable option in academia. Relationships are formed with colleagues and the mentee's peers serve as mentors. This form of mentoring provides the mentee with several colleagues to seek out for advice or assistance. Each individual in the group takes on the role of mentee and mentor at various intervals because of one's skills and area of expertise. This form of mentoring was introduced several years ago; however, it is not used often in academia (Johns and McNamara, 2014).

Group mentoring reduces the level of commitment for one individual in regard to time, and it provides a pool of knowledge and skills for junior faculty to select from for guidance. All involved parties contribute to the learning process in academia. This type of mentoring encourages the mentee to solicit help from a diverse group of colleagues (Zellers, Howard, and Barcic, 2008). If one mentor is unavailable, the mentee has other options from the pool of mentors to seek assistance. It is important for the needs of the mentee to be met and for the established goals to be accomplished during this relationship.

ADVANTAGES OF MENTORING

It is important to the growth and development of a department and university at large to ensure junior faculty are mentored. Obtaining promotion and tenure is not guaranteed for any faculty member. However, mentored faculty are better equipped with the skills and knowledge for application of tenure and promotion than faculty who have not been mentored. Academia is a competitive field and faculty are expected to conduct research and publish in professional, peer-reviewed journals, participate in grant writing, and service within the university and the community (Carmel and Paul, 2015). Participating in a mentoring program facilitates exposure to the required job responsibilities, support, advisement, and growth that otherwise may not be acquired in a timely manner for advancement and job stability, which equates to receiving promotion and tenure.

Recent research on mentoring suggests it is valuable to the success of faculty in higher education for those that desire promotion and tenure. Having a mentor has been found to positively influence one's career satisfaction and career choice. It provides opportunities for faculty to come together to collaborate on research interest, teaching philosophies, grant writing, scholarship, the culture of the university, and counseling (Simon, Bowles, King, and Roff, 2004; Montgomery, Dodson, and Johnson, 2014). Faculty are more likely to enjoy their new position once completely acclimated to it. The mentoring process alleviates adjustment difficulties many junior faculty experience in academia (Young and Wright, 2001). Mentored faculty reported having a chance to meet away from the workplace was important. These meetings furnish a safe place for junior faculty to openly discuss any concerns, without feelings of retribution (Diggs et al., 2009).

Mentored faculty report feeling connected and possessing feelings of ownership in relation to their department. Faculty who have been mentored are more likely to receive more promotions and have higher incomes than nonmentored faculty. Productivity increases drastically for faculty who are mentored. Being comfortable with required job responsibilities is more likely among mentored faculty, who report being more satisfied with their positions than nonmentored faculty. Mentored faculty possess feelings of loyalty toward their position, department, and the institution (Schrodt, Cawyer, and Sanders, 2003). Mentored faculty are so content with their place of work that they will remain on the job whether they needed the income or not. This type of loyalty is definitely a benefit for higher education, considering retaining faculty is vital to the education of students (Schrodt, Cawyer, and Sanders, 2003).

CONCLUSION

In my own experience, being mentored provided professional opportunities that I would not have had with the expertise of my mentors. Learning about their professional accomplishments in regard to publishing, research, and grant writing was motivation for me to excel in these areas. Knowing the process for submitting a manuscript for publication in a journal or to a publishing company is key to establishing yourself as a scholar and fulfilling job responsibilities in academia. On completion of a manuscript, submission to a publisher, acceptance from the publishing company, and seeing the final product in print brings on a sense of gratitude and excitement. After the first publication, I was left with a drive and motivation to continue on this journey, doing what I love to do, reading, writing, and research.

Another aspect of academia that is of equal importance is teaching our students and participating in service, whether it is on campus or in the surrounding community. My community service has also been instrumental in research interests, which led to a couple of my publications. Observing seasoned faculty conduct class was extremely helpful during my first few months on the job, which provided me with additional skills for use in the classroom. It is beneficial for a new faculty member to receive mentoring whether it is formal mentoring, informal mentoring, self-selected, or group mentoring.

The importance of a mentoring program in academia is obvious and a necessity for growth, development, and job security. Research, publishing, and grant writing is expected of faculty and conveys to the educational community the quality of faculty employed at the university. This speaks volumes to those interested in employment and in enrolling in the university. Prospective employees can research the university and read about the accomplishments of the faculty on staff. Higher education institutions seek employees with excellent credentials to join their team.

Potential students are able to make an informed decision on an institution based on a number of factors like majors offered, having accredited programs, and extracurricular activities. Researching the biography of current faculty teaching in their desired program of study is another determining factor taken into consideration when selecting an institution of higher education. Therefore, qualified faculty should be well-rounded in teaching ability, research, publication, and scholarship. Success in these areas are enhanced with the incorporation of a mentoring program. With the right mentor, junior faculty are destined to succeed and all parties involved win.

REFERENCES

Blood, E. A., Ullrich, N. J., Hirshfeld-Becker, D. R., Seely, E. W., Connelly, M. T., Warfield, C. A., and Emans, S. J. (2012). Academic women faculty: Are they finding the mentoring they need? *Journal of Women's Health, 21*(11), 1201–1208.

Boddy, J., Agllias, K., and Gray, M. (2012). Mentoring in social work: Key findings from a women's community-based mentoring program. *Journal of Social Work Practice, 26*(3), 385–405.

Borders, L. D., Young, J. S., Wester, K. L., Murray, C. E., Villalba, J. A., Lewis, T. F., and Mobley, A. K. (2011). Mentoring promotion/tenure-seeking faculty: principles of good practice within a counselor education program. *Counselor Education and Supervision, 50,* 171–188.

Bynum, Y. P. (2015). The power of informal mentoring. *Education Journal, 136*(1), 69–73.

Carmel, R. G., and Paul, M. W. (2015). Mentoring and coaching in academia: Reflections on a mentoring/coaching relationship. *Policy Futures in Education, 13*(4), 479–491.

Chandler, C. (1996). Mentoring and women in academia: Reevaluating the traditional model. *National Women's Studies Association, 8*(3), 79–100.

Corbett, F., and Paquette, K. R. (2011). An investigation of mentorship as perceived by university faculty, teaching associates, and graduate assistants. *Education, 132*(2), 285–295.

Crawford, K., and Smith, D. (2005). The we and the us mentoring African American women. *Journal of Black Studies, 36*(1), 52–67.

Diggs, G., Garrison-Wade, D. F., Estrada, D., and Galindo, R. (2009). Smiling faces and colored spaces: the experience of faculty of color pursing tenure in the academy. *Urban Review, 41,* 312–333.

Gibson, S. K. (2006). Mentoring of women faculty: The role of organizational politics and culture. *Innovative Higher Education, 31*(1), 63–79.

Girves, J. E., Zepeda, Y., and Gwathmey, J. K. (2005). Mentoring in a post-affirmative action world. *Journal of Social Issues, 61*(3), 449–479.

Griffin, K. (2012). Learning to mentor: a mixed methods study of the nature and influence of Black professors' socialization into their roles as mentors. *The Journal of the Professoriate, 6*(2), 27–53.

Holmes, S. L., Land, L. D., and Hinton-Hudson, V. D. (2007). Race still matters: Considerations for mentoring black women in academe. *The Negro Educational Review, 58*(1–2), 105–129.

Johns, R., and McNamara, J. (2014). Career development in higher education through group mentoring: A case study of desirable attributes and perceptions of a current programme. *Australian Journal of Career Development, 23*(2), 79–87.

Jones, T. B., and Osborne-Lampkin, L. (2013). Black female faculty success and early career professional development. *Negro Educational Review, 64*(1–4), 59–75.

Jones, T. B., Osborne-Lampkin, L., Patterson, S., and Davis, J. (2015). Creating a safe and supportive environment mentoring and professional development for recent black women doctoral graduates. *International Journal of Doctoral Studies, 10,* 483–499.

Leslie, K., Lingard, L., and Whyte, S. (2005). Junior faculty experiences with informal mentoring. *Medical Teacher, 27*(8), 693–698.

McLaughlin, C. (2010). Mentoring: What is it? How do we do it and how do we get more of it? *Health Services Research, 45*(3), 871–882.

Menges, C. (2015). Toward improving the effectiveness of formal mentoring programs: Matching by personality matters. *Group and Organization Management.* doi: 10.1177/1059601115579567.

Montgomery, B. L., Dodson, J. E., and Johnson, S. M. (2014). Guiding the way: mentoring graduate students and junior faculty for sustainable academic careers. *SAGE Open, 4*(4), 1–11.

U.S. Department of Education. Institute of Education Sciences, National Center for Education Statistics. (2015).

Savage, H. E., Karp, R. S., and Logue, R. (2004). Faculty mentorship at colleges and universities. *College Teaching, 52*(1), 21–24.

Schrodt, P., Cawyer, C. S., and Sanders, R. (2003). An examination of academic mentoring behaviors and new faculty members' satisfaction with socialization and tenure and promotion processes. *Communication Education, 52*(1), 17–29.

Simon C. E., Bowles, D. D., King, S. W., and Roff, L. L. (2004). Mentoring in the careers of African American women in social work education. *Affilia, 19*(2), 134–145.

Simon, C. E., Roff, L. L., and Perry, A. R. (2008). The status of women in social work education psychosocial and career mentoring: Female African American social work education administrators' experiences. *Journal of Social Work Education, 44*(1), 9–22.

Son, S., and Kim, D. Y. (2012). What makes protégés take mentors' advice in formal mentoring relationship. *Journal of Career Development, 40*(4), 311–328.

Tareef, A. B. (2013). The relationship between mentoring and career development of higher education faculty members. *College Student Journal, 47*(4), 703–710.

Thompson, C. Q. (2008). Recruitment, retention, and mentoring faculty of color: the chronicle continues. *New Directions for Higher Education, 143*, 47–54.

Vega, W., Yglesias, K., and Murray, J. P. (2010). Recruiting and mentoring minority faculty members. *New Directions for Community Colleges, 152*, 49–55.

Wilson, P. P., Pereira, A., and Valentine, D. (2002). Perceptions of new social work faculty about mentoring experiences. *Journal of Social Work Education, 38*(2), 317–333.

Young, C. Y., and Wright, J. V. (2001). Mentoring: The components for success. *Journal of Instructional Psychology, 28*(3), 202–206.

Zellers, D. F., Howard, V. M., and Barcic, M. A. (2008). Faculty mentoring programs: Reenvisioning rather than reinventing the wheel. *Review of Educational Research, 78*(3), 552–588.

EIGHT

Establishing Effective Mentoring Relationships, Part II

Martina Nieswandt

INTRODUCTION

"Hi, I am Don, how are you? You must be one of the new doctoral students." Who is this person and what is he saying? Is he talking in English?

"I am Martina. Uhm in Chemistry Education, Professor Hein is my Doktorvater, uhm."

"Right, you are one of Professor Hein's new students. What is your area of research? . . . Perth . . . Australia . . . Physics . . . "

This dialogue, in a mix of English and German, was my first interaction with Don, an internationally renowned scholar, and at the time of our interaction, a visiting professor at the research institute at which I had just started my doctoral studies in chemistry education. Little did I know, in this particular moment of stumbling in English, that Don would be one of my mentors throughout various stages in my academic career. I was just lost. My understanding of and ability to speak in English was minimal.

Over the years, Don's mentoring involved regular discussion about my research and career aspirations during his stays at our research institute, helping to navigate my first international science education conference, introducing me to many international scholars at national and international conferences, collaborating on a journal article, and writing reference letters when I was in the job market. Don was clearly one of the mentors who was highly influential in the development of my academic identity. Don and other mentors were also role models for how to advise my own students, and more recently, I have drawn on their examples to guide my mentoring of junior colleagues in doing research and developing strategies for tenure and promotion.

Interestingly, during my doctoral studies in chemistry education in Germany, most of my mentors were male, while during my academic career in science education, most of my mentors were and are female. The dominance of male professors in chemistry education at the beginning of my career in Germany may explain this pattern. Female professors were almost non-existent. In Germany, chemistry education is often located in a college of natural sciences with a majority of male professors. In contrast, science education in German universities tends to have a majority of female faculty and, similar to North American universities, is more often part of a college of education. Such structural differences may explain whether my mentors tended to be male or female. Other conscious or unconscious factors may have played a role in choosing or accepting a mentor as well, such as choosing a person who had access to the predominant culture of science education (Sosik and Godshalk, 2005), something that seems particularly of importance for doctoral students trying to find a place within the competitive academic environment.

In the following sections, I will discuss mentoring approaches for different groups: doctoral students and junior faculty within the college of education and particularly in science education. My arguments draw from my own experiences and the literature. This chapter is, however, not an overview of the mentoring literature; it does not compare various mentoring approaches and is not based on an empirical study of mentoring. This chapter is a reflection of my own mentoring journey: from a mentee to a mentor and an attempt to locate my mentoring approaches within the literature on mentoring.

WHAT IS MENTORING?

Mentoring is a multifaceted concept that I view as a process, "an intense interpersonal exchange" (Noe, Greenberger, and Wang, 2002) between a mentor and mentee. Such a relationship is reciprocal (Ragins, Cotton, and Miller, 2000) with different formats that depend on mentor's and mentee's needs and interests: from coaching and advising to emotional and psychological support, from one-on-one training to collaboration, and from role-modeling to facilitating goal accomplishment. An effective mentoring relationship is characterized by "mutual respect, trust, understanding, and empathy" (National Academy of Science, 1997, 2). Such relationships promote learning, professional development, and growth of mentee and mentor alike (Fletcher and Ragins, 2007).

MENTORING IN COLLEGES OF EDUCATION

The need for mentoring seems obvious in disciplines such as medicine, nursing, or public health, while less obvious in education, although various programs in colleges of education (e.g., teacher education, school counselors) are professional programs with internships or apprenticeship models that provide formal opportunities for mentorship. Various studies document the benefits of mentoring for mentees such as successful socialization into the profession (Gardner and Barnes, 2007), greater career satisfaction, more successful stress management, higher abilities to network and collaborate, more productive research careers, and better preparation in making career decisions (e.g., Boice, 1992, 2000; Borders et al., 2011, de Janasz and Sullivan, 2004; Kalbfleisch and Eckley, 2003; Schrodt, Cawyer, and Sanders, 2003; Wasburn, 2007).

The satisfaction of mentoring for mentors is often described as pride in disseminating their expertise and skills to the next generation of researchers or building a network of future professional collaborators. Tips for and models of mentoring are available through a quick Google search; some graduate schools provide guidelines for advising/mentoring of doctoral students, and the National Science Foundation (NSF) demands a mentoring plan for grant proposals that include postdoctoral researchers. Thus, mentoring seems an important aspect of academic professional life across all academic disciplines, and the vast amount of literature on mentoring indicates the growing value of mentoring (for an overview, see e.g., Howley and Trube, 2015). I don't know how my academic career would have developed without the different mentors at various times in my career, but being mentored was important.

MENTORING DOCTORAL STUDENTS:
CHALLENGES AND MODELS FOR SUCCESS

Various studies demonstrate the impact of mentoring relationships on successful student outcomes (e.g., Golde and Dore, 2001; Paglis, Green, and Bauer, 2006); in a recent NSF Dear Colleague Letter (2016), existing research awardees are encouraged to submit proposals for supplemental support to enhance professional development opportunities for students in PhD programs across science, technology, engineering, and mathematic (STEM) disciplines. Mentoring doctoral students is important and necessary to sustain the discipline and create new knowledge.

Historically, university systems in the United States and in Europe worked with close and sustained relationships between doctoral students and faculty advisors and mentors. In Germany such advisors are called *Doktorvater* or *Doktormutter*—doctoral father or doctoral mother—defining a relationship within the German university system that is multidimensional. This relationship is not without potential for conflict and contradiction: from strict to caring parent and from academic sounding board, collaborator and role model to employer and supervisor. Which role is more emphasized, the parent or the academic sounding board depends on the individual professor. My dissertation advisor, (Doktorvater) Professor Hein, was all of this at various times of my doctoral studies and depending on my needs. He wanted me to be successful, enabling me to make the transition from graduate student to independent researcher and effective academic. He acted as advisor in academic and personal matters and as a guide throughout the jungle of academia. The latter was particularly important for me. Coming from a working-class background, I was the first woman in my immediate and extended family to go to a university and continue my studies to pursue a career in academia.

I had no role model in my family, and until my master's studies, I also had no role model in my friends' families. The jungle of unwritten rules and norms of academic behaviors was foreign to me (Ryan and Sackrey, 1996); I lacked cultural capital (Bourdieu, 1986). This was particularly evident during my undergraduate studies where I was confronted with situations such as: getting access to chemistry research laboratories because I was interested in the work, but this wasn't part of the program of study. Being intimidated to articulate my thoughts about Bourdieu's work in a "by invitation-only" group of students and professors who met once a week to discuss the readings. Over time with support and encouragement from female peers (with the necessary cultural capital), working as a research assistant in a research project for a few years during my undergraduate and master studies and discussions with Professor Hein and other colleagues during my doctoral studies helped to develop more and more insight into the unwritten world of academia.

Professor Hein also acted as supervisor in my role as research assistant, as collaborator on publications and grant proposals, and as a role model in how to be a professor who is knowledgeable, generous with time and advice, and respectful to staff, students, and colleagues alike. Anderson and Shannon (1988, 40) defined mentoring as "a nurturing process in which a more skilled or experienced person, serving as a role model, teaches, sponsors, encourages, counsels and befriends a less skilled or less experienced person for the purpose of promoting the latter's professional and/or personal development." Professor Hein was clearly a mentor, a trusted counselor throughout my doctoral studies; unfortunately, he passed away shortly after I graduated.

Despite these excellent experiences with my Doktorvater, Professor Hein, I had to overcome some barriers as a woman in a mostly male-dominated research institute, and at the time of my doctoral studies, a mostly male-dominated discipline of chemistry education. Although I was used to demonstrating higher academic achievement across the board than my male peers to be visible and heard, it was still emotionally and cognitively exhausting to put in 200 percent effort throughout my doctoral studies, whereas the majority of my male peers received the same achievement, awards, and attention with what seemed like only 80 percent effort.

Making my presence in committees, meetings, and conferences normal and not the exception, demanded an enormous amount of time and a good portion of stubbornness and resilience, particularly when confronted with sexist interactions, such as: "You are smart and nice looking, why haven't you gotten a husband yet?" One of my chemistry professors made this comment during our discussion of a particular laboratory experiment that I did in his lab group—unrelated and totally out of the blue! Another male professor made the following comment at a social event at a chemistry and physics education conference: "You are very smart and have the potential for an excellent career, and I always supported you, so why do you need to fight and be outspoken for a position of a doctoral student on our board of directors?" In his view, I was insufficiently grateful for his support. I worked against the established structure of the professional association that viewed me as one of the promising new chemistry educators and had given me a seat at their table. My questioning the old boys' network, trying to open its traditional and conventional structures for doctoral students, seemed like a betrayal to him. Fortunately, other senior colleagues were more open to our group of doctoral students' demands, supported our motion, encouraged our efforts, and provided strategic tips; they informally mentored us and sooner rather than later the sexist comments faded.

Nevertheless, such negative, sexist, or racist experiences are still common for many female and racial and ethnic minority doctoral students, particularly in the STEM disciplines, which despite continuous efforts, are still viewed as having cultures and politics that alienate women and racial and ethnic minorities (Gibson, 2006). Matching doctoral students with a mentor of their gender and race or ethnicity has been promoted in various studies, although results show mixed results. For women in STEM, having a mentor of one's own gender was found to be somewhat important for success and for receiving more help, but it didn't make a difference for academic outcomes or confidence in females' own sense of "good fit" with science (Blake-Beard, Bayne, Crosby, and Muller, 2011).

Other research indicated that female mentees enjoyed same-gender mentoring relationships more than cross-gender ones (Lockwood, 2006) and experienced more psychosocial support when they had a female mentor (Lankau, Riordan, and Thomas, 2005). Tenenbaum and colleagues (2001) found gender relatively unimportant in graduate student–advisor relationships, and in Downing and colleagues' (2005) study, female students rated male advisors as significantly more influential in their pursuit of science than female advisors. Referring to Sosik and Godshalk's (2005) claim about the advantage of being mentored by the person who is perceived as having power, Blake-Beard and colleagues (2011) note: "The more a mentor has access to power and the predominant culture and its mores, the greater might be the rewards for the protégé." (626).

My Doktorvater, Professor Hein, had access to the predominant culture within Germany's chemistry education community. He was well-established and recognized as an excellent scholar among his peers, something that I wasn't aware of when I applied for the doctoral student position. Simply reading what he had written didn't provide enough insight into his status within the chemistry education community. I learned about this by being part of the community, being initiated into the community when I first attended and presented at the annual conference, when interacting informally with Professor Hein's colleagues, thus having access to its culture and norms. Over time, I came to perceive myself, and was viewed by its members, as part of the chemistry education community (Wenger, 1998).

Doctoral students in the United States apply to a program and often to a particular professor's lab or research team based on their interest. However, this initial professor is at first an advisor, mostly for the student's coursework. Taking classes with different professors, working with different professors as a research assistant on a project or as a teaching assistant in different classes should lead to choosing a mentor. It might be the initial professor, but it also could be another faculty member whose work may be more closely related to the doctoral student's developing interest. I strongly encourage my doctoral students to seek out other colleagues' research teams and classes to find the best professor who can support their research and be a mentor. At the same time, I try to be more than an advisor by initiating a one-on-one, mentor–mentee relationship.

I enhance such one-on-one relationships with collaborative group mentoring. Although such an approach has been used for faculty mentoring (several senior faculty members mentor a group of junior faculty; Pololi, Knight, Dennis, and Frankel, 2002), our collaborative group is comprised of all my doctoral students (and occasionally also master's-level students) and myself. My role during our regular meeting is either to facilitate discussion of student interest–driven topics or simply as a member of the group discussing the presentation of another group member. Clearly, it takes time to develop a collegial environment and atmosphere in which everyone is viewed as equally qualified to add his or her voice and knowledge to the table. Norms will need to be discussed and agreed on to establish an environment in which discussions are controversial without being judgmental, on a high intellectual level, and interspersed with laughter and humor; characterized by constructive feedback; and where learning is viewed as a social process influenced by our own cultural background and biases, with the latter being openly discussed and reflected upon.

Such collaborative mentoring has the potential to disperse latent power relations between faculty mentor and doctoral students and to create rich experience for both mentor and mentees. Collaborative mentoring is often less time-consuming than one-on-one mentoring, particularly when a faculty has a large group of doctoral students. Various topics are discussed with the whole group instead of with individual students, and more advanced doctoral students may support faculty in advising new doctoral students about program requirements and hidden curriculum of the department or the university.

For mentees, a collaborative mentoring approach creates opportunities to experience multiple perspective on departmental, college, and university politics; early initiation into the culture and norms of the department, college, the university, and the discipline of science education; and a safe and nonjudgmental practice field for conference presentations, dissertation defenses, or job interviews.

Regular meetings have different formats and topics, both dependent on needs and interests of all members. Typical formats and topics in a semester may be:

- More formal advising sessions (i.e., suggestions for courses based on students' interests and program requirements; timelines for different steps in the doctoral program);
- Discussions about students' ideas for research projects—formal with a structured presentation or more informal in a brainstorming session;
- Specific professional development activities on topics such as: how to write a conference proposal, curriculum vitae, or teaching philosophy;
- Discussions about suitable conference behavior and tips for networking at conferences;
- Job talk practice; and
- Discussion of specific topics based on common readings.

Despite such a collaborative mentoring approach, I still have one-on-one mentoring sessions with my doctoral students that may focus on emotional support related to their doctoral program or sometimes to their personal life. Knowledge of various university-based support structures (from psychological to health and academic support) is important to help my students accordingly and to clearly mark the boundary of the mentor-and-mentee relationship.

An important aspect of mentoring is providing students with experiences that enhance their competitiveness on the job market. Depending on their career aspirations, teaching experiences or research experiences may be more stressed or are equally important. I softly push my doctoral students to seek out teaching assistant positions or, if such positions are not available, to volunteer to be a teaching assistant (TA) in a course or to teach a course at another institution.

Collaboration with a colleague or myself on the development of a new course and on writing practitioner articles is as important as offering my doctoral students research assistant positions or encouraging them to apply for such positions in colleagues' research groups to develop insight and knowledge of different types of research. Similarly, I expect my doctoral students to submit and present their work at professional conferences. Supporting my students during their conference attendance and research presentations is taken for granted. Being in the room during their presentation, introducing them to colleagues in the field (like Don did for me), or making them aware of and encouraging them to join doctoral student groups in our professional associations are simple but effective components of my mentoring approach. I particularly encourage my students to develop professional relationships with their peers; these will be their future colleagues with whom they may collaborate on research and grants or may simply be friends and sounding boards during their careers in academia.

Mentoring is not only the sole responsibility of one faculty member, but it is the responsibility of a department and a college to mentor their doctoral students. Foley (2015) states: "Mentoring is a mindset" (220), and as such, it should be a vital and formal part of each doctoral program.

For example, a program has a one-credit required doctoral seminar—pro-seminar—for students across a department or college. Such a course can have many different formats but should foremost be guided by doctoral students' needs and interests. Topics may depend on when students take the course, enrich the one-on-one mentoring experience, or deepen collaborative mentoring experiences. Based on my experience teaching such seminars, a variety of topics were always highly appreciated and discussions particularly rich and informative when students from different educational subdisciplines provided multiple perspectives to the same topic: developing a program of study, forming an advising and dissertation committee, comprehensive exam expectations, navigating the dissertation research and writing process, or faculty personal experiences with writing for publication.

The described aspects of mentoring doctoral students do not address the specific challenge of mentoring a diverse set of doctoral students. Mentoring doctoral students from different cultures, races and ethnicities, social classes, and gender identities has the high potential to enrich one's own mind-set but only through an honest reflection on one's potential biases, conscious and unconscious preferences for one's own culture, or the dominant academic culture. As a White, female, lesbian, German immigrant scholar, socialized in a mostly male-dominated discipline who worked in various public and private universities in Canada and the United States with a majority of female and White colleagues, I am sometimes more sensitive and aware of the dominant White and male academic culture and question it, while at other times I have to be strongly reminded of my own preconceptions and biases. Having doctoral students from different countries, of different races and ethnicities, genders and sexual orientations makes me vigilant about the difficulties and barriers that they may experience and reminds me of discriminative interactions that I had experienced because of an unusual accent or an interaction style that is judged as awkward or too direct. Some of my students may be the only person of color in the room, which may make the student uncomfortable and insecure in how to interact or the majority of White students unsure how to interact with their peer.

Some of my students realize painfully that academic norms and values are different from their past experiences in educational institutions and lack behavior that is generally accepted. They also realize that nonconformity is not always accepted; academia has norms and expectations, and doctoral students are often expected to conform to them without questioning. Realizing how alienating this culture can be to some of my doctoral students, discussions about values and norms are important but should be carefully orchestrated. Apprenticing into the academic culture of one's own discipline should not be without questioning its current norms and values. I want my students to acculturate enough to join the academic community and at the same time feel empowered and being able to maintain sufficient perspective to change their community over time; similar to what my group of doctoral peers and I did in our professional association in Germany.

In summary, mentoring doctoral students should be an essential part of every doctoral program in a college of education. Mentoring is a process that should take place throughout the doctoral program facilitated by individual faculty and the faculty as group; it has multiple formats — from one-on-one mentoring to collaborative mentoring models; includes various elements, such as doctoral seminars, doctoral student groups; and is guided by diverse students' needs and interests while at the same time aimed toward developing capable and independent educators and educational researchers.

Mentoring Junior Faculty: Community of Scholars
versus Individualism and Competitiveness

In an ideal world, mentoring would be an ongoing process throughout a person's career in academia: from undergraduate to graduate to junior faculty to senior faculty. Mentoring junior faculty has been identified with successful academic careers (Leslie, Lingard and Whyte, 2005) and higher rates of retention and promotion (Ramani, Gruppen, and Kachur, 2006). Gardiner and colleagues (2007) found that pretenure female faculty who were mentored showed higher success in receiving external research grants, had higher publication rates, and better perceptions of self as an academic in comparison to a control group who did not receive mentoring. Mentoring does not only benefit individual mentees and their mentors but also the university through increased grant income and enhanced faculty reputation.

Starting your first tenure-track faculty position is stressful; many departmental, college, and university norms and expectations are mysterious, and from the first day, the burden of working hard toward tenure and promotion casts a shadow over other aspects of your personal and professional life. When I started my first academic position at a public university in the Southwest of the United States, I was at first more occupied with managing everyday life in this foreign country than paying attention to academia and worrying about what to do to receive tenure and promotion.

Navigating everyday life challenges (e.g., getting a driver's license, opening a bank account, and getting a credit card without having a credit history, understanding the health system, finding grocery stores that had food I liked, etc.) took up quite some time and energy as did some bouts of disbelief about social injustices in my new country of residence (e.g., health benefits only for the ones who can afford it). I had to grasp and make the culture and social norms my own, intertwine them with my German "I" and "Me," and to develop and mature into a new "I" and "Me" that was still true to my values. These socialization processes couldn't have been sped up, although I longed for fewer imbalances. Parallel to these everyday life challenges I slowly realized that I didn't know much about American universities, particularly when I was confronted with the strictly hierarchical structure of my department; something that I didn't expect in its entirety.

German universities' organizational structures impose hierarchies; job titles and formal interactions between faculty and faculty, faculty and staff, as well as doctoral students, staff, and faculty, support and make these hierarchies clearly visible. Everyone knows on which level he or she is within the system, which also makes it easier for newcomers to know rules and individual roles. Although I had some ideas about the organizational structures of American universities and identified its hierarchical configuration, the informal interactions between senior and junior faculty, faculty and staff, and university leadership and faculty made them less transparent and evoked an equality that is often not practiced and clearly wasn't reflected in my department. Based on my excellent doctoral training that included plenty of experiences in research, teaching in higher education, and in administrative work on various committees, I felt quite confident in managing my first academic job in the United States.

However, I had developed an academic identity that wasn't fully prepared for the cultural differences. I clashed, or, the culture clashed with me. Quite confident about my knowledge and expertise, I spoke out at department meetings, questioned procedures that were unclear to me, and asked my department chair for support in research, something that was promoted by the dean of our college and the president of the university during a new faculty orientation. Little did I know that as a junior faculty in my department, this was viewed as disrespectful and out of place—I was "mouthy," according to the departmental administrative assistant. My female department chair and some male and female senior colleagues told me clearly that junior faculty were supposed to listen to their senior colleagues; we were not supposed to ask for support—especially forms of support that may not have been available to them—and we clearly weren't allowed to question long-standing procedures and practices. I was used to speaking up when things didn't make sense to me, to articulate directly and clearly my thoughts, and provide reasons for suggested changes. I questioned my German socialization—maybe I should be less vocal; I wondered whether my experiences were typical for a U.S. university or only an exception because of my hierarchically structured department.

Looking back, I think it was a complex mix of all of these aspects. Depending on the departmental and college culture, expectations regarding pretenure faculty's role, their rights and responsibilities, and level of support prior to going up for tenure may vary. Junior faculty may accept set expectations, identify with their given role, or question expectations and roles. Gravett and Petersen (2007) stress the "hidden norms, values and rules" that "could be crucial elements for newcomers to negotiate in terms of their fuller participation and navigation in the discourse [of the department, college or university] community" (194).

Independent of how junior faculty engage with their academic community, guidance from experienced senior colleagues within and outside of the department will help to navigate these early career years. I had been assigned a mentor, a senior female faculty, who supported my questioning of roles, rules, expectations, procedures, and practices, and at the same time, cautioned me to be more patient and strategic in asking for change. An important additional support system was our group of junior faculty. I initiated regular, informal social gatherings of junior faculty from across the college of education. Besides making friends, venting about work-related issues, or simply having a good time, we articulated how to best ask for better or different support and changes in procedures and practices. Minimal changes and support happened in my and some of the other departments; yet, in one other department, the arrival of a new department chair and compassionate senior faculty resulted in substantially stronger support of junior faculty. I realized that changes can happen, but they are often dependent on individual efforts.

In the end, persistent lack of research support led me to go back on the job market, and I left to start a tenure-track position at a research-intensive university in Canada. This meant another immigration, and once again, the need to find a balance between the challenges of everyday life and professional life at a new university, in a new department. Resources such as start-up money, seed money, being part of a center in my field, a department chair who protected junior faculty from burdensome administrative responsibilities, and excellent students made this experience richer than my first position.

I worked with amazingly knowledgeable and talented colleagues in the science preservice teacher education program, who generously shared their knowledge and expertise about teaching and preparing future science teachers. Yet, something was missing. Beside colleagues who weren't interested in collaboration on research and personal challenges (a long distance relationship—my partner was a faculty member at a U.S. university), a lack of mentoring made these years difficult. Simply having monetary and administrative support for research isn't enough. As a junior faculty I needed guidance on what to do to achieve tenure and promotion successfully. Looking back, I realized that I would have profited from discussions with other colleagues about strategically pursuing shorter term research projects designed to yield results that then can be written up as publishable manuscripts. Tips about balancing research and teaching requirements, productive writing habits, or about which highly ranked journals also have a shorter turn-around time for reviews would have been as important as support in making connections to schools and teachers who are interested in collaborating on research. I would have benefited from a collaborative work climate instead of being part of a competitive group of colleagues who as a group were more interested in their own career advancement than in mentoring junior faculty. My experience can be best described with the following quote: "Young faculty are supposed to be independent; a lot of times they don't know what they are doing—teaching, committees, supervision of students, sole authorships—and there is very little support. It's sink or swim" (Wright and Wright, 1987, 207).

Eventually I found my way a few years ago to my current faculty position at a large, Research I, land-grant university. As a tenured senior faculty and who recently moved into the college leadership, I spend quite some time on mentoring junior faculty. Individual meetings discussing ideas for research projects, new course development, or strategies for successful writing and publishing are key elements of my mentorship work as are group workshops addressing topics such as "nuts and bolts of being a professor," "developing a research agenda that is fundable," "writing successful research grants," "mentoring research assistants," or "how to grow professionally—realistic goal setting."

However, creating a community of scholars that breaks the cycle of individualism and competitiveness that is inherent to many departments and colleges demands more than one person's commitment and engagement. Similar to my view of mentoring doctoral students, mentoring tenure-track faculty is not only the sole responsibility of one faculty member; as a mind-set (Foley, 2015); it is the collective responsibility of a department and a college. Depending on the needs of the faculty, mentoring may take different forms (e.g., peer mentoring, collaborative mentoring, or one-on-one mentoring), which as some studies show benefit faculty when conducted simultaneously (Cawyer, Simonds, and Davis, 2002; de Janasz and Sullivan, 2004; Sorcinelli and Yun, 2007; Van Emmerik, 2004). Of course, mentoring will only be successful in helping faculty meet their personal and professional goals when mentees are willing to commit time and effort for mentoring and to be open to reflection and constructive criticism.

Recently, I met Don at one of our professional meetings. I hadn't seen him for some time and we caught up for a while before I shared with him that I was writing this chapter, that I started it with a brief recall of our first interaction, and how important his mentoring was for my career development. Although he couldn't remember this particular interaction, he full-heartily thanked me for acknowledging him and also said: "But isn't this what we do in academia!"

CONCLUSION

Mentoring doctoral students or junior faculty is multifaceted but in general, guided by the mentor's interest in supporting her mentee's career and well-being. Mentor–mentee relationships are professional and personal. Boundaries of such relationships should be discussed, as should be potential power dynamics between faculty and doctoral student, tenured faculty and pretenure faculty. Often a mentoring style mirrors a mentor's own experiences as a mentee; yet, being open for and exploring various mentoring models in collaboration with the mentee may be more effective than staying within one's own comfort zone. Academic and professional development and growth is more likely when both mentor and mentee reflect critically their practiced approaches and are open for adjustments depending on mentee's needs or differences in culture, gender, race, or ethnicity.

REFERENCES

Anderson, E. M., and Shannon, A. L. (1988). Toward a conceptualization of mentoring. *Journal of Teacher Education, 39*(1), 38–42.

Blake-Beard, S., Bayne, M. L., Crosby, F. J., and Muller, C. B. (2011). Matching by race and gender in mentoring relationships: Keeping our eyes on the prize. *Journal of Social Issues, 67*(3), 622–643.

Boice, R. (1992). Lessons learned about mentoring. *New Directions for Teaching and Learning, 50,* 51–61.

Boice, R. (2000). *Advice for new faculty members: Nihilnimus.* Needham Height, MA: Allyn and Bacon.

Borders, L., Young, J., Wester, K., Murray, C., Villalba, J., Lewis, T., and Mobley, A. (2011). Mentoring promotion/tenure-seeking faculty: Principles of good practice within a counselor education program. *Counselor Education and Supervision, 50,* 171–188.

Bourdieu, P. (1986). The forms of capital. In I. Szeman and T. Kaposy. *Cultural Theory. An Anthology* (81–93). Oxford, UK: Wiley-Blackwell.

Cawyer, C. S., Simonds, C., and Davis, S. (2002). Mentoring to facilitate socialization: The case of the new faculty member. *International Journal of Qualitative Studies in Education, 15,* 225–242.

Dear Colleague Letter. (2016). Improving graduate student preparedness for entering the workforce, opportunities for supplemental support. NSF 16-067. Retrieved April 22, 2016, from http://www.nsf.gov/pubs/2016/nsf16067/nsf16067.jsp?WT.mc_id=USNSF_25&WT.mc_ev=click#EHR

de Janasz, S. C., and Sullivan, S. E. (2004). Multiple mentoring in academe: Developing the professional network. *Journal of Vocational Behavior, 64,* 263–283.

Downing, R. A., Crosby, F. J., and Blake-Bear, S. (2005). The perceived importance of developmental relationships on women undergraduates' pursuit of science. *Psychology of Women Quarterly, 29,* 419–426.

Fletcher, J. K., and Ragins, B. R. (2007). A window on relational mentoring. In B. R. Ragins and K. E. Kram (Eds.). *The handbook of mentoring at work: Theory, research, and practice* (373–397). Los Angeles, CA: Sage Publications.

Foley, G. D. (2015). Mentoring doctoral students. In A. A. Howley and M. B. Trube (Eds.), *Mentoring for the Professions: Orienting toward the future* (205–221). Charlotte, NC: Information Age Publishing, INC.

Gardiner, M., Tiggermann, M., Kearns, H., and Marshall, K. (2007). Show me the money! An empirical analysis of mentoring outcomes for women in academia. *Higher Education Research and Development, 26*(4), 425–442.

Gardner, S. K., and Barnes, B. J. (2007). Graduate student involvement: Socialization and the professional role. *Journal of College Student Development, 48,* 269–387.

Gibson, D. K. (2006). Mentoring of women faculty: The role of organizational politics and culture. *Innovative Higher Education, 31*(1), 63–79.

Golde, C., and Dore, T. (2001). *At cross purposes: What the experiences of today's doctoral students reveal about doctoral education.* Philadelphia: Pew Charitable Trusts.

Gravett, S., and Petersen, N. (2007). You just try to find your own way: The experience of newcomers to academia. *International Journal of Lifelong education, 26*(2), 193–207.

Howley, A. A., and Trube, M. B. (Eds.). (2015). *Mentoring for the professions: Orienting toward the future.* Charlotte, NC: Information Age Publishing, INC.

Kalbfleisch, P. J., and Eckley, V. K. (2003). Facilitating mentoring relationships: The case for new technology. *Informing Science,* 1581–1590.

Lankau, M. J., Riordan, C. M., and Thomas, C. H. (2005). The effects of similarity and liking in formal relationships between mentors and protégés. *Journal of Vocational Behavior, 67*(2), 252–265.

Leslie, K., Lingard, L., and Whyte, S. (2005). Junior faculty experiences with informal mentoring. *Medical Teacher, 27*(8), 693–698.

Lockwood, P. (2006). 'Someone like me can be successful": Do college students need same-gender role models? *Psychology of Women Quarterly, 30*(1), 36–46.

National Academy of Science. (1997). *Adviser, teacher, role model, friend. On being a mentor to students in science and engineering.* Washington, DC: National Academy Press.

Noe, R. A., Greenberger, D. B., and Wang, S. (2002). Mentoring: What we know and where we might go. *Research in Personnel and Human Resources Management, 21*, 129–173.

Paglis, L., Green, S., and Bauer, T. (2006). Does adviser mentoring add value? A longitudinal study of mentoring and doctoral student outcomes. *Research in Higher Education, 47*(4), 451–476.

Pololi, L. H., Knight, S. M., Dennis, K., and Frankel, R. M. (2002). Helping medical school faculty realize their dreams: An innovative, collaborative mentoring program. *Academic Medicine, 77*(5), 377–384.

Ragins, B. R., Cotton, J. L., and Miller, J. S. (2000). Marginal mentoring: The effects of type of mentor, quality of relationship and program design on work and career attitudes. *Academy of Management Journal, 43*(6), 1177–1194.

Ramani, S., Gruppen, L., and Kachur, E. (2006). Twelve tips for developing effective mentors. *Medical Teacher, 28*(5), 404–408.

Ryan, J., and Sackrey, C. (1996) *Strangers in paradise: Academics from the working class.* New York, NY: University Press of America.

Schrodt, P., Cawyer, C. S., and Sanders, R. (2003). An examination of academic mentoring behaviors and new faculty members' satisfaction with socialization and tenure and promotion processes. *Communication Education, 52*(1), 17–29.

Sorcinelli, M. D., and Yun, J. Y. (2007). From mentoring to mentoring networks: Mentoring in the new academy. *Change, 39*, 58–61.

Sosik, J. H., and Godshalk, V. M. (2005). Leadership styles, mentoring functions received, and job–related stress: A conceptual model and preliminary study. *Journal of Organizational Behavior, 21*(4), 365–390.

Tenenbaum, H. R., Crosby, F. J., and Gliner, M. D. (2001). Mentoring relationships in graduate school. *Journal of Vocational Behavior, 59*, 326–341.

Van Emmerik, I. J. H. (2004). The more you can get the better: Mentoring constellations and intrinsic career success. *Career Development International, 9*, 578.

Wasburn, M. H. (2007). Mentoring women faculty: An instrumental case study of strategic collaboration. *Mentoring and Tutoring: Partnership in Learning, 15*(1), 57–72.

Wenger, E. (1998). *Community of practice: Learning, meaning, and identity.* Cambridge, UK: Cambridge University Press.

Wright, C. A., and Wright, S. D. (1987). The role of mentor in the career development of young professionals. *Family Relations, 36*, 204–208.

NINE

Debunking Myths: Academic Community Members' Perspectives on Black Women Faculty

Crystal Renée Chambers

CRITICAL RACE FEMINISM

A derivation of critical race (Matsuda, Lawrence, Delgado, and Cren-shaw, 1993) and feminist approaches (hooks, 1984), critical race feminism acknowledges the endemic nature of racism within the United States while recognizing gendered manifestations of racism as well as racist manifestations of sexism (James, 2009). Critical race feminism centers analysis on the layers of racial and gender experiences. As espoused by Wing (2003):

> We . . . can no longer afford to think of ourselves or let the law think of us as merely the sum of separate parts that can be added together or subtracted from, until a white male or female stands before you. The actuality of our layered experience is multiplicative. Multiply each of my parts together, 1x1x1x1x1, and you have one indivisible being. If you divide one of these parts from one you still have one [emphases in the original]. (31)

As such, the experiences of Black women are not 100 percent congruent with Black men or White women and are worthy of independent analyses as testaments to the truth of both the similarities and disso-nances of their existence in academe.

To unpack this perspective, I begin with Paula Giddings's historical recounting of Black women from the colonial era through the twentieth century in *When and Where I Enter* (1984). Throughout, Black women are both supported and disappointed by the lack of support from allies in concomitant struggles for race and gender equity. The title of the Black feminist primer, *All the Women are White, All the Blacks are Men, But Some of Us Are Brave* (Hull, Bell-Scott, and Smith, 1982), perhaps best sums up the concomitant senses of both solidarity and isolation. Within the field of literature, Christian (1980) notes the estrangement of Black women's fiction from African American, Women, and mainstream literature. From this vantage, Black women's literary discourse reaffirms one existence as distinctive, giving voice to realities that are neither White nor male. Toni Morrison (1971) articulates this isolation, experienced both at work and in the community, "she had nothing to fall back on: not maleness, not whiteness, not ladyhood, not anything. And out of the profound desolation of her reality she may very well have invented herself" (63). Herein there is a value to Black womanhood while still connected to allies that is independent and distinct.

Morrison's articulation holds particular verisimilitude for Black women in academe more broadly. In examining content from 1916 to 1970, Murray (1970) found that the *Journal of Negro History* published only six articles dedicated to topics solely regarding Black women. Collins (1990) speaks to further marginalization of the intellectual contributions of Black women over time, and dubs Black women's existence in the academy as that of outsiders within: "The assumptions on which full group membership are based—Whiteness for feminist thought, maleness for Black social and political thought, and the combination for mainstream scholarship—all negate Black women's realities" (15).

BLACK WOMEN IN ACADEME

Black women comprise 3 percent of faculty in the United States and only 1 percent of faculty in predominantly White institutions (Wilder, Jones, and Osborne-Lampkin, 2013). In a rare nationwide study of Black women in academe, Gregory (1999) found that of the 182 women who met conditions of her study, 53 percent of Black women persisted in academe, while an additional 32.8 percent returned to the academy from positions outside academe. She found that Black women who stayed in academe were successful in their research, teaching, and service activities, overall highly satisfied with their work. Black women leaving academe, by contrast, were nontenured (including pretenure and nontenure-track faculty), tended to have worked at four-year institutions, and did not see themselves as being upwardly mobile within their institution. Women successful in Gregory's study attributed their success to God, familial support, and mentorship, which is a finding echoed in Cooper (2006). A collective of women of color in *From Oppression to Grace* (Berry and Mizzelle, 2006) shared narratives detailing workplace inequity in academe, exploring work–life balance issues, tokenism, mentorship, invisibility, and challenges to Black women's scholarship. Adding to Gregory (1999) and Cooper (2006), these authors found evidence of administrative creep, wherein administrative tasks were assigned to faculty as a component of their service load. For Black women, this trend is explored in Harley's (2008) "The Maids of Academe." Narratives within *Our Stories: The Experiences of Black Professionals on Predominantly White Campuses* further speak to both the limited support and hostility experienced by Black women in the academy (Taylor-Archer and Smith, 2002). Women here spoke to broken alliances with both Black men and White women.

Narrative is a significant strategy here as in the case of Black women's literary studies; it gives voice to the experiences of Black women in academe. Henderson, Hunter, and Hildreth (2010) find this form of storytelling as a strategy of resistance to oppression within the academy. Specific to the tenure process, Griffin, Bennett, and Harris (2013) found that Black women perceived race and gender influencing decisions on their tenure and advancement within the academy. However, the critique of this work and others is that it reflects the perspectives of Black women in the academy, but not necessarily the colleagues adjudicating tenure packages or others in the academy. The present work shifts the lens from the perceptions of Black women to the members of the broader academic community. In so doing readers "objectively" can read the expressed thoughts of colleagues and allies, seeing a glimpse of hegemonic and microaggressive forces Black women faculty experience.

RESEARCH METHOD

This study involves a critical content analysis of blogged responses to Schmidt's article in the *Chronicle of Higher Education*. "Many Black Women Veer Off Path to Tenure, Researchers Say." Content analysis is "a systematic reading of a body of texts, images, and symbolic matter" (Krippendorff, 2004, 3), a tradition which at its foundation holds that text is a cultural expression. As such, text is a reflection of social reality (Bos and Tarnai, 1999). Content analysis can employ quantitative and qualitative inquiry tools, numerically accounting for words and phrases as well as a qualitative dimension, ascribing meaning thereto (Ritsert, 1972)—in this case from a critical race feminist frame. As much of the experience of Black women are part of the subtext rather than tacit text of academe— what we do and who we say we are as compared to what we actually do—the present study brings testament to that subtext. More importantly, contemporary data and literature are employed to debunk myths expressed in the blog, which, if are widely shared, contribute to a suppressive if not oppressive work environment for Black women.

Positivists are welcome to challenge the groundings of this study in terms of the selection of the article, the representativeness of participants in the blogging exchange, and the extent of the pervasiveness of the sentiments espoused in the blogs. What cannot be denied are the facts of the event, the content of the blogged responses to a *Chronicle of Higher Education* post. Unlike responses to the *New York Times* and *Washington Post*, the regular readership of the *Chronicle of Higher Education* are typically members of the higher education community—faculty, administrators, graduate students, journalists, politicians, even critics. Of its subscribership of 245,000 persons, 68,000 are from academic subscribers (*The Chronicle of Higher Education*, 2011). In this vein, the blogged content proffered is from the academic community broadly defined and gives insights to the cultural air Black women faculty breathe. It exposes racialized sexism/gendered racism (Matsuda, et al., 1993; James, 2009) in an effort expose and undo power in this area (Krippendorff, 1995).

Data analysis began with multiple readings of the article and blogged responses. These readings were first of the whole and then of the parts. In particular, I sought connections between the article and blogged responses. In most cases there were none, with most responses seeming to come from the experiences and opinions of the bloggers. I then developed codes inductively (Miles and Huberman, 1994), calculating frequencies of words and phrases (Bos and Tarani, 1999) to develop themes. I used five peer debriefers (one Black female, one White male, and three White females), divided into two groups to increase the trustworthiness of results. In identifying themes, there was 97 percent thematic congruence across two groups for each theme, with 50 percent congruence across all three. The high level of congruence lends credulity to results.

RESULTS AND DISCUSSION

Results are presented in Figure 9.1. In order of frequency from highest to lowest, themes found were affirmative action, personnel processes, qualifications, pay/alternative opportunities, family "women's" issues, and workload. I discuss the first two themes in Chambers (2011/2012), using Sue and colleagues' (2007) taxonomy of macroaggressions, microaggressions, and microinvalidations. The present discussion focuses on perceptions of Black women's faculty qualifications and pay/alternative opportunities. Gender and race-neutral personal pronouns are used where appropriate, given the anonymity of the blogging format and insufficiency of cues, in many instances to infer gender identity. Where inferences from blogger content indicate race or gender identity, those pronouns reflect the identity communicated.

FACULTY QUALIFICATIONS

The conversation begins with five posts about the unfairness of reappointment, promotion, and tenure practices, psycho-social factors within academic units, and family/work–life balance concerns. Kat makes a comment about workload, the disproportionality in service work that is explored. This comment is followed by "Seen It":

> No one seems to be invoking the obvious explanation, Black women get into PhD programs on the basis of affirmative action preferences, not merit, at a higher rate than anyone else. They get jobs well above their ability on the same basis. After all, in affirmative action and quota terms, a Black woman is a "two-fer," and a highly desirable hire. Then, when held to something close to the same standards as everyone else for tenure, they can't meet the standards. I've seen it happen. Pretty simple and obvious explanation, really.

"Seen It"'s assertion was also coded under the affirmative action theme discussed in Chambers (2011/2012) and what is interesting here is how reactively the conversation turns to affirmative action. The *Chronicle* article does not discuss affirmative action, as "Seen It" initiates this thread. It is what he or she brings to the conversation. "Seen It" is correct in that affirmative action can help one secure a position but cannot help one keep it (Plous, 2003). And in fact, there are common perceptions of

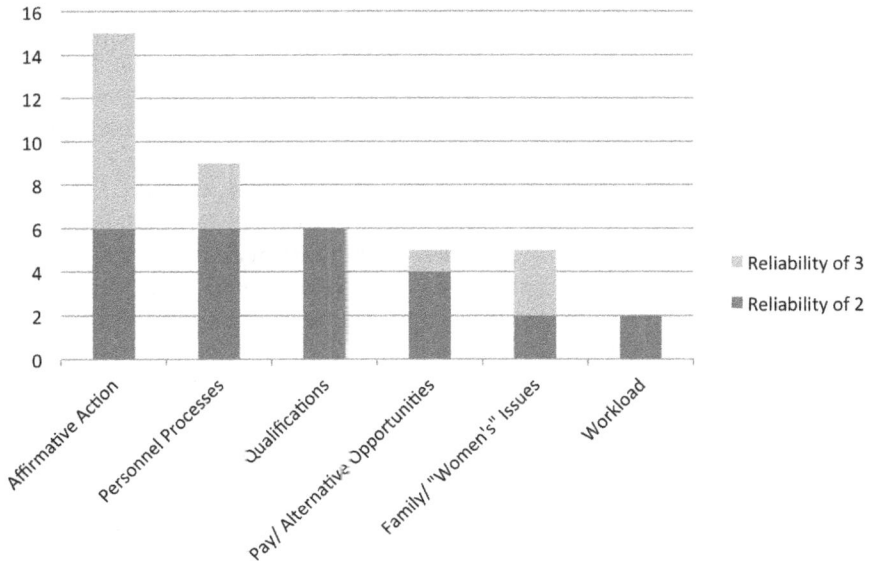

Figure 9.1.   Theme Frequency, Number of Blogged Response by Reliability.

affirmative action recipients as incompetent employees (Eberhardt and Fiske, 1994; Heilman, Block, and Lucas, 1992). Although this factor is more perception than reality (Taylor, 1994), the stigma in combination with workplace microaggressions can turn perception into reality (Leslie, Mayer, and Kravitz, 2014).

"Seen It"'s principal fallacy is the presumption that Black women are the primary beneficiaries of affirmative action. This may be true within the context of federal contracts (Kurtulus, 2016); however, in other sectors White women are found to be the principal beneficiaries (Leong, 2013/ 2014). Identifying who is and is not an affirmative action beneficiary is difficult. Beyond members of the search committee and administrators involved in the hiring process, few know what happens within the black box of employment decisions when it comes to picking the one candidate from a short list of otherwise qualified individuals. Moreover, a racial plus could be used for anyone. For example, a school of nursing may use affirmative action to hire a White male to increase gender diversity in the nursing profession.

Analyzing slightly more than two decades of data in the employment context, Moseley-Braun (1995) found that women significantly increased their presence across a number of professions: architecture (600 percent increase), medicine (100 percent increase), engineering (900 percent increase), and chemistry (300 percent increase). Among faculty, those numbers grew from 28 percent to 42 percent. In addition to not disaggregating by rank, as women are concentrated in pretenure and nontenure-track positions, these data are not disaggregated by race or ethnicity. However, as goes the definition of majority, a majority of these gains were made by White women. Looking at the intersections of race and gender in 2013, White women comprised 35.24 percent of all postsecondary faculty (instruction, research, and public service positions) and 88 percent of all women faculty. By contrast, Black women comprised 4.09 percent of faculty generally, 8.4 percent of women faculty. Black women hold the largest share of non-White women faculty positions (Snyder, deBray and Dillow, 2016). These data are presented as numerical counts in Figure 9.2. The reality then is that all women are underrepresented in faculty ranks; however, women of color are more underrepresented than White women. As such, it would be appropriate to extend affirmative action to both.

Yet, that does not mean that Black women who are hired were hired through affirmative action. It certainly does not mean that Black women are "two-fers." Sokoloff (2014) specifically debunks the two-fer myth, that is, that by hiring one Black woman, an employer increased its racial and gender diversity under the Equal Employment Opportunity Commission guidelines because no individual can be double counted.

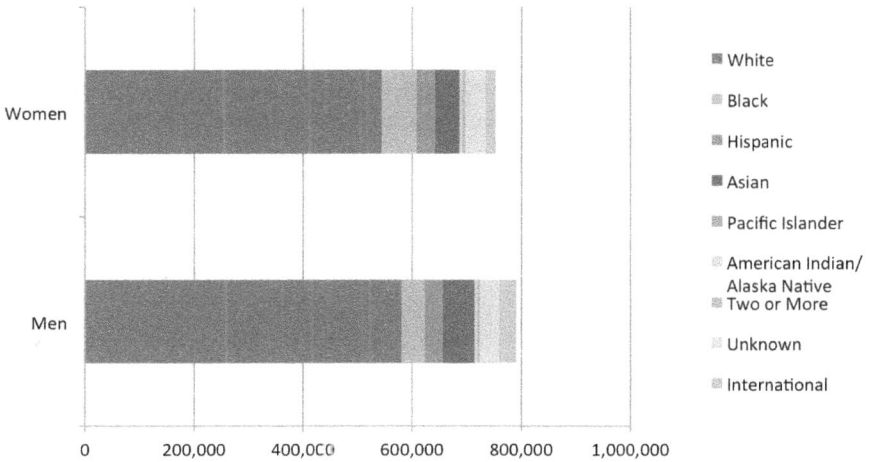

Figure 9.2. Number of Postsecondary Faculty by Race and Gender, Fall 2013. Data from the Nation Center for Education Statistics, Digest of Education Statistics 2014.

"Seen It" Was Rejoined by "Pretty Advantaged"

> "Seen It" — You must be blind lol. Your explanation is a bunch of do[g] poop. Black women don't get into PHD beca[u]se of Affirmative Action only. They must be qualified period.

"bb" resorts to name calling, labeling "Seen It" a bigot, while "Sarah" and "Unree" asked for data supporting "Seen It"'s assertion. "Stay on the Subject" cautions against ad-hominin attacks, and in support of "Seen It," cites his own experience at Hispanic-serving institution. "Stay on the Subject" was privy to announcements of minority research and travel fellowships and other support, but could not take advantage of it. From this, Stay on the subject extrapolates differential treatment to admissions and the educational experience:

> I saw WAY too many under- or marginally qualified minority students get pushed through the system. . . . If they did end up somewhere that didn't offer those "opportunities," then success would have been very difficult for them to obtain — not because of racism, but because they probably shouldn't have gotten a PhD in the first place.

He or she then goes on to postulate that doctorates of color obtain faculty positions and "ends up in a place that's over his/her head." "The 'Un-Diverse'" adds to the conversation, sharing his or her experience of being denied the opportunity to attend the PhD program of choice.

Both "Stay on the Subject" and "The 'Un-Diverse'" both write from a space of perceived loss, where they were not able to attain benefits extended to others, and they attribute this loss to their majoritarian status. Sokoloff (2014) finds that generally women have made workforce gains post-1970s, but these tend to be in woman-dominated fields such as nursing, education, and social work. Moreover, despite the progress made by the three disadvantaged race or gender groups (referencing White women, Black men, and Black women) in the technical fields, to talk about "losses" experienced by White men appears inappropriate when numbers in this group, as well as other groups, have grown substantially in the professions and technical areas. This is not a zero-sum situation; any such gains by women and Black men do not represent a direct loss for White men (Sokoloff, 53).

Or as captured by Malveaux in her foreword to Sokoloff's volume, the White male student who worried about his job prospects has, on the basis of race and gender, little to worry about if the trends from 1960 to 1980 continue. On the other hand, if the trends from 1960 to 1980 hold true, much more has to be done before women and minorities are represented in top professional jobs (2014, xi).

Within academe, White men hold the greatest share of faculty positions, 37.6 percent. Looking at Figure 9.2, this seems at near parity with White women. However, when one accounts for faculty rank, disparities widen. Using data reported by the American Association of University Professors (AAUP), 71 percent of full professors are men (Barnshaw and Dunietz, 2015; see Figure 9.3. Certainly, although perceived loss experienced at the individual level is hurtful, in the aggregate, the idea that people of color or White women are displacing qualified White men in academe is not borne out in the data.

The loss "Stay on the Subject" and "The 'Un-Diverse'" write from is probably best expressed in Kimmel's *Angry White Men: American Masculinity at the End of the Era* (2013). Kimmel asserts that White men, whether we are working-class plumbers or corporate financiers, "we're raised to expect the world to be fair—that hard honest work and discipline will bring about prosperity and stability. It's hard for us to realize that we've actually been benefiting from dramatic inequality" (xii).

Thus, when opportunities granted to others present themselves, it seems unfair, at the expense of White men, when in fact there is a lack of accounting for race and gender privileges experienced throughout their lives.

The point of balancing advantages is raised by "Madamesmartypants." To which "Stay on the Subject" retorts that "I don't see a whole lot of prejudice, at least in the sciences" to which "Jean" responds,

> It is no wonder you have not seen a whole lot of prejudice, at least in the sciences—you have not let almost ANY minorities into your elite club—you cannot "see" racism when you inculcate(sic) yourself in a world without difference.

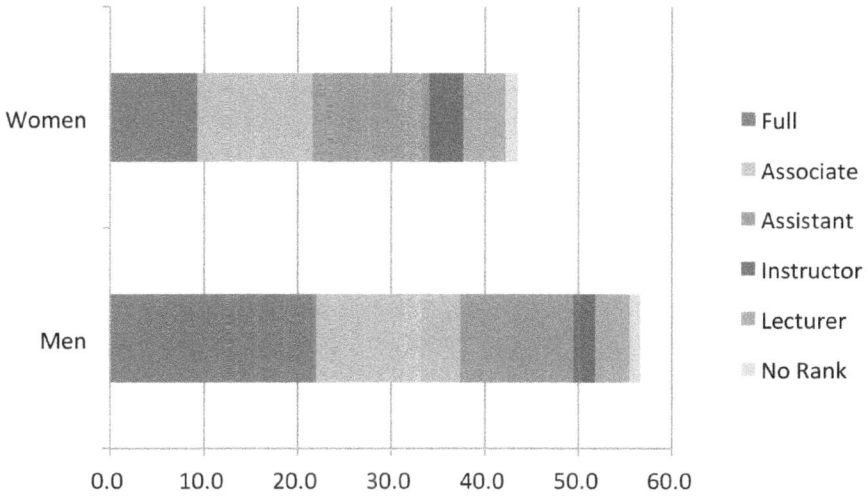

Figure 9.3. Faculty by Rank and Gender, Percentage. Data from the AAUP Annual Report on the Economic Status of the Profession, 2014–15.

Although the National Science Foundation (NSF) promotes Increasing the Participation and Advancement of Women in Academic Science and Engineering Careers (ADVANCE) grant competition to improve women's representation in science, technology, engineering, and mathematics (STEM) fields, racial gaps within science and engineering disciplines are greater than gender gaps. Whereas women were 24 percent of all STEM faculty in 2013, underrepresented minorities comprised 6.2 percent of STEM faculty (NSF, 2015). Overall diversity within the STEM fields are in need of improvement.

Responding to "Seen It" and others, "Max" shares her experience with affirmative action:

> I have worked 70 hour-weeks for YEARS, and EARNED two advanced degrees during that time. I am, finally, in a university that has made my job a tenure-track faculty position. Now I read, yet again, that as a "two-fer", I got the job due to "affirmative action." "Seen It" does NOT [know] how right that is. Affirmative action was started so that "two-fers" with two advance degrees could get jobs that white men without degrees have historically had HANDED to them.

Max's comments seem more congruent with administration than faculty ranks. Nevertheless her reflection rings true for me personally. In my own experience, I have been hired alongside White men as a summer law intern at an elite firm, graduate research assistant, and assistant professor, and in each instance, had greater education or experiential knowledge than my counterparts but was acknowledged through salary and other means as being equal. Although grateful for these opportunities, for Max and I both, affirmative action practically means that one has to be twice as good to go half as far.

Max goes further to address a contemporary perspective of postracialism: "You see, good people of all colors have been trying to convince me that "Seen It" had died in the nineteenth century. I knew better. Now everyone else does too." Postracialism presupposes that "racial minorities" societal gains combined with the presumed absence of contemporary discrimination against them render measures explicitly aimed at redressing racial inequality both unnecessary and counterproductive" (Carter, 2012, 1125). Unfortunately, this cultural narrative clouds racism in contemporary society, and by obscuring the issue, encourages retreat from remedial measures that could actually, in time, create a racially equitable society (Cho, 2009).

PAY AND ALTERNATIVE OPPORTUNITIES

> I would postulate that a significant cause of Black women falling out of the tenure-track is the pull of better paying positions outside of academia and the need for Black women (who are generally paid less than their white and/or male counterparts) to "do more" just to break even. . . . —DL

DL's perspective correlates with Max's comments, the idea that Black women do more in academe to be considered equal. Only DL takes it a step further, that Black women do more and receive less. Figure 9.4 displays salary differences by gender roughly over the past decade and a half. It is likely that the National Center for Education Statistics (NCES) did not include gender disaggregated salary at the assistant level and other ranks as differentials at those levels tend to be less.

There are significant differences, most pronounced at the full professor level. Some of these differences are explained by discipline and other factors (e.g., women faculty clustered in fields like education and social work); however, there are residual differences that are unexplainable (Lee and Won, 2014; Toutkoushian, 1998; Toutkoushian and Paulsen, 2016). From a labor economics perspective, that difference is gender discrimination. There is considerably less work on racial disparities in salaries, much less work parsing differences by race and sex at the intersections. However, it may be fair to infer that Black women share pay disadvantages with White women and other women of color. "Bill" suggests reasons for Black women's departures go beyond pay, refocusing the conversation to the topic of the *Chronicle* article. In "Bill's" words, "the real issue is that Black Women are not getting the tenure that many deserve":

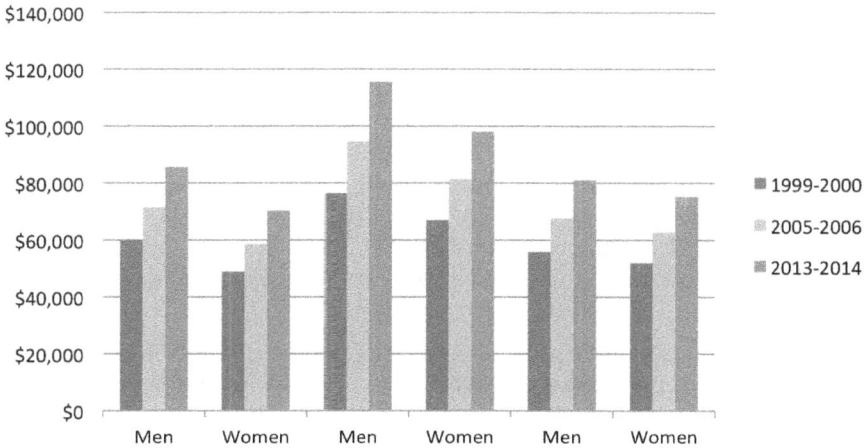

Figure 9.4. Faculty Salary by Gender, Select Years and Ranks, 2013–2014 Constant Dollars. Data from the National Center for Education Statistics, Digest of Education Statistics 2014

> Working on a state university campus for a number of years, what I have seen is Black Wom[en] leaving for a number of reasons. Some for [higher] pay in the private sector regardless of title. Some leave for family.

And several other bloggers discuss tensions between work and family experienced by many women faculty.

"Dan" posits that "black women have a better-developed sense of taste, . . . propriety, dignity, compassion, empathy, and human decency too." While there is some work on the distortions of Black women's character (West, 1999), there is no social science research that I could find documenting that Black women were any more moral or virtuous than anyone else. Black women certainly are not any angrier than anyone else (Walley-Jean, 2009). Although it is unclear the connection "Dan" is making with the article, he or she seems to indicate that leaving is an act of volition, an exercise of power in protest to hegemonic and oppressive systems in academe. "Brilliant Blonde" also speaks to the self-efficacy of Black women academics:

> Racism? Female-ism? Has anyone considered that it might have something to do with career opportunities in professional basketball? Black women don't need so-called researchers worrying over their fate in academia. They're perfectly capable of helping themselves and don't need affirmative action intervention to deal with "their" problems, you smug little twits.

The ad-hominin attacks notwithstanding, Brilliant Blonde's comment illustrates uneasy alliances (Dace, 2012; Frymer, 2010). Or as framed by

Martin (2013), "Some allies are more dangerous than enemies" (355). For most academics, considering alternative paths, basketball is not an option (Basalla and Debelius, 2014). In this vein, Black women do not differ from their peers, and to assert as much is a microinsult (Sue et al., 2007). Moreover, to assert that "Black women don't need so-called researchers worrying over their fate in academia," seems to suggest that Black women are not worthy of academic attention. And yet, Black women faculty experience the double tax of race and gender while performing their academic duties (Griffin, Bennett, and Harris, 2013).

Reflecting on race and gender bias in teaching evaluations, "PB" writes,

> If the subjective opinions of 18 year-olds continue to weigh in on our career paths, then tenure will remain not only elusive, but destabilizing. I for one am rethinking what my relationship to academe can/will be as much as for the political/social/personality vagaries and more in seeking fulfilling quality of life needs.

Crader and Butler (1996) in their meta-analysis of teaching evaluations literature finds that congruence between student expectations and faculty delivery is the key to higher evaluations. What they do not consider is that part of student expectancy relates to professor image (Weinberg, Fleisher, and Hashimoto, 2007; Worthington, 2002). In fact, an algorithm using RateMyProfessor.com predicts faculty gender by the language used in student evaluations and the influences of gender are strong (Schmidt, 2015).

So here, in real time, a faculty member expresses that he or she is currently contemplating leaving the profession. Even "DL" expresses his or her desire to explore other career options:

> If I can devote part of my time (career) to academia and part of my time to a non-academic job that pays better, then I get to have my cake (the satisfaction of teaching and helping students to learn) and eat it too (still make enough money to support my family. A PhD doesn't mean much outside of academia, so why go through the trouble unless I plan to make academia my full career.)

Miller, Chmiel, Whitehead, and Jet (2013), along with contributors to their volume and blog, give testament to there being life for doctorates after academia and that many people, across race, gender, and other diversities, feel let down by academe. Despite sacrifices of family, time, money, even sanity, there are many who meet their goals and still question whether academia is worth it. While I hope, as the editors do, that as the stories of social injustices across academe are told there is concerted action to restructure academe to be fundamentally fair; in the intermediate period, there will be people contemplating their prospects in academe and choosing to exit. The talent loss is unfortunate.

However, for someone like DL, the talent loss is not inevitable. There are aspects of her work that she enjoys and finds fulfilling. Yet, there is the sense that there is more that she would like to experience, contribute to society, and perhaps make a few more dollars in the meantime. Currently, most institutions have strict employment categories—tenure/tenure-track faculty and nontenure-track faculty. In most spaces, only non-tenure-track faculty have part-time opportunities. In fact, for many non-tenure-track faculty, part-time status is the only opportunity. However, what if tenured/tenure-track faculty had options to work concurrently, in a part-time capacity, had the opportunity to work with federal, state, and local agencies or nongovernmental organizations. Programs like the American Council on Education's (ACE) fellows allows senior faculty to experience executive level leadership in academe, but what if there were such programs were available through other nongovernmental organizations, like foundations, or in industries? This would allow faculty a break from the everyday of academe, as well as increase connections between the ivory tower and society.

Moreover, part-time options would be helpful for those raising families who want to continue to advance their career but would also like more time at home. They would also be of use to those caring for aging family members. In this way, faculty would not be faced with dichotomous choices of full-time work or supporting families in the way they would prefer. Such actions could enhance employee morale as well as stave off the number of persons leaving academe.

CONSIDERING THE UNIQUE CONTRIBUTIONS
OF BLACK WOMEN IN ACADEME

This discussion by bloggers trying to make sense of the headline "Many Black Women Veer Off the Path to Tenure, Researchers Say," as well as data availability by race or gender, speaks to the difficulty of centering discussions on discrete sets of individuals, like Black women. Black women are not just the "the sum of separate parts that can be added together or subtracted from, until a white male or female stands before you" (Wing, 2003, 31). Or as goes the title of the Black feminist reader, *All the Men are Black, All the Women are White, but Some of Us Are Brave* (Hull, Bell-Scott, and Smith, 1982).

Analyzing the entire blog, only one-third specifically related to Black women specifically, and half of these relate to the characterization of Black women as two-fers; the assertion and rebuttal thereof. The remainders speak to the unique value of Black women faculty in higher education. Bill asserts,

> We need to have these women in positions of faculty at universities
> and colleges for the African American students that are growing in

> numbers on campuses across the country. . . . African American wom-
> en have saved many students on campus from [losing] the dream.
> Without these women we will continue to see a high dropout rate
> among minority students that do not know how to navigate the higher
> education system, and have the social support and connections that are
> required to maturate in post secondary education.

Bill's assertion is congruent with Ladson-Billings' (1994/2013) depic-
tion of Black women, among others in the K–12 setting, as persons who
make hope tangible, enabling students to make their dreams come true.
And just as it is not solely Black women who are successful at aiding
Black children at the elementary and secondary levels, it is the case that
most Black women have the cultural capital to meet with students where
they are, and help them navigate to meet their highest aspirations. The
downside of this cultural knowledge is that Black women, in turn, are
taxed with not only the research and teaching responsibilities of all faculty, but also service, even administrative duties not commensurately
shared with faculty of their rank and faculty experience.

Says "Kat,"

> women and minorities often get slapped with all of the female or mi-
> nority student advisees, not to mention other service groups and pan-
> els that need "diversity" on them. If you're both a woman and a minor-
> ity, forget about it—you will end up with 40 advisees and you'll be on
> 4x as many committees as your white male counterparts. Service is of
> course considered for promotion, but it's more of "did you do the
> minimum?" checkmark. Doing extra, even if you're the only one ca-
> pable of filling the hole on certain committees, doesn't help you for
> tenure. And obviously spending 30 hrs a week on service and advising
> will mean a lot less time for research.

Kat seems to hit the nail on the head. If Black women were indeed
more likely to veer off the tenure path, it is because Black women are
indeed valuable to the higher education enterprise. The issue here, however, is that there are too few Black women in academe. And those who
are here, rather than protected and valued as a precious commodity are
(ab)used as workhorses. Or, as phrased by Harley (2008), are treated as
the maids of academe.

CONCLUSION

Although the premise of the *Chronicle* article is flawed, bloggers reflection
on why it could be the case Black women would veer off the tenure path
is telling. In the present chapter, I've presented findings under the
themes of faculty qualifications and pay and alternative opportunities.
Under the theme of faculty qualifications bloggers raised general questions about affirmative action regarding minoritized populations general-

ly, then specifically regarding Black women as mythological two-fers. In both, affirmative action with incompetency without regard for the fact that affirmative action is not specific to underrepresented racial and ethnic groups and is likely used with numerical majorities, White women. Given ongoing disparities in the workforce by gender, especially within STEM fields, this is a socially valuable policy directive. In addition, there seems less of a stigma of incompetence associated with affirmative action for White women. However, racial and ethnic disparities are starker than those by gender. Moreover, the persons with the most negative perceptions on affirmative action, tend to write from a space of loss, disjoined from the context of their privileges by race and perhaps also by gender.

Under the theme of pay and alternative opportunities, bloggers consider the reality of academic life for women generally, Black women specifically. Here unfair use of biased teaching evaluations, disproportionate service, and other factors come into consideration. However, as pointed out by Bill, Black women do have special value in academe and are able to reach many students otherwise unreachable. With increased accountability for retention and graduation rates, it stands to reason that rather than expending faculty assets until they are spent out, we can redouble efforts to create an academy with work structures that work better for all. Moreover, rather than fewer Black women in the academy, our aim should be to retain and promote the ones we have and continue to cultivate and make room for more.

REFERENCES

Barnshaw, J., and Dunietz, S. (2015). Busting the myths: Annual report on the economic status of the profession, 2014–2015. *Academe, 101*(2), 4–19.

Basalla, S., and Debelius, M. (2014). *"So what are you going to do with that?": Finding careers outside academia.* Chicago: University of Chicago Press.

Berry, T. R., and Mizzelle, N. D (2006). *From oppression to grace: Women of color and their dilemmas in the academy.* Sterling, VA: Stylus.

Bos, W., and Tarnai, C. (1999). Content analysis in empirical social research. *International Journal of Educational Research, 31*, 659–671.

Carter, Jr., W. M. (2012). The paradox of political power: Post-racialism, equal protection, and democracy. *Emory Law Journal, 61*(5), 1123–1152.

Chambers, C. R. (2011/2012). Candid reflections on the departure of Black women faculty from academe in the United States. *The Negro Educational Review, 62/63*(1–4), 233–261.

Cho, S. (2009). Post-racialism. *Iowa Law Review, 94*(5), 1589–1649.

Christian, B. (1980). *Black women novelists: The development of a tradition, 1892–1976.* No. 52. Santa Barbara, CA: Greenwood Press.

The Chronicle of Higher Education. (2011). About the Chronicle. Retrieved from http://chronicle.com/section/About-the-Chronicle/83.

Collins, P. H. (1990). *Black feminist thought*. New York: Routledge.

Cooper, T. L. (2006). *The sista' network: African-American women faculty successfully negotiating the road to tenure*. Bolton, MA: Anker Publishing.

Crader, K. W., and Butler, J. K. (1996). Validity of students' teaching evaluation scores: The Wimberly-Faulkner-Moxley questionnaire. *Educational and Psychological Measurement, 56*(2), 304–314.

Dace, K. L. (Ed.). (2012). *Unlikely allies in the academy: Women of Color and White women in conversation*. New York: Routledge.

Eberhardt, J. L., and Fiske, S. T. (1994). Affirmative action in theory and practice: Issues of power, ambiguity, and gender versus race. *Basic and Applied Social Psychology, 15*(1–2), 201–220.

Frymer, P. (2010). *Uneasy alliances: Race and party competition in America*. Princeton, NJ: Princeton University Press.

Giddings, P. (1984). *When and where I enter: The impact of black women on race and sex in America*. New York: Morrow.

Gregory, S. T. (1999). *Black women in the academy: The secrets to success and achievement* (Rev. ed.). Lanham, MD: University Press of America.

Griffin, K. A., Bennett, J. C., and Harris, J. (2013). Marginalizing merit?: Gender differences in Black faculty D/discourses on tenure, advancement, and professional success. *The Review of Higher Education, 36*(4), 489–512.

Harley, D. A. (2008). Maids of academe: African American women faculty at predominately white institutions. *Journal of African American Studies, 12*(1), 19–36.

Heilman, M. E., Block, C. J., and Lucas, J. A. (1992). Presumed incompetent? Stigmatization and affirmative action efforts. *Journal of Applied Psychology, 77*(4), 536–544.

Henderson, T. L., Hunter, A. G., and Hildreth, G. J. (2010). Outsiders within the academy: Strategies for resistance and mentoring African American women. *Michigan Family Review, 14*(1) Retrieved March 8, 2017, from http://hdl.handle.net/2027/spo.4919087.0014.105.

hooks, b. (1984). *Feminist theory: From margin to center*. Boston MA: South End Press.

Hull, G. T., Bell-Scott, P., and Smith, B. (1982). *All the women are White, all the Blacks are men, but some of us are brave: Black women's studies*. Old Westbury, NY: Feminist Press.

James, S. M. (2009). Racialized gender/gendered racism: Reflections on Black feminist human rights theorizing. In S. M. James, F. S. Foster, and B. Guy-Sheftall (Eds.) *Still brave: The evolution of Black women's studies* (383–391). New York: The Feminist Press.

Kimmel, M. (2013). *Angry white men: American masculinity at the end of an era*. New York: Nation Books.

Krippendorff, K. (1995). Undoing power. *Critical Studies in Mass Communications, 12*(2), 101–132.

Krippendorff, K. (2004). *Content analysis: An introduction to its methodology*. Thousand Oaks, CA: Sage.

Kurtulus, F. A. (2016). The impact of affirmative action on the employment of minorities and women: A longitudinal analysis using three decades of EEO-1 Filings. *Journal of Policy Analysis and Management, 35*(1), 34–66.

Ladson-Billings, G. (1994/2013). *The dreamkeepers: Successful teachers of African American children*. New York: John Wiley and Sons.

Lee, Y. J., and Won, D. (2014). Trailblazing women in academia: Representation of women in senior faculty and the gender gap in junior faculty's salaries in higher educational institutions. *Social Science Journal, 51*(3), 331–340.

Leslie, L. M., Mayer, D. M., and Kravitz, D. A. (2014). The stigma of affirmative action: a stereotyping-based theory and meta-analytic test of the consequences for performance. *Academy of Management Journal, 57*(4), 964–989.

Leong, N. (2013/2014). Reflections on racial capitalism. *Harvard Law Review Forum, 127*, 32–38.

Malveaux, J. (2014). Foreword. In N. J. Sokoloff, *Black women and white women in the professions: Occupational segregation by race and gender, 1960–1980*. New York: Routledge.

Martin, G. R. R. (2013). *A dance with dragons*. New York: Bantam Books.

Matsuda, M., Lawrence, C. R., III., Delgado, R., and Crenshaw, K. W. (1993). *Words that wound: Critical race theory, asscultive speech, and the First Amendment*. Boulder, CO: Westview Press.

Miles, M. B., and Huberman, A. M. (1994). *Qualitative data analysis: An expanded source-book* (2nd ed.). Thousand Oaks, CA: Sage.

Miller, K., Chmiel, J., Whitehead, L., and Jet (2013). *Moving on: Essays on the aftermath of leaving academia*. Seattle, WA: Amazon Digital Services LLC.

Morrison, T. (1971, Aug. 22). What the Black woman thinks about women's lib. *New York Times Magazine*, 63.

Moseley-Braun, C. (1995). Affirmative action and the glass ceiling. *The Black Scholar*, 25(3), 7–15.

Murray, P. (1970). The liberation of Black women. In M. L. Thompson (Ed.), *Voices of the New Feminism* (87–102). Boston: Beacon Press.

National Science Foundation. (2015). *Women, minorities, and persons with disabilities in science and engineering: 2015*. Special Report NSF 15-311. Arlington, VA: National Science Foundation.

Plous, S. (2003). Ten myths about affirmative action. In S. Plous (Ed.), *Understanding prejudice and discrimination* (206–212). New York: McGraw-Hill.

Ritsert, J. (1972). *inhaltsanalyse und ideologiekritik. ein versuch über kritische sozialforschung* [*Content analysis and critique of ideology: An essay on critical social research*]. Frankfurt, Germany: AthenaKum.

Schmidt, B. (2015). Gendered language in teaching reviews. Retrieved March 8, 2017, from http://benschmidt.org/profGender/.

Schmidt, P. (2008). Many Black women veer off path to tenure, researchers say. *Chronicle of Higher Education*. Retrieved from http://chronicle.com/news/articles/511/many-black-women-veer-off-path-to-tenure-research.

Snyder, T. D., deBray, C., and Dillow, S. A. (2016). Digest of education statistics, 2014. Retrieved March 8, 2017, from http://nces.ed.gov/pubsearch/pubsinfo.asp?pubid=2016006.

Sokoloff, N. J. (2014). *Black women and white women in the professions: Occupational segregation by race and gender, 1950–1980*. New York, NY: Routledge.

Sue, D. W., Capodilupo, C. M., Torino, G. C., Bucceri, J. M., Holder, M. B., Nadal, K. L., and Esquilin, M. (2007). Racial microaggression in everyday life: Implications for clinical practice. *American Psychologist*, 62(4), 271–286.

Taylor, M. C. (1994). Impact of affirmative action on beneficiary groups: Evidence from the 1990 General Social Survey. *Basic and Applied Social Psychology*, 15(1–2), 143–178.

Taylor-Archer, M., and Smith, S. (2002). *Our stories: The experiences of Black professionals on predominantly White campuses*. Cincinnati, OH: The John D. O'Bryant National Think Tank for Black Professionals in Higher Education on Predominantly White Campuses.

Toutkoushian, R. K. (1998). Racial and marital status differences in faculty pay. *Journal of Higher Education*, 513–541.

Toutkoushian, R. K., and Paulsen. M. B. (2016). Labor economics and higher education. In R. K. Toutkoushian and M. B. Paulsen (Eds.), *Economics of Higher Education* (323–369). Amsterdam, Netherlands: Springer.

Walley-Jean, J. C. (2009) Debunking the myth of the "angry black woman": An exploration of anger in young African American women. *Black Women, Gender and Families*, 3(2), 68–86.

Weinberg, B. A., Fleisher, B. M., and Hashimoto, M. (2007). Evaluating methods for evaluating instruction: The case of higher education. NBER Working Paper No. 12844. Retrieved August 5, 2013, from http://www.nber.org/papers/w12844.

West, T. C. (1999). *Wounds of the spirit: Black women, violence, and resistance ethics.* New York: New York University Press.

Wilder, J., Jones, T. B., and Osborne-Lampkin, L. T. (2013). A profile of Black women in the 21st century academy: Still learning from the "Outsider-Within." *Journal of Research Initiatives,* 1(1), Retrieved March 8, 2017, from http://digitalcommons.uncfsu.edu/jri/vol1/iss1/5.

Wing, A. K. (Ed.). (2003). *Critical race feminism: A reader.* New York: New York University Press.

Worthington, A. C. (2002). The impact of student perceptions and characteristics on teaching evaluations: A case study in finance education, *Assessment and Evaluation in Higher Education, 27*(1), 49–64.

TEN

Triumvirate of Academia

Rebecca Fredrickson, Sarah McMahan, and Holly Hansen-Thomas

INTRODUCTION

Entering into a new job, no matter what the job, is challenging. There are new opportunities. cultures, policies, and procedures that must be learned. It is no different in academia. Moving from being a graduate student or even an adjunct faculty member to a tenure-track position creates a significant learning curve for which most junior faculty find they are not prepared.

Often when junior faculty enter into the academy, they are expected to be job-ready on day one without really knowing or understanding what is expected of them (Pryce, Ainbinder, Werner-Lin, Browne, and Smithgall, 2011). This is especially important because the first year in a faculty member's tenure sets the tone of his or her productivity (Boice, 1992). Teaching, scholarship, and service are the mainstays that are required of the professoriate. Depending on the institution, one of the three may be held with higher importance than the others. Nonetheless, the expectation is that faculty will be productive in all three areas.

Excellence in teaching, sound scholarship, and a continuum of service to the profession and university are the three elements in which promotion and tenure are achieved. Indeed, this triumvirate is considered the holy grail of success in academia. Depending on the focus of the institution, the value of each is often viewed that one is significantly more important than the other. Scholarship is frequently the most valued in terms of promotion and tenure (Connelly and Ghodsee, 2011).

Institutions that focus heavily on research and have been granted the Carnegie Classification of Higher Institutions title of "Research I" place more value on scholarship than others, but in most academic institutions across the United States, scholarship is number one. The term *publish or perish* holds quite true for these types of institutions. This often leads junior faculty to focus on writing instead of investing time equally in all three areas. As faculty navigate the process, they may feel frustrated and confused about how to integrate all three elements into a productive line of scholarly inquiry all while maintaining excellence in teaching and notable service contributions.

No matter the gender of the academician, the job of a professor requires an extensive amount of time, dedication, and devotion to receive career advancement or tenure. Very often, however, females have a greater challenge. Studies have suggested that females in academia are often assigned a larger amount of teaching, advising, and service activities than that of their male colleagues. This often creates problems for women when it comes to matters of promotion and tenure (Boyd, Cintrón, and Alenander-Snow, 2010).

In addition to tenure-track demands on new faculty, females with young children at home also must balance the juggernaut of academia and "mommy-hood." Research by Mason and Goulden (2004) suggests that because women find it so challenging to balance family and tenure-track demands that being able to "have it all" is unattainable. Results from Mason and Goulden's work (2004) suggest that many female tenure-track faculty were leaving their institutions before tenure for much less distinguished positions. Further, their often-cited study suggests that balancing work and family demands is extremely taxing on female academics' personal lives. In their book *Professor Mommy*, Connelly and Ghodsee (2011) indicate that academia can easily take over women's lives, if not carefully crafted with demands of work and home life. The authors further maintain that women can make tenure while raising a family and give insightful suggestions on how to do both successfully.

Research suggests that academic "mommies" are often seen as "soft and kind" and as a result, are often preyed on by other senior faculty and administration (Connelly and Ghodsee, 2011). Women, especially those who are mothers, are perceived as "nurturing and nice." Although there may be some truth to this notion, it is often a term of endearment reserved for women/mothers in the academy. Because many women are considered to be "nurturing and nice," they are often asked to participate in more social service activities than their male counterparts. Moreover, female academics are often asked to do additional service work because it fits with their personality. Women are given "soft" committees in which to serve that are more prescriptive of their nature, while male colleagues are given more prestigious committee service.

Although this is not always the case, many female academicians are often perceived by male counterparts as not as important to the mission of the institution (Wilson, 2004). The prestige and acknowledgment that comes with "big committee work" is something that noted on promotion and tenure review processes. Glamorous work is highlighted in the academy, but as many academicians know, service alone (no matter how prestigious) will not get a person tenured.

As many in the academy know, it is extremely difficult for junior faculty members—no matter the gender—to say no when asked by a superior to serve on a college, university, or community committee. Junior faculty members are often the go-to person because they are bound by tenure ties to do it all. The idea of "saying no" is especially difficult for women with children for they fear they will look "unproductive" or "not focused enough" on their scholarship. This gender inequity is clearly noted by Williams (2004). "In fact, many academics are not given extensive teaching and service responsibilities their first year on the job; however, unofficial service requests often come up with no opportunity for a junior faculty member to say no" (18).

This chapter describes the trajectories of three female junior faculty members (all of whom are mothers to children younger than age eighteen) who entered into the academy within one year of each other and details how they have been able to navigate the personal demands of being a wife, mother, daughter, and community member (among other roles) all while working to meet the nexus of the academic triumvirate.

THEORETICAL FRAMEWORK AND METHODOLOGY

The theoretical framework used by the researchers was a combination of critical reflection and personal narrative analysis. The concept of critical reflection was used by the junior faculty members as they were working to develop their personal narratives (Patton, 2002). Aspects of the critical analysis tended to take a feminist perspective because the junior faculty members were all three females working to balance their personal lives with that of their academic persona. The personal narratives were then analyzed to see what themes and ideas emerged from the narratives provided by the three junior faculty members. Personal narratives are often used to draw understanding from subjects and their society (Maynes, Pierce, and Laslett, 2008).

BACKGROUND

On starting their positions, each of the faculty members were assigned to sponsor a student organization for future teachers. Two of them together sponsored a large student organization that served the majority of students enrolled in the department, and the other sponsored another, smaller student organization in her specific discipline. However, both organizations were within the realm of teacher education.

The three faculty members served on a nontraditional campus. Most of the students were first-generation college attendees, had families of their own, and were older. Because of this, the social aspects of sororities, fraternities, and additional social organizations do not have a profound presence on this campus. Because of this, student organizations, such as the ones these faculty members led, take on the additional aspects of serving as social organizations, service organizations, and career student organizations. The result is that sponsoring these organizations takes a great deal of time and commitment from the faculty sponsors. Due to the increased time spent working with these organizations, all three faculty members realized the importance of using this time spent as a way to inform not only their instruction but also their scholarship.

UNIVERSITY

The university where the three faculty members are affiliated is what can best be called a "teaching institution." Although the institution is classified on the Carnegie system as doctoral/research, it has traditionally been recognized as an institution in which faculty teach medium to heavy class loads (three to four courses per term) and are expected to serve on a minimum of three service committees (one at the department level, one at the college level, and one at the university level), as well as national/ international academic communities. The university is a medium-sized institution, with a population of approximately fifteen-thousand students. Unlike many other public institutions in the state, it is one of the very few that is not part of a larger university system. This equates to the university and individual departments having a good deal of autonomy; however, it negatively impacts the institution because it does not benefit from those established policies, dollars, or other resources that comprehensive institutions affiliated with larger systems enjoy.

FACULTY EXPECTATIONS

With regard to job expectations, faculty members have similar expectations of research, teaching, and service, when compared to other institutions. The expectation is that faculty on the tenure track excel in all three areas of the triumvirate: teaching, research, and service. In most cases, there is not a set rubric or defined criteria to be met; however, it is understood that to earn tenure and promotion, faculty will have sufficient publications in peer-reviewed journals, as well as other scholarly works, good teaching evaluations from the students, and development of courses, and a high level of service characterized by work in university committees and national/international academic committees.

MODELING FOR STUDENT SUCCESS

The institution where the researchers serve is diverse. It is a public institution with an approximately 87 percent female and 13 percent male student population Additionally, it has a population of 45 percent to 48 percent Latino(a) and African American students. In the researchers' department, the student demographics are reflective of that of the university. The majority of the students enrolled in the program are females — many of whom are mothers themselves. Some (approximately 24 percent of the undergraduate student population) are also first-generation college students, and of these, a large number are Latino(a) or African American.

Insofar as working with these student groups is a large time commitment, the three faculty members have all worked to make sure that their time spent working with these groups is not only a benefit to the students, but also to their own careers. They use the experiences that they gained through working with their organizations to help serve as a springboard to propel and shape their teaching and their scholarship, helping to round out the triumvirate.

VOICES FROM THE FACULTY

There is undoubtedly a balance that university faculty must find to be successful. This balance is delicate, especially as regard female academics with families, children, and responsibilities in the home. The multiple roles female academics must play are often at odds with one another. However, to be successful, it is critical that females find that balance and nurture it, so that the all-important academic triumvirate meets at its nexus and continues to flourish. In the following section, the researchers explain how (as academics) they have found that nexus, in part through their work with student organizations.

Faculty A

As a faculty member who has earned rank and just recently was awarded tenure, I have worked hard to integrate most of my academic activities in terms of teaching, research, and service in order to make the best use of my work-related time. My research agenda has remained relatively steady and streamlined, but I have had to be creative, independent, and self-sufficient in order to maintain it.

I teach in the language education component of the Department of Teacher Education. That is, I teach foundations and methods courses in language and pedagogy. The line of research I have followed has been that of language learners developing academic language in content areas, with a specific focus on mathematics and science.

I came to this university after having spent three successful years on the tenure track at a public research institution on the East Coast. There, I taught a light load of only graduate courses, which gave me time to dedicate to my research. I was also the charter sponsor of an international educational honor organization. As a result of my work on that student organization, I understood the hours involved in leading a student group, but I also knew of the rewards.

I learned when I moved to my current institution that I would be responsible for leading the student group in my component area, and since I had experience with such activities, I was confident in my ability to hold such a position. However, I also understood I would need to become rather more economical in my time, with a more intense teaching load and additional service requirements. As such, I began to tailor my research agenda to focus on professional development of in-service and pre-service teachers than specifically on students. I also worked to make connections with educators, administrators, and community members in my field through my work in schools.

Another responsibility I took on in my new affiliation was the role of project director and principal investigator on a federally funded teacher training grant. This experience was serendipitous, as the work we did with teachers in the grant aligned seamlessly with my research interests that I had previously embarked upon, starting with my research in graduate school, so this worked well.

With all these responsibilities, I knew I needed to budget my time so that I would at once maintain a cohesive and contiguous line of research, but also to keep up my teaching and work with students; not to mention the fact that I had a two-year-old daughter and another of just a handful of months who I greatly wanted and needed to spend time with and care for.

Flash forward several years later and not only are my little girls now both in elementary school, but I have accomplished a mission whose details and structure was previously unbeknownst to me. Along with the student group I lead, we developed a strong service component to the organization that had previously been absent.

Every year we engage in a partnership to promote biliteracy with a local dual-language school. In this two-way school, both native speakers of Spanish and native speakers of English learn content together in both languages. In this partnership, the stakeholders, including the school's administration, its teachers, me, and my students, first determine what kind of bilingual books the teachers want and need, then purchase those books for them. Our organization not only holds a fundraiser to raise money to buy the classroom books, but the students also read and very often teach a lesson related to the books, in advance of presenting them to the classrooms. It is a rewarding biannual effort, and the students gain a great deal of experience and exposure to the bilingual classroom through their work in the service program we have created and nurtured.

Through this, I have made and maintained connections throughout the independent school districts with which we worked with our organization and strengthened ties to the wider community organizations in my field. Our student group has been recognized at the university and the state level for its rich academic partnership, having won awards and garnered accolades. Additionally, my grant work, as well as my work with mainstream teachers and students, has afforded me opportunities to engage in research and publishing. Overall, I feel like I have made contributions to my field, my students, and my community, while still managing to pick up my children after school and take care of my home responsibilities, but I wonder, could I do more?

With regard to the question, can women, or specifically, junior women professors, "have it all"? I would say, maybe. But it depends where and when. I enjoy the flexibility I have at my institution. We must publish, write grants, teach well, and so on, but we are able to publish in a variety of journals, rather than simply top-tier, peer-reviewed ones. I am not sure if my work as a university student sponsor would be recognized or even count at a Research I institution, but it has served me well thus far.

Faculty B

I came to my institution with previous experience at a Research I institution in the Deep South; however, I only stayed one year at the institution because it was not a fit for me as an academician. Since I only stayed one year at the other institution, I started my tenure-track journey as I transitioned into my new position at this university. Within my first year on the job, I experienced several major life stressors. I got married, bought a new home, and had a child all within the first fourteen months on the job. These life stressors are major for any individual, but even more stressful for me since I just started a new tenure-track job. The only thing reassuring about this time was that I already established a research agenda.

As a component of my appointment, I was asked to cosponsor a professional student organization that was very active on the campus and community level. Even if I thought about saying no to the request, it was never an option because I had previous experiences with the parent organization as a classroom teacher before entering the academy. I knew that my professional organization was important and valuable to the profession and wanted to remain actively involved with it, while I was still a teacher just not a classroom teacher. Instead I was a college professor.

In addition to agreeing to serve as the cosponsor of the student organization, I was also expected to teach both undergraduate and graduate students in my program area and produce a definitive line of research, and contribute service at the university and national level—all while serving as undergraduate and graduate advisor to students. At first I thought I could manage it all without connecting my service activities to my research and teaching. I soon learned that I must find a way to integrate all three while being a first-time mom and a newlywed.

To be honest, the first year was a blur and I still don't remember how I managed to function, yet somehow I did it all while finding ways in year two of being strategic to incorporate my research in ways to prepare twenty-first–century teachers for the teaching profession. My previous research on effective school and community partnerships, as well as the mentoring of preservice teachers, was soon integrated into my work with my student organization.

Over the past four years, I have built a solid foundation that connected my research, teaching, and service to that of my work with the student organization. Several initiatives, including a summer reading program, were constructed that gave preservice teachers opportunities to bridge pedagogical theory into practice. The summer reading program began in year two and has since flourished in numbers, activities, and occurrences. I was able to carefully intertwine my research pursuits to that of the work within my student organization, especially through the school and community endeavors of the summer reading program. Although it might sound that it was an easy task, it was not. I had to be systematic and carefully connect all components of the academic triumvirate.

I still am searching for a balance between home and school life. I often spend countless hours at night frantically trying to write, grade, read, and think after my daughter goes to bed. It seems like I am always running as fast I can to do a stellar job during the daytime at school then transitioning into mommy mode for four to five hours each night. Once my daughter is in bed, I feel I must go back to work in order to keep abreast the demands of a tenure-track faculty member. Each year seems to get more hectic with responsibilities, and I get more and more wrinkles, less sleep, and incur more mommy demands. I recently finished my last manuscript on my scholarship agenda before tenure, yet I still feel robbed of a true balance. Maybe the authors (Connelly and Ghodsee) are right: We can't have it all, yet I chose to strive for it all by working hard both as a female academic and mommy.

Faculty C

Can we do it all? This has become a daily question in my life since I entered into my university tenure-track position. Unlike my colleagues, I came from a different background. I entered the university immediately upon graduation from my doctoral program. Although I served as a graduate and research assistant at the university level, I really had little to no formal knowledge of the expectations and demands upon junior faculty.

As I went through my master's and doctoral programs, my children spent a great deal of time at different universities. Since my children were in the fourth and fifth grades when I entered into the university, they only saw a modest shift in the demands and constraints on our time. That being said, I saw a huge impact in my life, time, and overall health. I worked very hard while I was at the university to get work done but still had additional work and responsibilities waiting for me when I returned home.

I entered into the university in the curriculum and instruction program in the Department of Teacher Education. As with most new faculty, I was eager to please and wanted to become helpful and valuable in any way that I could. When asked to cosponsor a student organization in our department, I was thrilled. Of course I would do it.

Coming from a public school background, there never was an option about things. If it was asked, it was expected without question. After I had spent more time at the university, I discovered that it is not always true, unless you were a junior faculty member. As I continued to gain an understanding of the climate and culture of the university, I quickly discovered that it was perfectly okay to say "no" to things, if one were a senior faculty member and tenured, otherwise, the expectation was to serve where you were asked to serve without question. Being as I am a pretty firm believer in servant leadership, this really did not cause me any issues or problems, but I watched it be a daily struggle for some of my other colleagues.

Time management eventually became my albatross. I really enjoyed my teaching and worked hard to make sure that my lessons led to increased student learning. I believed (and still do) that it is important that I model for my students the kind of behaviors and instruction that I would expect to see in their future classrooms. Teaching was really my focus as I worked through my first year. I also spent a great deal of time in service.

One of the best things that I got to do was to work with the student organization I co-lead and to really get to know the students and find ways to meet their needs. Through the student organization, we were able to do some pretty amazing things. We had a scholastic book fair every semester where our students were able to purchase children's texts for their future classrooms. We engaged in a great deal of community service where we were able to find ways to impact our community at large, as well as our university community. Probably the thing that was the most meaningful, and the most time-consuming, was the development of a weekly community reading program with a community partner. All of this was done not only for the betterment of our students and our program, but also for our community at large. While all of that was great and really made an impact, it also took a toll on my research agenda. I was at a loss for time and direction in my line of inquiry because I spent all of my time in teaching and service.

I quickly learned that I needed to make sure that my service and teaching should inform my research. Once I made that connection, I was able to more effectively shape and mold my line of inquiry into something meaningful that also shaped my instructional practices and service activities. Where none of this seems earth shattering or even original, it is what saved me when I felt I was barely treading water. By letting my triumvirate of teaching, scholarship, and service work together, I was able to not only meet the burden placed on junior faculty, but I was also able to exceed it.

I still do not have it all figured out. Where I was able, through my co-sponsorship with my student organization, to find a balance between my research, teaching, and service, but I still struggle with the time management between my family and my work demands. As I move closer to tenure, the compulsion to tip the balance in favor of work is often overwhelming. I am not sure that as junior faculty members we can have it all. I think that for me, it was probably easier than it was for my colleagues. My children are much older, and while they demand time, it is different than having a small child or even a baby in the house.

CONCLUSION

The personal narratives illustrate the demands junior women faculty with young children have on them. Their voices exemplify how women can be productive the first six years before tenure if they carefully craft and navigate balance (both at home and school). Several themes emerge as a result of their journeys in the academy.

The Mommy Role

It is evident in their stories the challenges they face being a working mom in the academy. All three women were solicited to serve the profession and university by sponsoring an active student organization. Often the student organization activities were outside the normal daily work time; hence the women were often faced with spending less time with their family in the evening hours at times. Another challenge each of the women faced was they were viewed by their senior colleagues as nurturing, caring, and kind, and as such were "good people to lead the student organizations." Although it was something the faculty members cherished, they were still asked to serve because of their devotion and personal interactive skills once they arrived at the university. Nonetheless, the junior faculty members were wary of potential subjective grudges they might face from senior colleagues if they did not participate in the service that was asked of them (Connelly and Ghodsee, 2011).

The women also expressed their emotions and difficulties of balancing the academic life even in a university community that was focused on women and very receptive and accepting of women with children in the academy. All women shared the notion that they felt they were running ragged because they had to balance their own children's activities, all while being dedicated faculty members who were engaged in several service projects. The sponsorship of the student organization was a large commitment and consumed a lot of time in the service component of the promotion and tenure requirements. The faculty narratives allude to the timely demands of female, tenure-track faculty members (Connelly and Ghodsee, 2011; Mason and Goulden, 2004).

Finding a balance between home and school demands is still not something the women find they are doing well. There is still the guilt in each of their voices that they are not doing enough on the home front; however, they feel that they must put in their time now to achieve success (success being defined as achieving promotion and tenure).

Gender Roles

Their stories not only speak of the mommy role, but also that of being a woman in a stressful academic position. Each of them are perceived as being young (younger than forty-five), energetic, and focused women with academic promise. Since they are outgoing and focused, they were chosen to fill service obligations because they were women and women are nurturing, kind, and social. Their male counterparts (whom also entered academia at the same time) were not asked to partake in such service activities; instead they were able to serve on other committee service requirements that did not constitute the time requirements as co-sponsoring active student organizations. Moreover, the inequities in gender roles are seen through these women's narratives (Wilson, 2004).

Similar to the literature on gender roles in the academy, these women served in less prestigious ways by co-sponsoring a student organization. Their male counterparts instead were viewed as serving on other more prestigious committees (Wilson, 2004). The gender role also had an impact on the networking opportunities within the university. While the women slowly networked with other constituents of the academy over the years, their names were not as high profile as their male counterparts because the women did not serve on as many university committees that comprised different disciplines.

Mentoring among Faculty

The women's stories illustrate that they were able to mentor each other because of their commonalities. The women not only collaborated with each other on student organizational projects, but also were committed to building one another up as they all understand the demands of working toward tenure with children at home. The mentoring relationship that developed was authentic and naturally reciprocal. Women felt that they could guide each other through the political infrastructure of the institution and college (Gibson, 2004). Since one of the women earned rank early in her arrival to the institution, she was able to answer questions and serve as a mentor to the other two assistant professors. She was not only well published, but also commended at the university level on numerous occasions for her outstanding work through her grant activities. This colleague helped the other women faculty by showcasing that she could be successful in terms of scholarship productivity all while being a mom to young children.

SUMMARY

Where to go from here? There is little in recent literature about the disparity between the genders in academia. Most of the literature focuses on information from the 1970s to 1990s and primarily emphasizes the pay disparity between males and females in academia. The problems in prestige and pay disparity between the sexes, have made some headway in the past twenty years, but are still woefully behind the times. Wilson (2004) noted that women faculty members more heavily predominate in the less prestigious institutions such as community and junior colleges (48 percent) and less at baccalaureate granting institutions (38 percent). Women as faculty members at research institutions that grant doctoral degrees only make up 28 percent of the faculty membership.

Another problem highlighted in this chapter is that which is illustrated by the "mommy" perspective. This concept is especially damaging to young women as they enter into the academic world. Often when evaluating the work of potential colleagues or examining a person for promotion or tenure, the focus does not tend to be on their accomplishments but on the contemplation of their future productivity (Wilson, 2004). When using this lens, it is much easier to put the "mommy hat" on younger, female professors. Additionally, young women often feel pressure due to the clash of their professional and family responsibilities—a phenomenon not as often faced by their male colleagues.

As many institutions have started taking steps in creating gender equity within the ranks of academia, there are still those who are willing to allow the sexism to go unchecked. Women in the academic world are often not content to sit idly by, but feel that their hands may be tied because it is difficult to prove that this is overt sexual discrimination.

The leitmotif of having it all that is so pervasive throughout discussions of female academics is unlikely to diminish in its importance. As corporate women continue to "lean in" (Sandberg, 2013) and female professors begin to "ask for it" (Babcock and Laschever, 2008), it is inevitable that academia will make way for more and more females to be successful in higher education, but this change may come slowly. Women may well need to continue to be creative and economical in their use of time and efforts, as the three described here have, but the institutions must also begin to recognize and acknowledge the work expended by such academicians as they develop their required triumvirate for success.

REFERENCES

Babcock, L., and Laschever, S. (2008). *Ask for it: How women can use the power of negotiation to get what they really want.* New York: Bantam Books.

Boice, R. (1992). *The new faculty member: Supporting and fostering professional development.* San Francisco: Jossey-Bass.

Boyd, T., Cintrón, R., and Alenander-Snow, M. (2010). The experience of being a junior minority female faculty member. *Forum on Public Policy Online, 2,* 1–23.

Connelly, R., and Ghodsee, K. (2011). *Professor mommy: Finding work balance in academia.* Lanham, MD: Rowman & Littlefield.

Gibson, S. K. (2004). Being mentored: The experience of women faculty. *Journal of Career Development, 30*(3), 173–188.

Mason, M. A., and Goulden, M. (2004). Do babies matter? The effect of family formation on the lifelong careers of academic men and women. *Academe, 88*(6), 21–27.

Maynes, M. J., Pierce, J. L., and Laslett, B. (2008). *Telling stories: The use of personal narratives in the social sciences and history.* Ithaca, NY: Cornell University Press.

Patton, M. Q. (2002). *Qualitative evaluation and research methods* (2nd ed.). Newbury Park, CA: Sage.

Pryce, J. M., Ainbinder, A., Werner-Lin, A. V., Browne, T. A., and Smithgall, C. (2011). Teaching future teacher: A model workshop for doctoral education. *Journal of Teaching in Social Work, 31*(4), 457–469.

Sanberg, S. (2013). *Lean in: Women, work, and the will to lead.* London, UK: Ebury Publishing.

Williams, J. C. (2004). Hitting the maternal wall. *Academe, 90*(6), 16–23.

Wilson, R. (2004). Where the elite teach, it's still a man's world. *Chronicle of Higher Education, 51*(15). Retrieved March 8, 2017, from http://chronicle. com/article/Where-the-Elite-Teach-Its/35450/.

ELEVEN

Academic Advancement and Leadership

Keisha M. Love

INTRODUCTION

Before discussing my experiences as a department chair, I think that it is important to provide a brief overview of my journey in the academy. I begin this chapter by providing a context for my experiences and perspectives while both preparing for the academy in graduate school and while in the academy as a junior faculty member. I believe that these experiences are relevant to my advancement in the academy and directly affect the leader that I am today.

After working a dead-end job as an unlicensed master's-level clinician for a couple of years, I decided to pursue a terminal degree in counseling psychology. Because of its emphasis on multiculturalism and prevention, counseling psychology has always been appealing to me. Within this profession, I found my voice as an African American woman and a profession through which I could have a positive impact on society, especially for marginalized and oppressed groups. I hadn't decided upon my ultimate career goal; I just knew that I couldn't keep doing what I had been doing. I considered private practice, working in a college counseling center, and doing consulting work with school districts, but none of these outlets felt right.

As an advanced doctoral student, I received an opportunity to teach a graduate-level, career-counseling course one summer. Teaching this course ignited my passion for teaching, which wasn't surprising given that I came from a long line of K–12 educators. Although I aspired to enter the academy, I was very intimidated by the thought of conducting research. My dissertation chair, a Caucasian woman, challenged this fear by reminding me that I had a first-authored publication in a top-tier journal. With her affirmation and support, I realized that I actually could conduct research. My research focused on African Americans; I enjoyed using my publications as a way to give a voice to a historically underrepresented group in the literature. After conquering my fears, I committed to pursuing a career in the academy—so my journey began.

BEGINNING A CAREER IN THE ACADEMY

Toward the end of graduate school, I interviewed at a variety of universities, ranging from small, undergraduate liberal arts schools, to large, research-extensive universities. I ultimately accepted a tenure-track assistant professor position in counseling psychology at a large, research-extensive university located in a small college town in the South. I selected this university for two primary reasons: its proximity to my hometown and the strong support network that existed among the African American faculty on the university's campus. African American faculty represented less than 5 percent of all faculty (total faculty was roughly 2,200), but their network was strong and supportive, which was important for me as I looked for opportunities to collaborate with peers, sought out mentors, and strived to start my own research program.

There is a saying in psychology that "research is mesearch," meaning that we tend to research our own experiences or issues that are salient to us as individuals. My primary research interests in graduate school stemmed around attachment relationships in families of color and psychological adjustment among college students of color—two lines of research that I sought to continue as an assistant professor. However, as I began to network with other women in the academy, both at my university and outside my university, I noticed that many of us shared a collective experience as women and women of color. As such, I became interested in women's experiences in the academy, to the extent that I decided to pursue research in the area. Therefore, in addition to my other research on attachment relationships and psychological adjustment among college students of color, within the last few years I have begun to conduct research on women in the academy.

SUMMARY OF THE RESEARCH

Two of the most researched topics in the literature related to women in the academy and their experiences with promotion and tenure, namely, the added barriers that women face, and the underrepresentation of women in leadership positions, especially in executive positions (Cooper et al., 2007; Madsen, Longman, and Daniels, 2012). The literature has consistently found that sexism, racism, alienation, discrimination, or the confluence of these issues have historically posed significant barriers to promotion and tenure for women and have hindered them from achieving executive positions in the same percentages as their male counterparts (Harley, 2008).

MY EXPERIENCES IN THE ACADEMY
IN RELATION TO THE LITERATURE

As I immersed myself in the academy literature, I began to question how my experiences as an African American woman aligned with the literature. Unfortunately, many of my experiences were consistent with those in the literature. For instance, my dean and evaluators considered my research focus primarily on African Americans "narrow," yet, research conducted primarily or solely on Caucasians wasn't considered narrow. In addition, my evaluators were unfamiliar with many of the prominent tier-one and tier-two African American journals and student affairs journals in which I had published my work. As such, my work was deemed as not having a "significant" impact on the field. I found myself fighting to validate the quality of the journals in which I had published, which was consistent with reports in the literature (Harley, 2008). While I did not have the expectation that they, administrators with backgrounds in higher education and teacher preparation, would be familiar with psychology journals, the fact that they assumed the journals were of a low quality (simply because of their own ignorance) was frustrating and disheartening.

Second, as one who operates from a social justice, multicultural perspective, I infuse issues of diversity into all that I do—teaching, research, and service alike. Although I refused to teach our "multicultural" classes because I did not want to be stuck teaching the classes, I taught "mainstream" courses from a diversity perspective.

I found that students, the vast majority of whom were White, who rejected my infusion of diversity into my classes tended to give me relatively low teaching evaluations. Students rated me low at times not because I was not a knowledgeable, effective instructor, but because they were not ready to confront the complex and sensitive issues related to race, ethnicity, gender, sexual orientation, ability, and many other diversity topics that I covered in my classes. In essence, I made them uncomfortable because I opened their eyes to White privilege and issues of oppression among minority groups. Despite this issue, my evaluations were fine because although some students rated me low, many rated me very high, which balanced my teaching scores in the high average/average range. Nevertheless, as a woman of color in an untenured position, working in a university that was not oriented toward social justice, I was concerned about how these evaluations would affect my attempt to receive promotion to associate professor with tenure.

Another example from when I first entered the academy: I was considering starting a family. Numerous female colleagues strongly advised me to wait until I had achieved tenure. They shared their horror stories with me surrounding their fight to get their promotion and tenure clock suspended, or extended, because of childbirth or adoption. Many also shared the unwillingness of their department chair to modify their schedules to adjust to having a new child, or in some cases, children. They shared how harshly their male and some female colleagues judged their decline in research productivity due to childbirth or adoption. Despite the warnings, I proceeded with starting a family, having two children pre-tenure.

Being proactive, I met with my department chair and negotiated a modified teaching schedule the semesters that I had both my children. I was fortunate to have a department chair who was supportive and helpful, which I think made a big difference in my ability to remain productive. In addition, thanks to a then newly adopted administrative policy, when pregnant with my second child, my promotion-and-tenure clock was suspended for one year due to the birth of a child. Despite having two children, I successfully received promotion to associate professor with tenure a year early. I was aware of the written and unwritten rules related to promotion and tenure, especially as a woman of color, so I worked three times as hard to ensure that my materials had no room for error. Through this process, I had earned a reputation as being organized, assertive, and driven, yet personable, or "safe" for White people, so, when the position of department chair became available, several of my colleagues nominated me for the position.

ADMINISTRATION: THE FIRST INSTITUTION

I had never given administration much thought because I enjoyed being in the classroom working with students, so I really did not know how to respond to my colleagues' nomination for department chair. Several of my veteran African American colleagues encouraged me to accept the nomination, stating that I had "what it takes" to be a successful department chair: tact, critical-thinking skills, problem-solving skills, organizational skills, and communication skills. On the one hand, department chair seemed like a great opportunity to lead the change that I wanted to see in my department, for it was an opportunity for me to bring new leadership to the department. On the other hand, given my previous experiences, I wondered how my department and college would respond to an African American woman being a department chair. I wondered if issues of racism, sexism, and discrimination would limit my ability to be successful and effective. I also wondered if people would respect me as their chair, being not only African American, but also a woman. Despite having known my colleagues for years, being peers with them is different from being their department chair. As chair, I would be evaluating them, leading them, advising them, which is a very different relationship from the one that we had to date.

After much debate and consultation, I accepted the nomination. It turned out that not many faculty were interested in serving as chair because the heavy workload associated with the position, so there were not many faculty who accepted the nomination for the position. Competing against full professors with more leadership experience, I was not optimistic that my colleagues would vote for me. However, I was surprisingly mistaken; I won the nomination.

My first experience with discrimination came as I was negotiating my chair salary. Having thoroughly done my research, I was fully aware of salary increases that two Caucasian women had received as newly appointed chairs within the last two years. My initial offer was dramatically lower, to the point that I was personally insulted. I was given the same rhetoric that I was told when negotiating my salary as an incoming assistant professor, "That's all that I can do" said my dean. Being ignorant about the negotiation process back then, I pushed for a little, which I received, but I didn't get what I desired.

Interestingly, for the next three years, White colleagues joined my department and their salaries far exceeded mine. So, how is it the dean could do for them, but couldn't do for me? Sadly, the experience negotiating my chair salary just validated all of the experiences that I had read about from women of color who commonly reported that they made less money than their male colleagues and their Caucasian female counterparts (Robinson and Clardy, 2010). After nearly a month of negotiations, I decided to "walk" from the chair position. I met with my dean to give her the news in person. Naturally, she asked why; I explained my significant concern about the inequity in the financial compensation that she had offered me to take the chair position. I shared my knowledge of the raises that those before me had received and explained that I was questioning why my offer was not comparable, making it clear that I had no interest in the position unless I would be fairly compensated. She asked for additional time to "see what I can do." She came back with an offer that was acceptable—with that, I accepted the position.

My first semester as chair came with a steep learning curve. Relating to my colleagues as their chair was an adjustment for them and for me. In addition, my leadership style, which is democratic and participatory, was in stark contrast to my predecessor's laissez-faire style, which meant significant changes on many levels. Colleagues' responses to my new position were bimodal. Some were supportive and appreciated me being their chair, whereas others constantly challenged me and worked hard to circumvent my authority. The latter issue became one of the biggest challenges that I encountered. There were certain individuals who, no matter what I did or said, always sought validation or verification of my responses or decisions from White associate deans or the dean, suggesting that they didn't trust my decisions or information.

My honest opinion is that racism, and in some instances, racism and sexism were fueling these faculty members' actions. I had a "chip on my shoulder" due to these experiences and knew that I would have to work extraordinarily hard to win some of my colleagues' respect. A participant in a recent research study that I conducted summarized my experience well by stating, "A White man can walk into a room and instantly demand respect; a woman, especially a Black woman, has to earn it" (Love, Thomas, Lloyd, and FitzGerald, 2012, 12). This statement had definitely been true in my experience. I attempted to discuss these issues with my dean, for which I received limited support. My general sense was that she was oblivious to the issues with which I was dealing, or if she was aware, did not know how to address them; so I was on my own. In addition to personnel issues, there was the budget to learn, course scheduling, student issues, promotion and tenure, faculty evaluations, and the list goes on. It was overwhelming at times, but I survived the challenge.

In addition to the challenges described, my administrative role also presented internal struggles and challenges. Being chair provided me with a front-row seat to discriminatory practices and acts of covert racism, sexism, and heterosexism on a scale that I had never imagined. For instance, the discrepancies in starting salaries for faculty of color was disheartening and the inequities in the ways that the rules were bent for some but not others was alarming. The struggles that some women of color encountered with promotion and tenure was sickening.

However, I understood that I was within a system that had enabled such practices for decades, but never before had I seen the full extent of it, nor had I ever been so close to it. The stories that I had read about in the literature were coming to fruition right in front of me. Over time, the exposure became psychologically oppressing and depressing, as the problems became more pervasive. I had been part of the system for years, and knew of such issues, having even experienced some of them personally, but seeing them as a department chair was different. I eventually concluded that I could no longer work for an institution that engaged in such overt and covert practices.

In all fairness, I believe that it is important to discuss the positive aspects of being a department chair at my first institution. Although there were challenges, there were also successes, which is a part of what kept me motivated to serve in the role. For instance, three colleagues were promoted or tenured while I was chair. It was exciting to be able to guide them through the process, advocating for their advancement, and being able to celebrate with them when they received the good news of their promotion or tenure. I was able to recruit two highly qualified tenure-track African American faculty to our department and secured one openly gay male lecturer, all of whom turned out to be excellent hires. With the addition of our new hires, our department led the college in relation to faculty diversity, an accomplishment of which I was most proud.

Moreover, committed to my new colleagues' success, I was intentional in my efforts to mentor them and offer guidance related to surviving in the academy. I truly enjoyed our individual mentoring meetings and providing them with feedback on their research projects and courses. Clearly outlining the promotion and tenure guidelines for the tenure-track faculty and helping them develop a plan for success was fulfilling. As well, focusing on teaching excellence with the lecturer in hopes of him being promoted to senior lecturer was rewarding. I was truly invested in my faculty's professional development, and I worked to support them in any way that I could in relation to teaching, research, and service. Therefore, despite the challenges endured, I enjoyed the work and realized that I had a niche for administration given the positive feedback that I had received from several colleagues. . . . I just needed to do it in another setting.

ADMINISTRATION: THE SECOND INSTITUTION

Therefore, I hit the job market. I applied for department chair and associate dean positions all over the country, but given my experiences at my previous institution, I looked at universities in more progressive locations with more progressive, open leadership. I finally accepted a chair position in the psychology department of a large, master's-granting comprehensive university in a large, metropolis. When interviewing, I was candid with hiring committees about my commitment to diversity and my leadership style.

The university with which I became affiliated was not surprised or intimidated by my direct comments and questions related to diversity and inclusion, explaining how diversity and inclusion were part of their strategic plan. Their commitment was not just rhetoric, for they gave me several concrete examples of how they were operationalizing diversity and inclusion. Moreover, I was awed by the number of women that I saw in leadership positions, from department chairs to directors to senior vice-provosts. I was even more impressed that several women in these positions were women of color. The atmosphere at my new institution was a stark contrast to the environment that I had left, and for the first time in a long time, I felt optimistic and excited about being a woman of color in the academy. I do not intend to portray my new institution as utopia—sure, issues of discrimination, racism, and sexism exist, but on a much smaller scale. I believe that this contrast is attributed to administrators' intentional focus on fostering a culture that minimizes the isms (racism, sexism, heterosexism, ableism, etc.).

I have been in my new position six months; however, I have been extremely busy. I came to my new institution during a time in which it was going through significant changes such as adding more master's- and doctoral-level graduate programs, shifting its identity to place a greater emphasis on research and creative activity, getting a football team, and a host of other changes. With nearly thirty-one thousand students, my new institution is the third-largest public university in the state and continues to grow. The vision of excellence and positive outreach that the president has for the university is both inspiring and positive. I welcomed the opportunity to be part of such miraculous change and was excited about the opportunity to lead my department to greatness.

A few of my new colleagues did not appreciate the changes happening at the university, including my appointment as chair; however, the majority have been extremely welcoming and supportive. My first few months have been spent redesigning our program to add a minor; outlining our new vision, mission, and strategic plan; petitioning for additional faculty "lines"; advocating for faculty resources with the dean; and meeting with faculty individually to discuss their goals, projects, and activities but most important, brainstorming ways that I can support them. I actively look for ways to motivate my faculty, encouraging them to strive for excellence. To no surprise, I have had a faculty member from the majority group challenge some constructive feedback that I provided. However, having experienced this type of exchange numerous times at my previous institution, I believe that I have handled the situation well and resolved the situation. I know that more issues will emerge, but I am prepared.

For my own professional development, I connected with an organization called the Women's Leadership Council. This organization consists of women in the academy and women in corporate settings from the local metropolitan area who are committed to women's advancement and success. Being part of this organization has been a wonderful experience. I have had the opportunity to network with some very prominent, professional women throughout my campus and city, which has opened a variety of doors for mentoring, networking, consultation, and collaboration opportunities. I am now connected with judges, detectives, CEOs, CFOs, psychologists, provosts, and others. As women in leadership positions, we share a common bond. We are able to share our experiences with one another, brainstorm coping strategies and solutions, and perhaps most important, collaborate to conduct research and enhance teaching and consultation efforts. Consistent with the literature, I believe that having a support network in the academy is critical for academic success—and sanity.

SURVIVING THE ACADEMY

Numerous authors have written about women's experiences in the academy. However, not much attention has been given to the coping strategies that women use to survive in the academy, which is a focus of my research. As mentioned previously, mentoring has received attention as a strategy that women use to cope with being in the academy. Research suggests that mentoring has positive impacts on outcomes such as promotion and tenure, job satisfaction, and retention among women in the academy, but studies are limited; additional research is needed for further validation. Personally, I find connecting with other women in the academy, especially those in similar leadership positions, to be therapeutic because the relationships provide a source of support and guidance. Therefore, in addition to other strategies, mentoring and engaging with a professional support network are primary coping strategies for me.

HOW I SURVIVE

Love and colleagues (2012) found that the number one coping strategy for women of color in the academy was prayer. I too use prayer as a primary coping strategy. When the challenges seem like they are too much to handle, I take prayer time to relax, release, and strategize. My faith teaches me that life will never put more on me than I can bear. I hold this saying to be true when times get tough. I also strongly believe in work-life balance. I joke with friends that I'm a wife and mother who moonlights as a department chair. Keeping the roles that I occupy in life in their proper order and perspective keeps me from getting too serious and engulfed in my work. As such, spending quality time with my family and having time for personal hobbies such as baking, interior design, and exercising keep me physically and mentally balanced. I also have very close friends who are in the academy and understand my struggles. Being able to share my experiences with them is invaluable. Therefore, using a support group is my second-most utilized strategy. Consistent with my personal experience, among Caucasian women in the academy, Love and colleagues (2012) found professional friends to be the number one coping strategy, followed by the engagement in activities/hobbies outside of work.

Being a licensed psychologist, I am very interested in self-discovery and self-exploration. To that extent, I completed an assessment, the Myers Briggs Type Indicator, to learn about my personality style. The information that I gleaned from this assessment was very helpful. The feedback provided me with an understanding of my personality style, namely, how I am likely to relate to others in the workplace given my style. Moreover, I had a context for understanding how my interactions with colleagues may vary based on differences or similarities in personality styles. This information has also been helpful in guiding difficult dialogues with colleagues and managing interpersonal conflict among my faculty.

I also took an assessment to learn about my leadership style, which is Democratic and Participatory. As a Democratic leader, I value the input of my faculty and solicit their feedback and ideas when making decisions; however, they and I know that the ultimate decision resides with me. Being participatory, I like working with my faculty, meaning that I keep abreast of activities in which my faculty and departmental committees are engaged. I lend support and participate when possible. Knowing my leadership style allowed me to evaluate the level of fit between my prospective institutions and myself to make an informed decision. For instance, I would probably have a difficult time fitting with an institution that was dictatorial or laissez-fare, as they don't blend well with my leadership style. I believe that finding a strong fit has significantly contributed to my increased level of job satisfaction, commitment to my current institution, and ability to lead successfully. I also occasionally participate in leadership and conflict management seminars and workshops, which has been helpful in teaching me how to facilitate difficult dialogues and manage difficult employees.

MY RECOMMENDATIONS

Based on my experiences and knowledge of the literature, here is what I would recommend for women in the academy. First, I think that it is imperative to pick an institution that is a good fit. Look for an institution that is aligned with your values and goals. Determine your leadership style and pick an institution, or perhaps college or school within an institution, that is compatible with your style.

Longing to be closer to my family, I made proximity to my hometown a major variable when selecting a university. In hindsight, I realize this choice was a mistake. Next, make self-care (i.e., taking care of yourself mentally, physically, and spiritually) a priority by budgeting time for positive activities outside of work. Having outside interests can minimize the risk of burnout and help facilitate a healthy balance between work and your personal life. Seek mentoring from trusted colleagues and professionals who can offer support and guidance. Also, engage in your own self-discovery to determine who you are as a leader and how your leadership style, along with your unique identity as a woman, or woman of color, will interact with your colleagues. Last, participate in relevant professional development activities to hone your leadership skills.

CONCLUDING THOUGHTS

I hope that the academy will eventually advance to a stage in which women are treated equally in all regards, especially as it relates to promotion, tenure, compensation, salary, job duties, and respect. I welcome the day that women are seen for their accomplishments and credentials, not their gender or race. I would like for women to reach a point where they are no longer underrepresented in leadership positions, especially executive positions. I hope that by hearing my story you have received a first-hand account of my experience in the academy as an African American woman. More important, I hope that my recommendations provide you with tools that help facilitate your advancement through the academy.

REFERENCES

Carnegie Foundation for the Advancement of Teaching. (2010). Retrieved from http://carnegieclassifications.iu.edu/.

Cooper, J., Eddy, P., Hart, J., Lester, J., Lukas, S., Eudey, B., and Glazer-Raymo, J. (2007). *Handbook for achieving gender equity through education.* Mahwah, NJ: Lawrence Erlbaum Associates.

Harley, D. (2008). Maids of the academe: African American women faculty at predominately White institutions. *Journal of African American Studies, 12,* 19–36. doi: 10.1007/s12111-007-9030-5.

Love, K., Thomas, D., Lloyd. H., and FitzGerald, K. (2012). The experiences of African American women in higher education. Unpublished manuscript, Department of Educational, School, and Counseling Psychology, University of Kentucky, Lexington, KY.

Madsen, S., Longman, K., and Daniels, J. (2012). Women's leadership development in higher education: Conclusion and implications for HRD. *Advances in Developing Human Resources, 14,* 113–128. doi: 10.1177/1523422311429734.

Robinson, C., and Clardy, P. (2010). *Tedious journeys: Autoethnography by women of color in the academy.* New York: Peter Lang.

TWELVE

Injustice Revealed

An African American Female Faculty Member Dealing with De-professionalism, Inequalities, and Prejudice at One Appalachian Regional University

Doris L. Crawford

INTRODUCTION

Before I can begin my story properly, it is important to trace the meaning of *de-professionalism*. The academic literature understands this concept as the shifting of an individual from a professional role to less professional responsibilities or the reduction of one's professional responsibilities to less professional job characteristics. Oftentimes, the professional individual pursues alternative responsibilities, and in some cases, even changes positions (Kritzer, 1999; Hodges, Tippins, and Oliver, 2013). The experience of de-professionalism, and all the shame and distrust it entails, lies at the core of my narrative.

As a newly minted doctoral degree holder, I was elated to accept my first full-time, tenure-track faculty position at a regional Appalachian university. However, my appointment made me the only person of color in my department, and I experienced a few reservations about accepting a faculty position in an all-White setting. Nevertheless, I was upbeat about joining the faculty and making a significant contribution to both my department and the university as a whole. Being hopeful that my experience would prove to be valuable and progressive, I set off the first week to make every day a positive and productive one.

During my doctoral studies, I read many journal articles and books about intersectionality (Crenshaw, 1991; McCall, 2005; Yuval-Davis, 2006); Black faculty identity conflicts and discrimination against women of color faculty in the academy (Butner, Burley, and Marbley, 2000; Gregory, 2001; Smith, 2004; Stanley, 2006); Black feminist thought (Collins, 2013); and gender inequality in the professorate (Hensel, 1991; Husu, 2000; Okpara, Squillace, and Erondu, 2005). Despite this background awareness, I maintained that I would be a respected partner among my peers. Unfortunately, I experienced many of the same conditions that I encountered in the literature on discrimination against African American female faculty.

After my first month of teaching, I began to experience disrespect and irrational bias from several of my White counterparts. In the subsequent months, I was subjected to harsh criticism, constantly required to defend my actions and decisions. The eyes of my White peers followed me ceaselessly, and to worsen matters, both my department and the college met my concerns with complacency. It appeared that no one cared that I experienced overt and covert racism on a regular basis. Being the only African American teaching in my department, I naturally had no companions to turn to when the problems started to mount.

Cruelly and bluntly, my faculty peers dismissed and treated me as if I was a service worker instead of a faculty member, repeatedly telling me, for instance, to make copies for them and to move my classroom whenever they wanted to hold a meeting in my space. This was an attempt to de-professionalize me and reduce my role as a tenure-track faculty member. The following accounts recapture the highlights of my experience.

UNFAIR TREATMENT

For starters, I entered a work setting without a proper office, deprived of supplies, a telephone, a desk, and a computer. I was told by my superior at that time to go to the surplus store on campus (e.g., junk storage store) to find items. My dingy office space appeared to be an old storage room with dirty carpet and an outdated storage cabinet. I was told by the superior that the department did not spend money on office furniture. I immediately sent an email to the associate dean of the college complaining about this treatment, noting that I was the only faculty in the college who was not offered a functional office. All faculty routinely received fully accommodated and furnished offices. This initial issue would eventually become emblematic of a series of unprofessional responses I encountered in this all-White environment.

When I was prepared to begin work, I was given no job description, formal induction, orientation, or training as other new faculty. I was told to go to another faculty member whom the superior entrusted with the responsibility of giving me basic advice and an outline of my job responsibilities.

Over the course of the academic year, I was given fewer administration tasks, committee assignments, and courses to teach. Furthermore, I was unsuccessful in obtaining a graduate-level course to teach, despite numerous attempts, which made it clear that I would struggle to satisfy the requirements for tenure and promotion. Ultimately, I taught courses that I was not technically assigned to, and a graduate assistant was never assigned nor did I receive a stable classroom assignment (I often had to find an empty classroom to use). I discussed my concerns with my supervisor; however, my supervisor treated me with isolation and made me feel unwanted.

FINDING RELIEF AT THE
NEW FACULTY ENGAGEMENT ACADEMY

During the academic year, I found support from the New Faculty Engagement Academy (NFEA), a peer faculty group for the first-year teacher. The academy provided new faculty of color with helpful tips on how to navigate the academy and successfully acquire the skills needed to advance in one's department and discipline. The NFEA was designed to promote faculty development and address challenges that faculty members would face during tenure, promotion, and post-tenure. The academy proved to be a safe haven, providing me with empathic support from other faculty on campus. The academy not only sponsored activities that helped me improve my research and teaching skills, but it was also instrumental in helping me build networks with senior faculty. The NFEA provided resources that included web-based learning resources, faculty-to-faculty mentoring, cultural competence training, and book discussion exercises.

Throughout our monthly meetings, I quickly discovered that my African American colleagues, as well my faculty of color peers at the NFEA, were experiencing racial injustices. Our mentor and other tenure-track presenters all spoke of a culture of racial discrimination and toxic environments on their campuses. I was appalled that this type of environment was tolerated and accepted as the norm. As new faculty we were all somewhat afraid and confused. We did not feel safe sharing our concerns with our supervisors and White colleagues because we thought they might think that we were unprepared to do our jobs.

I observed well-deserving African Americans being overlooked for positions and denied for advancement, despite being more than qualified. Many Whites with mediocre work backgrounds and subpar work practices were rewarded, and in some cases, given promotions specifically created for them, outside the demands of an employment search. In my department, I discovered that there was no professional accountability for producing scholarly research, innovative scholarship, or active teaching. Cronyism seemed to be the norm.

COMPLACENCY OF UPPER ADMINISTRATION

The departmental chair and the individuals who supervised me were like paperweights: They suppressed my creativity and prevented me from growing professionally. There were numerous occasions, for instance, when I was treated with disrespect by my male peers. One such occasion happened when I was asked to teach a math course that had been taught by one of the male teachers. I taught the course and worked with the students to ensure that they were understanding the content and enjoying the class assignments. One day, several students came to me and expressed dismay at hearing the male teacher berate me in front of his class, telling them that it was a mistake for me to teach the course in question. According to the students, he claimed I could not teach this subject better than he could. With proof in hand, I reported this to the authorities, only to learn that nothing was done to resolve this matter. I was told that an investigation would be conducted and I would be informed of the results. Such results were never revealed to me. Quite frankly, I am not convinced an investigation ever took place. The upper administration was made aware of my concerns; however, they took a cynical view of complaints and nothing was done to provide me with relief from the hostility I experienced.

The point stands: Working in a hostile environment can be mentally draining and physically numbing; I would often leave the campus feeling as if I had been in a battle. This hostility left me feeling as if no one cared about my situation. Failing to receive help from those in charge of my department, I sought the assistance of the provost. At first, the provost listened with great interest, asking questions for clarification and showing signs of empathy. The provost volunteered to be a listening post and to "look into this matter." The provost even shared her cell phone number with me and encouraged me to call her at any time if I experienced unprofessional treatment. I left the provost's office feeling that, at last, I found an avenue that would advocate for me and address the issues that confronted me.

But I was surprised once again.

A couple weeks later, the provost announced that there would be some personnel changes taking place in my department. A letter was circulated explaining that a reorganization of the department would occur at the end of the semester. An unprecedented decision was made to eliminate my faculty position and apply my salary to the new administrative position. I was shocked, distressed, and upset that the provost had decided to eliminate my faculty position in response to my complaint. I protested, explaining that I was being victimized by this decision, while pointing out to the provost and department chair that I had not been given any due process. I was a tenure-track faculty member in the college and had yet to even receive an annual faculty evaluation up to that point. To my continued surprise, I was told that I had performed in an outstanding manner and demonstrated superior teaching skills, but that the decision was solely based on a reorganization decision. I asked for a reassignment, only to be told that I could apply for any future faculty openings on campus or at other universities in the region. I was flabbergasted.

I filed a complaint with the Equal Employment Opportunity Commission (EEOC) and Affirmative Action office. I provided evidence of my mistreatment, including dated emails of discussions with individuals who were major players in creating a hostile and unprofessional work environment. I further indicated that, as a tenure-track faculty member, I was unfairly discharged and did not receive due process according to university faculty policies. Several weeks after I was discharged, I received a letter outlining the investigation's findings. The EEOC and Affirmative Action office reported that they found no evidence of wrongful actions. Astounded by these findings, I quietly reflected on the situation. I determined, however, that the treatment I experienced was blatant and deliberate racial discrimination. The most painful possibility was that the university had been complicit and covered up the truth.

LESSONS LEARNED

I learned that, as a new, tenure-track, African American, female faculty member, I was not judged solely on my ability and performance but was instead subjected to racial stereotyping and hostility. My colleagues made their own rules, rather than abided by the university's faculty guidelines, which should allow for the successful pursuit of educational endeavors and activities in a humane, respectful, and considerate work environment. The following sections outline the core lessons I learned from their hostility and disdain.

Bullying

Being the only person of color in a predominantly White environment created complications: Nothing I did seemed to be appreciated, nor did I receive any credit for my innovations. Painfully, I watched as my colleagues received praise and recognition for what appeared to be the most routine activities. Eventually, I realized that I was a victim of bullying by my superiors. It is a heartbreaking reality to be bullied, implicitly or explicitly, by the "role models" who are in place to assist you in your occupation. This behavior damages the faith you place in the system and in people of authority.

My personal experience has taught me that when you are a victim of bullying, you should focus on individuals' conduct. Generally, you, as the professional, are not the problem; instead, the bully is likely having personal issues and has subjected you to their irrational behavior. In response, remain courteous. Rather than lower yourself to their level, keep detailed notes on the date, place, and time of their cruel behavior. Also, maintain a list of others who might have been exposed to the demoralizing experiences directed toward you. Develop a keen understanding of institutional policies so that you can remind those behind the hostility that their actions may result in increased university liability.

Mentoring

To my fault, I did not locate a mentor; I became too preoccupied with trying to adjust to my first faculty position and the accompanying responsibilities. But the old adage, "No mentor, no success" rings true: I realize now that the first thing I should have done was seek out a respectful senior mentor who was willing to accept me as an apprentice.

Simply stated, I recommend that tenure-track or tenured faculty should seek a mentoring relationship. The seasoned advice will help you understand how to navigate your way through the system, even in the face of vague statements and unfavorable assignments. Make sure to locate a senior mentor who will help you understand the culture of the department. A mentor would have helped me gain an informal social network among my colleagues, as well as overcome the social isolation and gain the appropriate coping skills that are essential for new faculty to persist in the college. A mentor could have explained, for example, that senior faculty sometimes resent new faculty, and therefore, subject them to unequal treatment and unpopular assignments. For me, personally, a mentor would have provided considerable psychological relief by being someone to share my thoughts and anxieties with in confidence.

Personal Care

During these stressful encounters at work, I experienced an array of attitudes: anger, disappointment, betrayal, and feelings of combativeness, to name a few. The idea that I was charged and ready to launch my career, only to have it temporarily halted by unforeseen happenstances, was painful to say the least. These setbacks can be taxing—on body, mind, and soul—which is all the more reason to focus on maintaining your health. Personally, I sought various ways to reduce the mounting stress: I tried long walks, but that exercise just resulted in a longer contemplation of the situation. I read more books, listened to music, traveled to fun destinations, but nothing alleviated my feelings about myself and my situation.

One day, a colleague made a life-changing suggestion after hearing my regrets: He advised that I start practicing mindfulness meditation on a regular basis. To my surprise, I found that this technique helped me achieve inner stability and helped to reframe my professional purpose in life. Each evening, I spend about thirty minutes in a relaxing, upright position in a chair in a quiet room; I close my eyes and become aware of my breath—its feel, its sound, and its warmth—which helps to awaken me to the present moment. There is, of course, much more to be said about the techniques used in this form of meditation; however, there are already a number of great resources on YouTube and TED Talks that can explain the process more thoroughly. I simply want to share that practicing mindfulness meditation has provided several benefits, such as improving my mental and physical health, helping me to sleep and concentrate better, and deal with daily activities without judgment.

Spirituality

Part of the reason that meditation worked for me ties back to my spirituality. During those times when I was humiliated, I would retreat to my office and commune with the higher power. The more criticism that rained down on me, the more I was drawn to a quiet place to pray. Spirituality played an important role in my life during this time, giving me the energy to continue with my work, even amidst hostility and disrespect. My initial reaction to the treatment I experienced was to retaliate with the same degree of meanness. However, the spiritual quiet time gave me a deeper consciousness and stronger emotional intelligence; it renewed my personal values and purpose.

Student Learning

During these trials, I also learned how valuable it is to focus on your students and their needs. I was hired to expose my students to the most innovative and active learning environment that I could provide to transform their lives. Thus, I dedicated myself to giving my students the best experience I could, committing my time and energy to their development rather than my own complaints. I motivated and inspired my students to search for the truth, to explore and investigate beyond the resources and subjects that we examined in class. I strove to learn about each student's ambitions, and then weave their personal interests into the curriculum. I also tried to create a warm and welcoming environment where they would be comfortable learning. For example, I asked them to give me some limited personal information, such as their birthplaces and birthdates and would then surprise them with a personalized birthday card and a class greeting.

In response, my students were wonderful, supportive, and invested in their educations. Most of them expressed to me that I was their first faculty of color. To some extent, I believe they wanted to show me that they respected my role in the classroom, and their diligence was reflected in their clear motivation to learn. The students were by far the most enjoyable aspect of my experience in the college. If I had been supported by my superiors and peers, I am certain that I would have been able to advance my students' learning even further. I regret to think that the isolationist treatment from my peers and the complacent actions of the college might have, if only in some small way, hampered the advancement of future students by mitigating my classroom effectiveness.

CONCLUDING THOUGHTS

The chilly work environment that I entered was unhealthy. There were some who, in privacy, expressed that my experiences were not right; however, they never spoke out on my behalf. As for the others who deliberately engaged in de-professionalizing conduct, I can only speculate that they suffer from some psychological and social conditioning that blinds them to their own harshness when engaging people of color.

But the blame does not lie purely with the people; I also realized that it was the cultural norm at my college and department that allowed covert and overt racism to exist. The college has a poor record of hiring faculty of color. The faculty that are in the college are predominately White, they are close friends with each other, and they tend to have a close professional society among themselves. I tried without success to become an accepted member of the faculty. They failed in collegiality. Generally speaking, I understand that individuals identify with their own racial or ethnic group, even if the group norms hurt people outside their group. And true to this model, even those White counterparts who quietly proffered support for my cause never took a stand to show visible solidarity with me. The silence was reflective of their rejection.

However, in regard to the intersection of race, gender, class, age, and other social differences, I now have a much better understanding of how underrepresented individuals and groups are denied the opportunities to advance in the academy. Little did I know during my graduate studies that I would one day live out my own case study, unraveling my authentic phenomenological story on inequity that arose within the complex maze of oppression and injustice. Amidst the marginality, microaggression, and invisibility that plagued my experience, I am drawn to the immortal words of Maya Angelou's poem: "You may write me down in history with your bitter, twisted lies, you may tread me in the very dirt. But still, like dust, I'll rise" (Angelou, 1978).

And rise I shall.

REFERENCES

Angelou, M. (1978). *And still I rise*. New York: Random House.

Butner, B. K., Burley, H., and Mabley, A. F. (2000). Coping with the unexpected: Black faculty at predominately White institutions. *Journal of Black Studies, 30*(3), 453–462.

Collins, P. H. (2013). *Black feminist thought: Knowledge, consciousness, and the politics of empowerment*. New York: Routledge.

Crenshaw, K. (1991). Mapping the margins: Intersectionality, identity politics, and violence against women of color. *Stanford Law Review, 43*(6), 1241–1299.

Gregory, S. T. (2001). Black faculty women in the academy: History, status, and future. *Journal of Negro Education, 70*(3), 124–138.

Hensel, N. H. (1991). *Realizing gender equality in higher education: The need to integrate work-family issues*. Washington. DC: School of Education and Human Development, George Washington University.

Hodges, G. W., Tippins, D., and Oliver, J. S. (2013). A study of highly qualified science teachers' career trajectory in the deep, rural south: Examining a link between depro-fessionalization and teacher dissatisfaction. *School Science and Mathematics, 113*(6), 263–274. doi: 10.1111/ssm.12025.

Husu, L. (2000). Gender discrimination in the promised land of gender equality. *Higher Education in Europe, 25*(2), 221–228.

Kritzer, H. M. (1999). The professions are dead, long live the professions: Legal prac-tice in a post-professional world. *Law and Society Review, 33*(3), 1–33.

McCall, L. (2005). The complexity of intersectionality. *Signs, 30*(3), 1771–1800.

Okpara, J. O., Squillace, M., and Erondu, E. A. (2005). Gender differences and job satisfaction: a study of university teachers in the United States. *Women in Manage-ment Review, 20*(3), 177–190.

Smith, W. A. (2004). Black faculty coping with racial battle fatigue: The campus racial climate in a post-civil rights era. In D. Cleveland (Ed.), *A long way to go: Conversa-tions about race by African American faculty and graduate students* (171–190). New York: Peter Lang Publishing, Inc.

Stanley, C. A. (2006). Coloring the academic landscape: Faculty of color breaking the silence in predominantly White colleges and universities. *American Educational Re-search Journal, 43*(4), 701–736.

Yuval-Davis, N. (2006). Intersectionality and feminist politics. *European Journal of Wom-en's Studies, 13*(3), 193–209.

THIRTEEN

Brown Girls in the Ivory Tower: Reflections on Race, Gender, and Coming of Age in Academia

Janaka B. Lewis

INTRODUCTION

In my forthcoming manuscript *Civil Discourse: Black Women's Narratives of Freedom and Nation*, I analyze the narratives of formerly enslaved educators Lucy Craft Laney (who went from Macon to my hometown of Augusta, Georgia, by way of Atlanta University) and Anna Julia Cooper (whose career path took her from Raleigh, North Carolina, to Washington, D.C.), not only as autobiographies of teachers but also as lessons taught by students of freedom themselves. Furthermore, I examine how they reflect on enslavement and transitions into freedom to translate lessons about what freedom should look like in its lived experience(s) for their students. Since I encountered Cooper's *A Voice from the South* (1892) while writing my dissertation, I have been shaped by her quote, "We look back, not to become inflated with conceit because of the depths from which we have arisen, but that we may learn wisdom from experience" (27).

Arguing that "we can give ourselves" (281), Cooper writes Black women into conversations of racial "uplift," but she is as concerned with past efforts of racial progress as with future opportunities for Black men and Black women. After gaining her freedom, Laney went on to start the first Black kindergarten and the first nursing school for Black women in Augusta, Georgia, in addition to a reputable school, Haines Industrial and Normal Institute, in 1886, that was recognized by such figures as

W. E. B. DuBois and Booker T. Washington.

Through speeches and essays, Laney also reflected on the distance from which Blacks had come in just a short period of freedom and instructed mothers on how to build their children up at home to be successful and productive as the first generation of free adults. By setting up both personal narratives and ideals of social progress as curricula for life, Cooper and Laney argue for education and institutional opportunities as means for women (and in effect, men as well) to achieve real social progress.

In my career as a scholar, I have read, reread, and taught the stories of these and other African American women who lived and wrote in the nineteenth century. Their stories have inspired me and helped me to realize that it was not the institution of slavery that defined their lives, but instead, the ways in which they saw themselves as free.

This chapter explores, through personal reflections, my experiences at a large state school as a junior professor, wife, and mother from hiring through mid-tenure review through preparation for tenure. It addresses several "well-intentioned" comments and assumptions said aloud to me throughout my career about my age and family choices, including "it must be so hard," and even more often, "but can you get it done?" My personal narrative is a response to these comments as, like women who lived, worked, and wrote before me, I negotiated strategies within my department, college, university, community, and home.

I did not feel that I was "born" to be an academic. As a matter of fact, I didn't know anything about teaching college until my first semester at Duke University, when there was an option to take a class called "Designs for Black Women's Living." I wondered if perhaps the course name was a mistake, although it was in a Women's Studies Department (another field that I knew nothing about). How could there be a whole course on how to live as a Black woman? Who would or could teach such a course?

I soon found out that the course was taught by Charlotte Pierce-Baker, PhD, part of the powerhouse couple of renowned English professor Dr. Houston Baker and Women's Studies and English professor Dr. Charlotte Pierce-Baker, who had come to Duke from the University of Pennsylvania and who were the first two married African American academics that I would know. After just one or two days in the course, I was fascinated, not just with what Dr. Pierce-Baker ("Charlotte" as I came to know her) taught, but with her career path. I knew that I wanted to be an educator, but I decided as a first-semester freshman that I wanted to be a professor of African American women's writing.

Fortunately, the entire universe, it seems, was conspiring with my career plans at that time. Our vice president for student affairs, Janet Smith Dickerson, was a Black woman (also the first African American named to that position in 1991), as was Dr. Martina J. Bryant, the first academic administrator at Duke that I met (African American Firsts at Duke University). Dean Bryant, as she was known across campus even after her retirement, was named the first Black female dean of Duke's Trinity College in 1977 and was also from my hometown of Augusta, Georgia, where her sister (who attended our family church) still lived.

Both women were my mother's sorority sisters (and later became mine as well), so I truly felt that I was going from a home into an academic family. Dean Bryant called my dorm room as soon as I got to Duke and announced herself as my "home girl" (which she was, and which I still call her, post-retirement). This world of educated and powerful Black women were my introduction to Duke, and I came to document a whole two years of my African American experience in pictures with friends and speakers, including the illustrious Maya Angelou in the Duke Chapel, before I got too busy to scrapbook. Friends from back home who saw my books were surprised that there were "so many Black people" at such an elite (also read 'White') institution. But in reality, I didn't even question the privilege to be able to choose.

It wasn't until my closest group of girlfriends and I were finishing up, all of us accepted to doctoral, medical, and law programs (some of us even using professional programs as "back-up" plans until we figured out what we really wanted to do), that I even started to think about the privileges of being a Black woman in the academy. Because many of us came from households with professional parents and joined organizations with professional women, we knew what middle-class (even if they struggled to reach it) existence looked like. I won't say that there weren't challenges at Duke, such as when we staged a protest at the administrative building in response to a racist ad and article in the student newspaper, but even in that moment, there was a cadre of Black faculty and staff who spoke with us and wrote on our behalf. This would happen again after we left in response to the Duke lacrosse incident, which resulted in the mistreatment of some of those faculty members and the subsequent departure of some who we depended on to help us through our times of need.

I never questioned, however, what it took to be that faculty member. To balance one's own life and work with what was going on in the world, with students who looked like me depending on me to help make sense of issues of race and gender, and class and sexuality, and the list goes on. Outside of my household, the only discussions about existence as a Black woman were in my eleventh-grade classroom, where to her credit, my high school teacher led a group of only slightly diverse (two Black women of a few women overall) teenagers through *Their Eyes Were Watching God*, a book that deterred some with its language but to which I clung to every word and wrote all of my college admissions essays about.

I lost the first Black woman educator I ever knew in my paternal grandmother, in the eleventh grade, and I sought to negotiate through all

of my writing that relationship of Janie Crawford and her grandmother
Nanny who just sought to protect her through marriage. What would my
grandmother have wanted me to do? She earned her college degree and
raised two children while my grandfather, her husband, served overseas
in the Army. Once I learned what feminism meant, she represented it for
me, along with my maternal grandmother, a manufacturing employee-
turned-baker at a country club in a major Georgia college town who,
divorced for more than a decade, opened up her own baking and catering
company. Because of these women and my mother, a career registered
nurse who decided to stay in the home once my siblings and I were in
school to be our primary source of care while our father (a cardiologist)
worked, I never doubted that I could do anything I set out to do. Again,
now I realize that that was also a privilege that not everyone had.

Finally, I never questioned the support of my college boyfriend, an
African American male and student athlete who was subject to stereotypes regarding his academic performance as well, as I announced my
plans to move from Durham to Chicago and begin a doctoral program,
while he stayed and played another season of football at Duke and then
looked for jobs. When the job search did not bring him to Chicago, we
maintained a long distance relationship from Durham to Chicago, to Mia-
mi (his first job) to West Virginia, where he began graduate school, and
then to Atlanta, where I moved at dissertation stage and also found employment at Georgia Institute of Technology, and then at Spelman College.

There are important moments that this overview doesn't cover: the
support of the women in my church in Evanston, Illinois, the power of
seeing young(ish), African American faculty members at Northwestern
University who gave me tough love but who encouraged me through my
degree, the dozens (well at least more than a dozen) of friends in various
programs who looked like me and finished with doctorates across fields
as well. Through our entire story, my now husband and I had the privilege of knowing that we would be together, and that I could and would
work in a professional career, and that at some point for us, which was
after three years, a new job, and a finished dissertation, as I was told, we
would have a family.

With all of this said, however, I never questioned what it meant to be a
Black woman in the academy. I had seen Black women in the academy. I
asked what it took to get there. They told me. I did it. And so, at the age
of twenty-eight, I landed my first tenure-track job in Early African
American Literature at the University of North Carolina at Charlotte. I
had "made it," with the hands of and on the strong shoulders of men, but
especially of women, who came before me, and then it got "real."

As I reflect on what an intersectional experience (in terms of race,
gender, and class) looks like for me, it also includes age. I did what I
thought I was supposed to do. I pursued a relationship while I did the

work. I sought the job to make the transition as soon as I finished the degree. Yet, even seven years in, the comment I receive most from within the academy, although it is often offered as a compliment outside, is that I look "so young." This is a comment that I don't believe is meant to offend, yet it's one that I am most curious about how to respond.

Finding a tenure-track job coming out of doctoral programs is a goal for many, but it also comes with a set of timelines that some take to be prohibitive of a life outside of the academy. I entered my job not so newly married (two years) and was often made to feel, even with well-meaning comments, that I either should not have a personal life or certainly should not display one. I was warned of the divorce rate within the field at large when I was just trying to figure out how to transition from being an individual graduate student "in a relationship" to a married professional couple. But what was I "too young" for? Marriage? Children? A career that others had been in for decades?

Each of these milestones can be goals set for when coming out of doctoral programs, yet each also comes with a set of timelines that some assume to be prohibitive of a life outside of the academy. As I think about equity, there is a huge gap here as male academics are assumed to have children and someone else who assumes primary care. In more recent cases, men have assumed care during parental leave, but I also got comments from male colleagues about how they were able to use their leave to get a lot of writing done. Not nursing, not maintaining the household, and so on, I don't fault these colleagues for a system that works in their favor even in the name or pursuit of equality, but even the lack of leave or the choice not to take it, for those who don't, is a choice when women literally need that time to recover from the childbirth process.

As my husband and I made decisions together as to when to start a family, which we had been planning as soon as we were living in the same city (at that time, again, two years), we decided on the timing best for us. I didn't publicize or inquire about what would be the best time for my job because I didn't and still feel like I shouldn't, have to, although I did consult carefully the family leave policy to make sure my support and benefits would continue on one semester of leave. I had my first child, a son, the summer after my first year and returned the following winter.

I continued to check the necessary boxes, teaching, submitting publications, and we planned for an additional child, again, without what I felt was unnecessary input from others. In the meantime, I had the most well-meaning colleagues ask after not just our child but about my ability to get work done, which continued into my second pregnancy two years later. Some of the comments were direct. "Why now?" or, "I didn't know you were trying again." I maintained my face in my responses. Was I supposed to broadcast on the listserv? But I also felt like maintaining our family privacy was read as secrecy even though, I was and am still a grown and independent adult.

If I had known then what I know now, I would have spent more of those first few months bonding with my children instead of choosing activities at which to be present to appear still involved. I would not have felt guilty about enrolling my first in a half-day program on nonteaching days since I was waking up at 4:00 or 5:00 a.m. to stay caught up. I would have taken a bit more summer time without the stress of feeling like I should be working. But some would read this as not wanting the job I worked for so many years to get.

Guilt is also "real" as a Black woman in academia, but it comes from the fear that we are not working hard enough when we are often overworking; that we aren't spending as much time being visible when we are helping others to establish themselves. As an advanced assistant professor nearing tenure, I would tell my early junior scholar self that I was enough—doing enough, being enough, capable of enough. Fortunately, I have stayed in academia long enough to hear these messages from others. Unfortunately, some are pushed out before they hear it from anyone.

Mentorship and sisterhood collaborations have been most responsible for creating an environment in which I could thrive at my current institution. When I began, I was assigned a mentor in one of my affiliate departments, Women's and Gender Studies. This was a beneficial relationship in that it gave me insight from outside of my primary department. Additionally, my mentor was married and had a child, which although not a requirement, was extremely helpful as I made my own choices about family life.

I also met more senior colleagues through affiliate departments that became good friends and sister collaborators. I celebrated with them through tenure and the publications of their books, even early in my own career. We bonded over dinners and conversations, and one became a more formal mentor as well. I find that women can be made to feel as if they should not discuss what they find to be challenging even if there is room for change, but my peer relationships with other African American women scholars at my university became positive spaces to navigate the challenges that those at my rank, regardless of race, may face.

My concern, as I enter the next state of my career, is to address publicly and in writing the assumptions of inability to "get it done" as a young African American woman, as a spouse, as a parent, as a junior faculty member, when all of these identities come together. I will discuss the mentality that we have to endure silently to triumph. Rather than being prescriptive, I hope to show the possibilities not only for responding to challenges but also for conversation about why they exist.

Both Frances Ellen Watkins Harper's shorter novel *Minnie's Sacrifice*, which appeared in the African Methodist Episcopal–sponsored *Christian Recorder* in 1869, and her longer and most-well known novel, *Iola Leroy*

(1892), feature mixed-race female characters who are raised as White women and have to decide how to live their lives once they discover they are Black.

Minnie and Iola choose to educate fellow members of their race as their contribution to African American freedom. *Iola Leroy* is historical fiction; it addresses post-Emancipation issues such as the reconnecting of families, but more generally, what Black people should do "on the threshold of a new era" (Harper, 1892, 271). In Iola's decision to "teach in the Sunday-school, help in the church, [and] hold mothers' meetings to help these boys and girls to grow up to be good men and women," Harper's text is fiction about the virtues of education and also proof of how Black women can be instrumental race leaders (276).

The work of Black women, such as Laney, is also evidence of success. She did not just educate young pupils, but she created a kindergarten that was modeled throughout the country. She did not just establish a school, but one with a classically based college preparatory curriculum for a range of ages. During the time that many noted African American colleges were established, Laney also incorporated similar curricula into elementary through high school classrooms. Laney's curricula have been discussed in several theses and dissertations, including "'Tell Them We're Rising': Black Intellectuals and Lucy Craft Laney in Post Civil War, Augusta, Georgia" by Mary Magdalene Marshall (1998); Lucy Craft Laney: The Mother of the Children of the People: Educator, Reformer, Social Activist by Gloria T. Williams-Way (1998); and "'The Burden of the Educated Colored Woman': Lucy Laney and Haines Institute, 1886–1933" by Britt Edward Cottingham (1995).

The final chapter of my first academic book reads ways in which Frances Ellen Watkins Harper represents the freed woman's role in reconstructing her community through fiction. As her character Iola Leroy in the book of the same name states, "My life-work is planned. I intend on spending my future among the colored people of the South . . . they need me" (1892, 234). Sacrifice and education are the means articulated in Harper's fiction for women to take up the responsibility of racial leadership.

Neither Cooper nor Laney is frequently mentioned among the "Women's Era" writing of the 1890s, perhaps because their writing was not considered "popular" literature. Yet, as Mary Helen Washington asserts, these women were *activists* and *intellectuals*, "more committed to the idea of uplift than to their own personal advancement, partly because they could not isolate themselves from the problems of poor Black women" (1987, 1).

After being born into slavery in Macon, Georgia, and having her freedom bought by her father, Laney was encouraged to pursue an education and graduated ranked first in her class from Atlanta University in 1873 (McCluskey 2006, 407). She taught in Georgia's public schools for years before opening Haines Normal and Industrial Institute. As McCluskey discusses, the school was named in honor of Francine F. Haines, president of the Woman's Department of the Presbyterian Church, who gave Laney funds after the church rejected her first appeal. They later became a sponsor.

During this period, Reconstruction ended and Black Americans were faced with more opposition because of the removal of troops from the South. They were charged with continuing to construct and reconstruct their own communities with little outside or governmental support. As discussed in the introduction to Laney's "Burden of the Educated Colored Woman," on BlackPast.org: An Online Guide to African American History, Laney succeeded in this task, however, drawing more than thirty teachers and nine-hundred pupils to Haines by 1914. This was an incredibly difficult task, especially given the South's difficulty in emerging from Reconstruction.

After participating in W. E. B. DuBois's Atlanta University conferences, farmer's conferences in Tuskegee that began in 1890, and becoming active in the National Association of Colored Women organized in 1896, Laney was eventually invited by DuBois to the Amenia Conference in 1916, which McCluskey described as an "interracial conclave of leaders assembled to discuss future of the race" (81).

Laney did not only describe the problems in Black communities, but she also offered solutions. At the Second Atlanta Conference, Laney presented topics such as "Mothers' Meetings," "Need of Day Nurseries," and "Need of Kindergartens" to the Women's Meeting attendees. McCluskey writes:

> Each speaker proposed some special way in which African American women could or should be more useful to their communities. Dubbed the "mothers' meetings," these became the media for bringing effective instruction and practical strategies to the masses in matters religious and moral. (McCluskey, 2006, 82)

Laney also endorsed the idea in the conference of "day nurseries" for children while mothers worked, which likely led to her establishment of the first kindergarten for Black children in Georgia.

As an observer, educator, and scholar, Laney's rhetoric focused on religion, marriage, and the maternal role as she discussed ways to enhance the institutions that withstood slavery and could potentially grow much stronger in freedom. She is also proof that everyone had a role to play in building up the community, from men and women improving their own domestic environments to other individuals supporting collective efforts of uplift.

Laney chartered Haines Institute in 1886, only five years after Washington (then married to first wife Olivia Davidson Washington) founded Tuskegee (McCluskey, 2006, 76). Laney's model of a preparatory institution did not mirror Washington's, however, as she offered more academic than industrial courses. Mary McCleod Bethune apprenticed with Laney in 1896 before opening her own school in Daytona in 1904 (76). DuBois, who admired Laney for her "principled, uncompromising advocacy on behalf of Black people," visited Haines in 1917 to lecture on the difference between industrial education and preparation of the "talented tenth" for race leadership. In an editorial in *The Crisis*, he wrote:

> There is fighting in Augusta . . . a lone, little Black woman waging war, not only against entrenched prejudice . . . but also with traitors and hypocrites in her own race; men who know how to work with tourists for tidy sums by cringing and kowtowing. Yet, Lucy Laney triumphs even when her school is poor and half equipped. (McCluskey, 2006, 80)

Laney is recognized for overcoming on her own, but the community for which she works is also her greatest resource.

Her early conference talks culminated in the 1899 "Burden of the Educated Colored Woman" at the Hampton Negro conference, where she addressed the need for more Black women in teaching positions. The "educated colored woman," Laney argued, had different challenges to deal with than her White counterparts. As a former enslaved woman who used education to locate herself amongst the best and brightest minds of her time, Laney's insight into what an educated Black woman should do was both personal and practical advice.

The work with which she challenges Black women as they move ahead as free people and into the twentieth century was to teach young children "and [save] many lives from shame and crime" (Laney, 1899, 4). Although rhetoric of African American uplift had been heard in other narratives by the time of Laney's speech, the morals she encourages Black women, especially teachers, to instill, set a precedent for the progress of an entire younger generation.

If these women "of culture" can "daily start aright" these children, they can put them on a strong educational path and prevent them from succumbing to crime. There is also pervasive rhetoric of respectability — with a good start, they can also be kept from shaming themselves and their families who have such high hopes for their opportunities.

Educational models established by Black women were able to develop students in ways that other institutions alone could not. Only years removed from an enslaved status herself, a formally educated Laney analyzes the hindrances of Negro families from reaching their full potential and prescribes the women, especially in the role of teachers of young students, as the answer to instilling right moral guidelines. Laney was very interested in improving the quality of domestic life (which was thought of primarily as the women's sphere) but believed such improvement would change African American lives overall. As an adult, Laney promoted Black control of schools in addition to homes, control which depended on access to education.

The legacy of Lucy Craft Laney, whose name is on a high school and the museum of African American history in my hometown of Augusta, is a reminder of the goals that I have had as a brown girl, and now woman, in the ivory tower. My research on African American women and freedom and also on lessons taught and learned in Black childhood in the nineteenth century, I have certainly translated from my work to my life. Laney, Cooper, and other women create a curriculum of freedom that circulates by means of formal education but has distinct applications for African Americans. In my current scholarship, I continue to examine the lives and liberties of Black women and girls through discipline and play, which is also connected to larger conversations taking place at the Anna Julia Cooper Center, located at Wake Forest University and directed by acclaimed scholar Melissa Harris-Perry, and through other organizations that examine policies and practical solutions for both.

As Harper concludes in "Two Offers" (1859), "true happiness" is found for women in "full development and right culture of [their] whole natures" (Harper, 1994, 114 [reprinted in Foster, 1990]). Although Harper's text is a fictional account about the virtues of education and proof that Black women can be instrumental race leaders, it is also representation of options for women (76).

CODA: REPRESENTING RACE

In Harper's first novella *Minnie's Sacrifice* (1869), Minnie argues: "When I found out that I was colored, I made up my mind that I would neither be pitied nor patronized by my former friends; but that I would live out my own individuality and do for my race, as a colored woman, what I never could accomplish as a White woman" (Harper, 1994, 72).

Sacrifice and education are the means articulated in Harper's fiction for women to take up the responsibility of racial leadership. Both Minnie and Iola choose to educate fellow members of their race as their contribution to African American progress. Once they discover their racial origins, they invest themselves in promulgating knowledge in a very passionate way; literally implanting the seeds of racial elevation.

The representation of Minnie is an intellectual enterprise in this text because Harper uses an "imaginary" figure to show the effects of female commitment and dedication to working for racial progress. Harper is also specific in how she sees this work playing out: first, the woman must identify herself as part of a collective body; Minnie, like Iola decades later, "sacrifices" the possibility of White privilege to suffer the plight of racial oppression. Then, the woman must, through education, present a way out.

Harper suggests one must cling to her race and use her talents to serve them rather than denying community for personal elevation. Education becomes the gift with which Harper endows her female characters, and it is evidenced by an unshakable commitment to spreading knowledge to others. Iola Leroy then becomes a culmination of the possibilities of female intellectual influence. Like Minnie, the education Iola receives in the text is not for her own benefit, but so that she can reach and teach others. Also set in the Reconstruction period, Iola dedicates herself immediately after Emancipation to becoming a teacher in one of the country's new schools for Black people. By interpreting Iola's lessons as Harper's lessons, one can see the virtues and visibility of Black female intellectualism.

The best "brain and heart of the country," Harper suggests in Iola Leroy, can be found in Black women just as well, if not more so, than in anybody else. "True reconstruction" is issued in this text as "the surrender of the best brain and heart of the country to build, above the wastes of war, more stately temples of thought and action" (1859, 236). I analyze the "brain and heart of the country" through my continued research as I continue to establish myself as a Black female scholar and emerging leader at my own institution.

REFERENCES

African American firsts at Duke University. Retrieved March 8, 2017, http://spotlight.duke.edu/50years/african-american-firsts-at-duke-university/.

Cooper, A. J. (1982). *A voice from the South.* New York: Oxford University Press, 1988.

Cottingham, Britt Edward. (1995). "The burden of the educated colored woman: Lucey Laney and Haines Institute, 1886–1933." Master's Thesis, Georgia State University. Ann Arbor, MI: ProQuest/UMI.

Foster, Frances S., ed. (1990). *A brighter coming day: A Frances Ellen Watkins Harper reader.* New York: The Feminist Press at the City University of New York.

Harper, F. E. W. (1859). *The two offers and our greatest want.* New York: Anglo-American Magazine.

Harper, F. E. W. (1892/1987). *Iola Leroy, or shadows uplifted.* Boston: Beacon Press.

Harper, F. E. W. (1994). *Minnie's sacrifice—sowing and reaping—trial and triumph: Three rediscovered novels by Frances E. W. Harper.* Ed. Frances Smith Foster. Boston: Beacon Press.

Laney, L. C. (1899). *Burden of the educated colored woman.* Report of the Hampton Negro conference. Retrieved March 8, 2017, from http://www.Blackpast.org/?q=1899-lucy-craft-laney-burden-educated-colored-woman.

Marshall, Mary Magdalene. (1998). "Tell them we're rising": Black intellectuals and Lucy Craft Laney in post Civil War, Augusta, Georgia. Doctoral Dissertation, Drew University. Ann Arbor, MI: ProQuest/UMI.

McCluskey, A. T. (2006). "Manly Husbands and Womanly Wives." In *Post-bellum, Pre-Harlem: African American Literature and Culture, 1877–1919.* Eds. Barbara McCaskill and Caroline Gebhard. New York: New York University Press.

Washington, M. H. (1987). *Invented Lives: Narratives of Black Women, 1860–1960.* Garden City, NY: Doubleday.

Williams-Way, Gloria T. (1998). *Lucy Craft Laney—the Mother of the Children of the People: Educator, Reformer, Social Activist.* Doctoral Dissertation, University of South Carolina. Ann Arbor, MI: ProQuest/UMI.

Conclusion

Pam Parry and Sherwood Thompson

All power tends to corrupt; absolute power corrupts absolutely.
–Ben Moreell

This well-known quote describes the roots of patriarchy and can account for much of the discrimination in society, culture, politics, government, religion, sports, entertainment, the military, and even in higher education. In his book *The Gender Knot: Unraveling Our Patriarchal Legacy*, Allan G. Johnson posits that patriarchy is not inherent to human nature, so it is a system that people invented in order to maintain "power and control" over other people (2014, 64–65). Or more precisely, how some men have gained and maintained power and control over some women and others who are powerless. Early in his work, he defines patriarchy: "A society is patriarchal to the degree that it promotes male privilege by being *male dominated, male identified, and male centered*" (5). (The emphases are in his book, and he explains in a footnote that his notion of privilege is influenced by Peggy McIntosh's "White Privilege and Male Privilege: A Personal Account of Coming to See Correspondences through Work in Women's Studies.")

Higher education unquestionably is patriarchal by Johnson's definition, because male professors are given privileges over their female counterparts and the entire system of academe is male dominated, male identified, and male centered. This is not to say that men should be excised from the system, but rather, it is past time that the system level the playing field, equalizing standards for women and minorities. It is also important to note that many men have been working to solve the problem. This is not "us-versus-them" in academe, but rather, we are all responsible for perpetuating a system of male privilege, and therefore, we are all responsible for fixing it as well. Academe can and should be better than this.

The preceding chapters are replete with gripping personal narratives, academic studies, statistical support, and expansive literature that testify to the truth that higher education remains patriarchal even in the twenty-first century. The stories of women faculty members are disheartening, and at times, shocking. That the so-called ivory towers still discriminate so openly and completely should appall everyone.

171

But the preceding chapters also proffer hope—a hope that there are strategies for surviving the system, thriving in the system, and maybe even incrementally changing the system. These women's stories are not one of defeat, but of triumph. In the end, these academicians have offered several lessons on how to overcome and change the patriarchal system of academe. One step toward improvement is heeding their words. Some of the overarching lessons we can glean from the preceding chapters include:

THE UBIQUITY OF THE PROBLEM

In reading this book, one thing is certain that the discrimination rampant in higher education is everywhere despite the type of institution (private or public, two-year or four-year, research or teaching, colleges or universities). The contributors to this book range from a senior lecturer to a retired full professor, and they have experienced similar discrimination in higher education. Women have to overcome higher expectations with often larger workloads, while sometimes encountering double standards in terms of recognition and reward. Although there are pockets of improvement throughout higher education, the problem of discrimination remains virtually everywhere. The issue of gender and other types of discrimination are systemic and pervasive.

THE IRONY OF THE PROBLEM

Higher education advances knowledge and is often criticized by some for its progressivism. So, it is ironic that the same societal force that answers the great questions of the day cannot solve this systemic problem. Even more discouraging, it sometimes seems like academe is not trying to solve this problem. Of all the cultural, societal, political, and other institutions that grapple with patriarchy, academe ought to be able to discover a solution to the problem. Great minds work in higher education, and the level of discrimination in the face of such intellectual capacity is startling. Smart people know better, so why do they perpetuate patriarchy? The answer is simple: power and control (Johnson, 2014). Even in the bastion of intellectualism, power and control keep academics from eradicating or sometimes even improving the inequities at their respective institutions. This book challenges us to share the power and relinquish the control.

THE INSTITUTIONALIZATION OF PATRIARCHY

Too many universities and colleges provide lip service to diversity, but they do not make it a central tenet of their institutions, even if diversity is espoused as central to the organizational mission and vision. This is not because universities and colleges are bad institutions, but because so many other urgent matters provide a distraction. Higher education is constantly combatting budget cuts, changing demands, student recruitment and retention, power rankings, and many other matters that seem more urgent than the ever-present discrimination inherent in our institutional systems. Discrimination has always existed and it probably always will—a thought that might make diversity efforts at universities seem defeating and pointless. The school needs to focus on gaining students, educating students, graduating students, and cultivating alumni; it also cannot spend money, energy, and time ensuring all faculty, staff, and students receive equal treatment. That's exhausting, so we'll talk about it and hope for the best. When we get time, we'll address it more extensively. But time is limited. It seems like a problem that cannot go away, so we do not even make a real effort.

PATRIARCHY IS NOT COLOR-BLIND

Several contributors shared how racial and ethnic discrimination makes the situation even harder on women who feel they are asked to do more for less. Women of color have to overcome additional stereotypes and disrespect in their classrooms that their White counterparts do not. Asian, Latina, and African American authors write about how difficult that racial discrimination makes their situations, including the fact that they are incorrectly perceived as angrier than other powerless colleagues because they "complain" about the discrimination if they point it out. Patriarchy is not just a system that discriminates against women, but others outside the traditional power structure.

INDIVIDUAL STRATEGIES

All the authors provided methods for overcoming the discrimination they face. From pedagogy and mentoring to taking care of oneself, the strategies can help faculty to overcome the obstacles. Mentoring is one of the most important strategies mentioned by the authors—finding a reputable person who is invested in the faculty member's success is key to navigating tenure and promotion. A strong mentor can help the faculty member with research, service, and other expectations of academe. A successful mentor–mentee relationship makes a difference, and everyone should find one. Additionally, it is important to be a little selfish and to take care of oneself. Whether it be exercise, a hobby, self-reflection, faith, family, or friends, faculty members need to make sure that their entire lives are not wrapped up in the job and the demands of tenure and promotion. A holistic approach to the job will help sustain you during those difficult times of high productivity. Take care of yourself, and you will better navigate the pitfalls of academe.

COURAGE REQUIRED

The women in this book had similar stories. Even as the situation and context might be different, they encountered ridiculous expectations and outrageous misbehavior from some colleagues—even sometimes well-meaning colleagues. But the thing that sustained them all was an element of courage. To combat discrimination in higher education, we must all be courageous and be willing to speak up. We must be willing to look inward as well as outward to discover the source of our problems. Once we find solutions, we cannot let the business of the day—grading papers, advising students, faculty meetings, annual reports, and so on—keep us from implementing them.

Each woman in this book has expressed her story with courage, a necessary component for addressing diversity in academe. As we move forward, let's all be courageous.

REFERENCES

Johnson, A. G. (2014). *The gender knot: Unraveling our patriarchal legacy*. Philadelphia: Temple University Press.

Moreell, B. Power corrupts. *Religion and Liberty*, 2(6). Acton Institute for the Study of Religion and Liberty. Retrieved November 24, 2016, from http://www.acton.org/pub/religion-liberty/volume-2-number-6/power-corrupts.

Contributor Bios

INTRODUCTION AND CONCLUSION

Sherwood Thompson, EdD, has attained distinction through a lengthy and productive career, directing campus-wide diversity programs for three major Carnegie Foundation Divisions I public research universities, as well as one regional polytechnic university. In this capacity, he has worked as a leader for university-wide diversity initiatives and multicultural programs, and he led an array of leadership positions in departments that served the academic needs of diverse students, faculty, and staff. He is a professor in the College of Education at Eastern Kentucky University. He is the editor of two books: *Views From the Frontline: Voices of Conscience on College Campuses* and a two-volume *Encyclopedia of Diversity and Social Justice*. He has published sixty-five articles, essays, and papers all variously concerned with education reform and social justice, and 752 downloads. His diversity and social justice training areas include faculty and staff diversity training, inclusion and diversity strategies, global citizen's awareness, school climate and culture, and organizational leadership, and appreciative inquiry diversity summits.

Pam Parry, PhD, APR, is the incoming chair of the Mass Media Department and associate professor at Southeast Missouri State University in Cape Girardeau. In 2016, she received the Applegate Award for Excellence in Research from the Kentucky Communication Association. She is the author of *Eisenhower: The Public Relations President*. She is the lead co-editor of a book series, *Women in American Political History*. She has freelanced for *The Baltimore Sun* and "The McLaughlin Group" television show. In 2009, she was named Teacher of the Year by an interest group within the Association for Education in Journalism and Mass Communication.

CHAPTER 1

Ginny Whitehouse, PhD, is professor of journalism at Eastern Kentucky University where she teaches and researches in the areas of media ethics, media law, and the emerging journalism in social media. She earned her doctorate from the University of Missouri School of Journalism and is the "Case and Commentaries" section editor for the *Journal of Media Ethics*.

Krista Kimmel, MA, is senior lecturer of communication studies at Eastern Kentucky University. Her research interests include instructional communication, first-generation college student success, and communication education. She holds a master of arts in communication from the University of Kentucky and a master of arts in adult and higher education from Morehead State University.

CHAPTER 2

Simone C. O. Conceição, PhD, is professor of adult and continuing education leadership and chair of the Department of Administrative Leadership at the University of Wisconsin-Milwaukee School of Education. She has been a faculty member with the Department of Administrative Leadership since 2001 and teaches courses and conducts research in the areas of learning design, curriculum development, adult learning, online education, and the impact of the use of technology for teaching and learning.

CHAPTER 3

Dr. Karen Christopher is associate professor of sociology and women's and gender studies at the University of Louisville. Her research explores the intersections of gender, race, and class in the family and labor market. She has published in many journals, including *Gender and Society*, *Advances in Gender Research*, and *Feminist Economics*. Her current research project explores work-life conflict among nurses and nursing aides.

CHAPTER 4

Dr. Shirley O'Brien, PhD, OTR/L, FAOTA, is professor of occupational science and occupational therapy at Eastern Kentucky University in Richmond. Dr. O'Brien is a Fellow of the American Occupational Therapy Association and has been recognized as the 2016–2018 EKU University Foundation Professor. She has teaching and research expertise in policy development/leadership, online learning and student engagement, and sensory processing challenges. She is recognized for her application of inter-professional practice in community settings.

CHAPTER 5

Dr. Carolyn A. Lin (PhD, Michigan State University) is faculty in the Department of Communication at the University of Connecticut. Her research and teaching areas focus on the content, uses and effects of information technologies, digital informatics, risk communication, marketing communication, and cross-cultural/international communication. She is the recipient of a University Distinguished Research Faculty award and the founder of the Communication Technology Division at the Association for Education in Journalism and Mass Communication. Professor Lin was head of the communication program and associate dean of the University of Connecticut Graduate School.

Dr. Diana I. Rios (PhD, University of Texas, Austin) is faculty in the Department of Communication/El Instituto at the University of Connecticut. She conducts research and teaching on mass media and cross-cultural communication. Her writings include Latino-Black communication, socio-cultural functions of telenovelas and TV serials, and women faculty in higher education. She has been chair of the Standing Committee on Teaching for the Association for Education in Journalism and Mass Communication, chair of the Feminist Scholarship Division of the International Communication Association, director of the Institute of Puerto Rican-Latino Studies, and president of the UConn chapter of the American Association of University Professors.

Dr. Ruth A. Washington is executive director for faculty and graduate student retention, inclusion, and success at Kent State University. She received her BS in biology from Stillman College, Ph.D. in the biological sciences from Wayne State University and conducted postdoctoral research at the University of Michigan. Her recent awards include the 2013 Ella T. Grasso Distinguished Service Award and the 2014 American Medical Women's Association Mentoring Essay Award. Her research interest focuses on understanding the biology of pericytes in the cardiovasculture. Because of her experiences in diversifying STEM, a second area of studies concentrates on increasing diversity in the STEM fields.

CHAPTER 6

Dr. Edith C. Fraser is a retired professor and social worker. Prior to her retirement, she was professor and chair of the Social Work Department at Alabama A&M University, in Normal. Before her tenure at A&M, she was at Oakwood University, where she held several positions: director of field instruction, chair of Social Work Department, and had a dual appointment as professor in the Social Work Department and director of faculty development and research. In addition, Dr. Fraser has been an adjunct professor and the Bertha Reynolds Senior Fellow at Smith School for Social Work from 1991–2009. Dr. Fraser has also been a Fulbright Scholar to Egypt, China, Thailand, Myanmar, and the Republic of Georgia.

CHAPTER 7

Donna Gibson McCrary, PhD, LGSW, is a licensed graduate social worker in the state of Alabama. She is employed with Alabama A&M University as the BSW coordinator in the Department of Social Work, Psychology, and Counseling. She has ten years of experience as the field coordinator. The past six years she has been teaching undergraduate and graduate social work courses on HBSE, child welfare, assessment, crisis intervention, and social work with groups, as well as death, dying and bereavement with the Gerontology Certificate Program. Gibson obtained her bachelor of arts degree, master of social work, and a PhD in human services. She has several years of experience in child welfare. Publications and research interest include topics on dementia, bullying, domestic violence, and emotional intelligence.

CHAPTER 8

Martina Nieswandt, PhD, is associate professor of science education and interim associate dean for research and engagement in the College of Education at the University of Massachusetts, Amherst. Her research focuses on the relationship between motivation, affects, and learning associated with K–16 science concepts and various instructional contexts utilizing mixed-methods approaches.

CHAPTER 9

Dr. Crystal Renée Chambers is associate professor of educational leadership at East Carolina University in Greenville, North Carolina. Dr. Chambers is a graduate of Spelman College and holds a JD as well as a PhD in education policy from the University of Virginia. She is the 2003 first-place winner of the American Association for Higher Education's Black Caucus Doctoral Student Award and a 2005 recipient of the Association for Institutional Research's Research Grant. Dr. Chambers published works are numerous and include *From Diplomas to Doctorates: The Success of Black Women in Higher Education and its Implications for Equal Educational Opportunities for All, Support Systems and Services for Diverse Populations: Considering the Intersection of Race, Gender, and the Needs of Black Female Undergraduates*, and *Black female undergraduates on campus: Successes and challenges*. Her newest work *Law and Social Justice in Higher Education* is part of the Core Concepts in Higher Education Series edited by Ed St. John and Marybeth Gasman.

CHAPTER 10

Rebecca Fredrickson, EdD, is associate professor in teacher education at Texas Woman's University. Her research interests include professional practice and pedagogy, certification testing, and best teaching practices.

Sarah McMahan, PhD, is associate professor of teacher education at Texas Woman's University. Her research focus is in the area of school/ university partnerships and preservice/novice teacher induction and mentoring.

Holly Hansen-Thomas, PhD, is associate professor in English as a second language and bilingual education at Texas Woman's University. Her research interests include issues of second language learners' teaching and learning in schools.

CHAPTER 11

Keisha M. Love received her PhD in counseling psychology from the University of Missouri-Kansas City and she is a licensed psychologist. Dr. Love is chair of the Department of Psychology at Kennesaw State University in Kennesaw, Georgia. Prior to her appointment at Kennesaw State University, she was chair of the Department of Educational, School, and Counseling Psychology at the University of Kentucky. Her research interests include women's issues in the workplace, college students' mental health, and attachment relationship among families of color. She teaches a variety of graduate and undergraduate courses in psychology, and serves as a mentor for several students. She founded a private practice in which she primarily conducts psychological assessments, provides individual therapy, and advocates for women of color.

CHAPTER 12

Dr. Doris Lynette Crawford is a national education consultant for Ideal Educational Concepts and Solutions, LLC. She is former assistant professor, response to intervention coordinator, and former director of secondary schools. Dr. Crawford was a fellow in the Fulbright U.S. Scholar Program in Japan and a Mississippi Teacher Fellowship Program Scholar. In the capacity of a cabinet level district administrator, Dr. Crawford has expertise in the areas of teacher performance, student achievement, closing the achievement gap, school reform, diversity and inclusion, and effective school leadership. She holds a BS in mathematics from Rust College, an MED degree in K–12 Educational Leadership from the University of Mississippi, and an EdD degree in Educational Leadership from Eastern Kentucky University. She is a 2016 graduate of the Harvard's Women in Education Leadership Program, a 2013 recipient of the American Association of School Administrators Educational Administration Scholarship Award for leadership, and she was selected as a 2013 fellow in the Leadership Institute for Superintendents at Harvard University Graduate School of Education. She is a published author and a frequent presenter.

CHAPTER 13

Janaka B. Lewis, PhD, is assistant professor of English at University of North Carolina at Charlotte, with a research specialty in nineteenth-century African-American women's writing. She earned her BA in English and African and African American studies from Duke University and MA and PhD in English, specializing in African-American literature, from Northwestern University. She has published articles and chapters on Black women and freedom and on African-American sports culture, is researching narratives of Black childhood and best practices in teaching early African-American literature, and her book, *Civil Discourse: Black Women's Narratives of Freedom* is under contract with McFarland Press. She is also the author of children's book *Brown All Over* (2012), which helps caregivers and educators talk to young children about race.